# THE EUROPEAN EMERGENCE

TimeFrame AD 1500-1600

THE AMERICAS

RUSSIA

EUROPE

TimeFrame AD 1500-1600

THE MIDDLE EAST AND INDIA

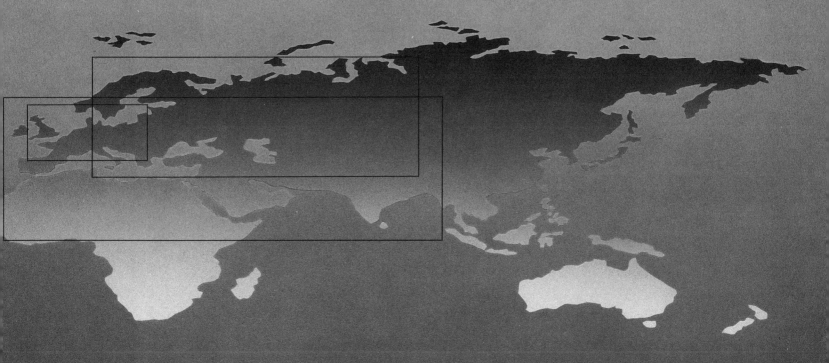

TIME® LIFE BOOKS

# THE EUROPEAN EMERGENCE

## TimeFrame AD 1500-1600

BY THE EDITORS OF TIME-LIFE BOOKS

TIME-LIFE BOOKS, ALEXANDRIA, VIRGINIA

Time-Life Books is a division of Time Life Inc., a wholly owned subsidiary of **THE TIME INC. BOOK COMPANY**

**TIME-LIFE BOOKS**

*Managing Editor:* Thomas H. Flaherty
*Director of Editorial Resources:*
Elise D. Ritter-Clough
*Director of Photography and Research:*
John Conrad Weiser
*Editorial Board:* Dale M. Brown, Roberta Conlan, Laura Foreman, Lee Hassig, Jim Hicks, Blaine Marshall, Rita Thievon Mullin, Henry Woodhead

PUBLISHER: Joseph J. Ward

*Associate Publisher:* Ann Mirabito
*Editorial Director:* Russell B. Adams
*Marketing Director:* Anne Everhart
*Director of Design:* Louis Klein
*Production Manager:* Prudence G. Harris
*Supervisor of Quality Control:*
James King

EUROPEAN EDITOR: Sue Joiner
*Executive Editor:* Gillian Moore
*Design Director:* Ed Skyner
*Assistant Design Director:* Mary Staples
*Chief of Research:* Vanessa Kramer
*Chief Sub-Editor:* Ilse Gray

Correspondents: Elisabeth Kraemer-Singh (Bonn); Christina Lieberman (New York); Maria Vincenza Aloisi (Paris); Ann Natanson (Rome). Valuable assistance was also provided by: Jaime Florcruz (Beijing); Jane Walker, Trini Bandrés (Madrid); Elizabeth Brown (New York); Ann Wise (Rome); H. C. Hwang (Seoul); Dick Berry (Tokyo); Traudl Lessing (Vienna).

**TIME FRAME**
(published in Britain as **TIME-LIFE HISTORY OF THE WORLD)**

SERIES EDITOR: Tony Allan

Editorial Staff for *The European Emergence:*
*Editor:* Charles Boyle
*Designer:* Lynne Brown
*Researcher:* Caroline Lucas
*Sub-Editor:* Frances Willard
*Design Assistant:* Rachel Gibson
*Editorial Assistant:* Molly Sutherland
*Picture Department:* Amanda Hindley (administrator), Zoe Spencer (picture coordinator)

Editorial Production
*Chief:* Samantha Hill
*Traffic Coordinator:* Emma Veys
*Editorial Department:* Theresa John, Debra Lelliott

**U.S. EDITION**

*Assistant Editor:* Barbara Fairchild Quarmby
*Copy Coordinators:* Anne Farr, Colette Stockum
*Picture Coordinator:* Leanne G. Miller

Editorial Operations
*Copy Chief:* Diane Ullius
*Production:* Celia Beattie
*Library:* Louise D. Forstall

*Computer Composition:* Gordon E. Buck (Manager), Deborah G. Tait, Monika D. Thayer, Janet Barnes Syring, Lillian Daniels

*Special Contributors:* James Chambers, Roderick Conway-Morris, Neil Fairbairn, Ellen Galford (text); Sheila Corr (research); David E. Manley (index)

**CONSULTANTS**

**General and Germany:**
GEOFFREY PARKER, Professor of History, University of Illinois, Urbana-Champaign, Illinois

**General and India:**
CHRISTOPHER BAYLY, Reader in Modern Indian History, St. Catharine's College, Cambridge University, Cambridge, England

**The Americas:**
JOHN HEMMING, Director of the Royal Geographical Society and author of *The Conquest of the Incas*

**England:**
DAN O'SULLIVAN, Head of History Department, Prior Purseglove College, Guisborough, England

**Russia:**
R. E. F. SMITH, Fellow of the Institute for Advanced Research in the Humanities, University of Birmingham, England

**Ottoman Empire:**
ROBERT IRWIN, author of *The Middle East in the Middle Ages*

**Library of Congress Cataloging in Publication Data**

The European emergence: AD 1500-1600 / by the editors of Time-Life Books.
    p.   cm. — (Time frame)
    Includes bibliographical references.
ISBN 0-8094-6450-0.—ISBN 0-8094-6451-9 (lib. bdg.)
    1. Europe—History—1492-1648.
    2. Sixteenth century.
I. Time-Life Books. II Series.
D220.E97 1989   940.2'3—dc20       89-20328
                                    CIP

# CONTENTS

1 **The Church Divided** 8

Essay: An Emperor's Fading Dream 32

2 **The Conquest of the New World** 36

3 **Elizabeth's England** 58

Essay: The Gunpowder Revolution 85

4 **Russia's Ruthless Czar** 94

5 **The Ottoman Zenith** 116

Essay: The Proud Display of Privilege 139

6 **The Moguls Ascendant** 148

Chronology 168
Acknowledgments 170
Picture Credits 170
Bibliography 171
Index 173

# THE CHURCH DIVIDED

On foot and on horseback, a steady stream of peasants and villagers crowded the rutted roads into the small German town of Jüterbog. They appeared to be going to market, and it was true that they had scented a bargain. But it was not livestock or farm produce that they were coming to buy. The celebrated Dominican preacher Johann Tetzel had set up in the marketplace a rostrum surmounted by a great cross decorated with the arms of Pope Leo X; Tetzel's credentials, a document of authorization from the pontiff himself, lay on a gold-embroidered cushion. And beside the rostrum, a representative of the Augsburg banking house of Fugger superintended the chest into which the credulous would be invited to deposit their florins.

"As soon as the coin in the coffer rings, the soul from purgatory springs," ran the catch phrase attributed to Tetzel. His sermons employed a harsher rhetoric:

> How many mortal sins are committed in a day, how many in a week, how many in a year, how many in a whole lifetime? They are all but infinite and they have to undergo an infinite penalty in the flaming punishment of purgatory. Yet in virtue of these confessional letters, you shall be able to gain, once in a life, full pardon of these penalties.

The money paid for the letters, which were known as indulgences, would, Tetzel promised, instantly remit punishment due for sins committed, or to be committed in the future. And this applied not only to the subscriber but also to his dead relatives.

Among Tetzel's audience on that day in April 1517 was Martin Luther, a thirty-three-year-old lecturer in biblical studies from the nearby University of Wittenberg. During the course of his training, Luther had become convinced that the sale of indulgences had no basis in the teachings of Christ. Six months after hearing Tetzel, Luther's anger was to burst forth in a letter of protest, addressed to his archbishop, in which he set out ninety-five theses directed against the concept of indulgences. These reiterated with the force of hammer blows Luther's scorn for a corrupt doctrine. Thesis number twenty-eight read: "It is certainly possible that when money clinks in the collection box, greed and avarice can increase; but the intercession of the Church depends on the will of God alone." A number of the theses were cast in the form of prescriptions for what the Church should be teaching, thereby implying its present failings: "Christians should be taught that the pope's pardons are useful only if they do not rely on them, but most harmful if they lose the fear of God through them."

Years later, a colleague of Luther's, Philipp Melanchthon, wrote that Luther had also nailed his theses to the church door in Wittenberg—a story that gained wide currency in later times. Whether or not Luther made such a dramatic gesture, within weeks the theses were circulating in print throughout Germany and beyond. Luther

In a detail from *Ship of Fools*, painted in the 1470s by the Netherlandian artist Hieronymus Bosch, the sin of lust is symbolized by a nun and a monk gamely trying to bite off pieces from a swinging pastry ball. At the turn of the sixteenth century, many priests and monks had concubines and illegitimate offspring, and they attracted widespread contempt. Financial corruption further tarnished the Church of Rome and opened the way for the reforms of the German monk Martin Luther, reforms that changed Christian worship across Europe and reshaped Europe's web of political alliances.

had set in motion a train of events that would lead to a breach with Rome and shatter the centuries-old unity of the Catholic church. New forms of worship would be established, and as the Christian community of the Western world became divided between the old and the new faiths, the political map of Europe would be redrawn.

The Germany in which Luther grew up consisted of a patchwork of principalities, duchies, and other territories within the overall compass of the Holy Roman Empire. Some of these units—in particular the sixty-five imperial cities, which were governed on a daily basis by their own municipal councils—enjoyed considerable autonomy,

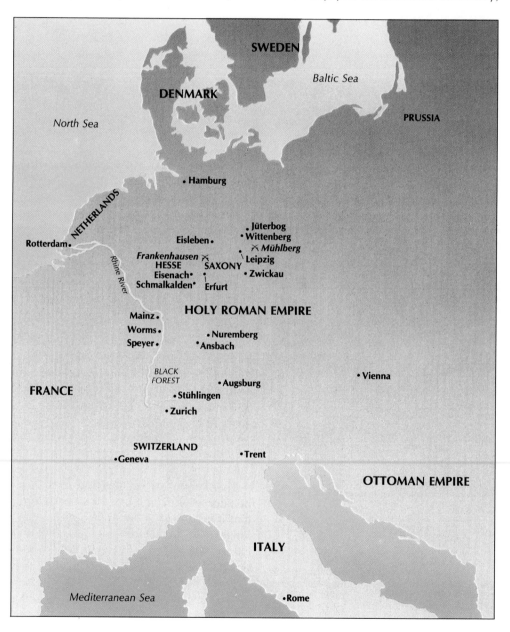

During the first crucial phase of the Reformation, from 1517 to 1525, the issues were fiercely debated in Saxony and neighboring north German principalities within the borders of the Holy Roman Empire and in south German lands near the Swiss city of Zurich. They then spread across all of Europe. The Scandinavian countries were among the first to adopt Lutheranism; in 1534, England established its own national church; in the 1540s, the doctrines preached by John Calvin in Geneva started gaining wide acceptance in France and other countries. By the 1560s, only Italy, Portugal, and Spain remained unaffected by Protestant doctrine.

By the time Martin Luther sat for this portrait in 1529, the immediate dangers to which his criticisms of Church doctrines had exposed him were over. Having abandoned his monk's habit and settled into domestic life with his wife and children, Luther nevertheless continued to influence the progress of the Reformation both through his numerous writings and through his sermons and teaching at the University of Wittenberg. Among his colleagues in this city was the artist Lucas Cranach the Elder, who painted this portrait and also made woodcuts for Lutheran publications that were sold in Cranach's own bookshop.

but all were at least nominally subject to the Holy Roman emperor. The latter was regarded as the pope's temporal counterpart, the leader of Western Christendom, and it was against the authority of pope and emperor jointly that the diverse grievances of the German people in the early sixteenth century came to be directed.

Over the previous century, the spirit of intellectual inquiry that was one of the chief legacies of the Renaissance had led to a widespread questioning of tradition in many fields, including religion. Desiderius Erasmus of Rotterdam, the most respected scholar in Europe, had argued that many of the current practices of the Church were based on superstition; other theologians in France, Italy, and England had also voiced stern criticisms. In Germany, scholars had examined the origins, both legendary and historical, of the German-speaking peoples, and had promoted nationalist feeling at the same time as they challenged many of the long-established doctrines of the Church. In 1492, at the inaugural ceremony for the University of Ingolstadt, the poet Conradus Celtis had called upon all German people to resume "that spirit of older time wherewith you so often confounded and terrified the Romans. . . . Let us feel shame, yes, shame, I say, to have let our nation assume the yoke of slavery."

Even uneducated citizens could see that the Church was deserving of criticism. Many parish priests were illiterate and hardly knew how to perform the ordinary services. Although the Church prescribed celibacy, a large number of clergymen lived with women, and their bishops preferred to let matters stand rather than lose the income derived from imposing fines for concubinage. Many monks and nuns flagrantly violated their vows of poverty and chastity. But the Church retained a strong hold over its poorer congregations, who remained bound by superstition and ritual. Belief in the healing properties of sacred relics was common. Fear of hellfire was stronger than hope for redemption—a fear enforced by the Church's continuous emphasis on the price to be paid in the afterlife for sins committed in this life.

Luther himself possessed a deeply personal sense of sin that he was never to lose. There were times during his early years, he confessed, when he even hated a God who made rules that seemed impossible to obey and who then condemned those who broke them to eternal damnation.

Luther was born in 1483 in the little town of Eisleben in what is now East Germany. His father, Hans, had started life as a peasant but had gravitated to ironstone mining and had subsequently risen in the world. He had high ambitions for his gifted son and sent him to college to study law. He was therefore greatly disappointed when, in 1505, two months after starting his law course, his son decided to give up the law and enter an Augustinian monastery in Erfurt. According to one account, Luther was returning to the university after a visit to his parents when he was struck to the ground by a flash of lightning. In terror he cried out to his father's saint, the patroness of miners: "Saint Anne, help me and I will become a monk!"

There was no more determined novice than Martin Luther. "I was a good monk," he later recounted, "and I kept to the rule of my order so strictly that I may truly say that if ever a monk got to heaven by his monkery it was I. . . . If I had kept on any longer I should have killed myself with vigils, prayers, reading, and other work." Nevertheless, this intense dedication was motivated at least in part by Luther's private doubts and feelings of unworthiness, which were reinforced on the occasion of his first celebration of Mass after he was ordained. After the ceremony, which had drained him emotionally, he sought reassurance from his father, whom he had invited to attend. But Hans had still not forgiven him for abandoning his legal studies and reproached his son for leaving his parents unprovided for in their old age. And when Martin explained that he had been called by a voice out of the thundercloud, Hans spoke the terrible words, "God grant that it was not an apparition of the Devil!"

Luther became increasingly skeptical of many of the practices by which, according to the Church, God's will was to be fulfilled. During the winter of 1510-1511, he traveled to Rome on business for his order and visited sacred places; in one of these, so that a soul might be released from purgatory, he was required to recite the Lord's Prayer in Latin on every step of a holy staircase. But, as he later related, at the top of the stairs he was only half-convinced of the power of his prayers, and a question formed itself in his mind: "Who can tell if it is so?"

On his return to Germany, he was appointed a lecturer at the new University of Wittenberg, which had been founded by Frederick of Saxony. Here, while studying and lecturing on the Bible, Luther achieved his great theological insight. He became convinced that salvation was to be secured not by what people did but by what they believed. He interpreted a text in Saint Paul's Epistle to the Romans, "By faith are ye saved," as meaning, "By faith alone are you saved." From then on, he no longer saw God as an accountant to be bartered with, a stern judge who must be continuously propitiated by good works. Christ had come to save sinners; salvation was not to be achieved through one's own puny efforts but only through faith in him.

From this standpoint, many of the prevailing doctrines of the Church appeared to Luther to be both irrelevant and blasphemous. Particularly suspect were: the notion that God was expected to reward a Christian in proportion to the number of prayers said, of pilgrimages undertaken, of contributions made; the cult of saints and their relics, with its odor of polytheism; and the sale of indulgences.

The last provoked Luther's special ire. According to the doctrine of penance, a sinner had first to feel remorse for his sin and then confess it to a priest; when the sinner performed a "satisfaction" to prove his sincerity—such as reciting certain prayers or going on a pilgrimage—the priest could grant absolution. By 1300, the pope had arrogated the right to dictate the nature of these satisfactions and to grant an indulgence—a certificate of absolution—to repentant sinners. In return, the recipient was expected to make a contribution to Church funds according to his means.

A final development concerned the concept of purgatory that, though not explicitly mentioned in the Bible, had evolved during the Middle Ages partly in answer to the problem of why one should pray for the dead. If the dead are in hell, no entreaty can redeem them; if in heaven, they hardly need our intercession. If there was an intermediate state, however, impure souls might there wash off the residue of earthly sins and thus qualify for heaven. Toward the end of the fifteenth century, Pope Sixtus IV, one of the less reputable pontiffs of the Renaissance period, succumbed to an urgent need for money and combined the two doctrines of penance and purgatory by issuing an indulgence whose purchasers were assured that their deceased loved ones would be immediately transferred from purgatory to heaven.

According to the preacher Johann Tetzel, those who purchased indulgences did not even need to be in a state of repentance for them to be effective. To make matters worse, a web of financial corruption surrounded Tetzel's sales drive, and it involved the very archbishop to whom Luther wrote his letter. Officially, Tetzel was engaged in raising funds for the rebuilding of Saint Peter's Basilica in Rome, an ambitious new edifice that would cover the site of the martyrdom of Saint Peter and contribute greatly to the glorification of the papacy. Tetzel, however, was also employed by

The spirit of intellectual and artistic adventure that emerged in Italy in the fourteenth century and became known as the Renaissance was grounded in an unwavering confidence in humankind's capabilities and essential goodness. In their keen pursuit of this humanistic ideal, scholars set about rediscovering and interpreting, sometimes after centuries of obscurity, the achievements of the great civilizations of ancient Rome and Greece.

The scholar who was chiefly responsible for introducing this new learning to northern Europe was Desiderius Erasmus, born in Holland around 1466. He wrote theological treatises, social criticism, and satire and made a pioneering Latin translation of the New Testament from the original Greek. His work provided ammunition for critics of the Church doctrines that had no scriptural authority.

Although Erasmus fiercely attacked philandering and corruption among the clergy, his dislike of violent reform made it impossible for him to give anything but qualified support to Martin Luther. He remained steadfastly loyal to the Church of Rome and wrote: "I laid a hen's egg; Luther hatched a bird of quite a different species."

engraving by the German master Albrecht ...er shows Erasmus writ... at his desk surrounded by books and flowers.

ceeds from the indulgences. Albert was in debt to the banking house of Fugg
10,000 ducats, money that he had borrowed to pay Leo for a dispensation allo
him to hold three bishoprics at once. In this way, the credulity of the faithful h
finance the greed of ambitious clergy and bankers alike.

Luther was probably unaware at the time of these financial ramifications, b
believed that indulgences were profoundly dangerous. Those who continued
because they felt secure from punishment, having purchased absolution, were
view being fatally misled by the Church. It was a question of life and death.

Even the indolent and pleasure-loving Pope Leo X—who is reported to have
on gaining the papal tiara, "God has given us the papacy; now let us enjoy it"-
forced into action when the archbishop of Mainz forwarded to him Luther's N
five Theses. It was first decided that Luther should be disciplined by his own
the Augustinians. He was summoned to a convention of the order, at whi
justification of the theses was widely supported. He was then instructed to tra
Rome, but wisely refused. Despite rumors that he was to be arrested, he did ag
meet a representative of the pope, Cardinal Cajetan, at Augsburg. The only re
this encounter, however, was that Cajetan's emphasis on the need to obey the p
in the matter of indulgences led Luther to question the entire basis of papal aut

By the time he returned to Wittenberg toward the end of 1518, Luther had be
in the eyes of the Church, a dangerous heretic who must be suppressed.
Frederick of Saxony he had a powerful protector, and while the pope maneu
Luther was granted crucial time in which to develop his ideas and gain supp

Frederick, the head of one of the largest states within the Holy Roman Empir
conventional religious views and took pride in a collection of 17,000 holy
These included a piece of Moses' burning bush, thirty-three fragments of th
cross, and even a vial of milk from the Virgin's breast. Although he probably c
share Luther's radical ideas, he was persuaded by his chaplain—a close fri
Luther's—that his bright young protégé should be given shelter in Saxony and n
to Rome for judgment. And when Maximilian I, the Holy Roman emperor, c
1519, Frederick's status as one of the seven secular and ecclesiastical rulers wh
the right to elect the new emperor made the pope reluctant to antagonize hi

Even after the election of Charles V later that year, Frederick remained ar
ential figure, under whose protection Luther was transformed from an obscure
er into a national celebrity. One event contributing to this process was a
disputation he undertook in Leipzig in 1519 against a professional debater, J
Eck. Such contests, which often went on for weeks, attracted large and voc
audiences. During the eighteen days of their debate, Eck managed to man
Luther into the damaging admission that he fully agreed with the views of Ja
a Czech preacher who had been condemned by the Church as a heretic and I
in 1415. In fact, Luther never considered himself a heretic, but rather a defer
the one true Church from which the papacy, not he, had deviated; and th
important difference between Eck and Luther was over the respective role
assigned to tradition and the Bible. The Catholic argument was always that, b
God watches over his people, any doctrine that had evolved over the centuri
had been accepted by the whole Church—such as the concept of indulge
could not be erroneous; otherwise God would have long since revealed the fra
Luther would have none of this sanctification of history and insisted on goin

to the Bible. He would take the word of a pope or a theologian only when it agreed with the Scripture. Inevitably, the debate was inconclusive.

In 1520, Luther published twenty-four books and pamphlets. In "The Address to the German Nobility"—written not in Latin, the language of the Church, but in German, so as to reach a wide audience—he demanded that a general council of the Church be convened to examine papal abuses. At the same time, he denied that there existed a privileged sphere of religious activity reserved exclusively for the clergy, and he appealed to his compatriots to institute ecclesiastical reforms. His arguments were based upon "the priesthood of all believers," one of the most revolutionary of all his ideas. "If a little company of pious Christian laymen were taken prisoners and carried away to a desert," he wrote, "and had not among them a priest consecrated by a bishop, and were there to agree to elect one of them, born in wedlock or not, and were to order him to baptize, to celebrate the Mass, to absolve, and to preach, this man would as truly be a priest as if all the bishops and all the popes had consecrated him." Luther concluded that this "would not be possible if we were not all priests."

In the same tract, Luther attacked the greed of the papacy, which he referred to as "the greatest thief and robber that has appeared or can appear on earth," and he demanded the abolition of indulgences and of pilgrimages to Rome. He proposed that clergy be allowed to marry: "It is not every priest that can do without a woman, not only on account of human frailty but still more for his household." And he called for an end to religious holidays and saints' days, customarily celebrated with great processions and merrymaking: "With our present abuses of drinking, gambling, idling, and all manner of sin, we vex God more on holy days than on others," wrote Luther, noting also that such intemperance left the commonfolk "unfit for labor."

Even more significant theologically was a work called "The Babylonian Captivity of the Church," whose title linked the pope's rule of the Church with the enslavement of the Israelites described in the Old Testament. It was written in Latin and intended for academics. In it Luther argued that the papacy had perverted Christianity with beliefs and practices that were man-made rather than springing from the Word of God. He attacked, in particular, the Church's seven sacraments—such religious ceremonies as marriage, ordination, and extreme unction for the dying, which could be performed only by priests and which supposedly transmitted spiritual power. Four out of the seven he rejected on the grounds that they were nowhere mentioned in the New Testament. This left baptism, the Mass, and penance. (Within a year he was to reject penance also.) Again Luther was calling into question the whole concept of tradition, the idea that God would not lead the Church into error.

To his opponents, Luther's most outrageous comments were on the Mass. He was angered by the way the Church used the words of the ancient Greek philosopher Aristotle to express the doctrine of transubstantiation. Aristotle had said that all things have both an "essence" and "accidents." The former makes a thing what it is; the latter consists of sensory qualities available to our experience. According to the Church, during the Mass, the accidents of the bread—its taste, texture, and appearance—remain what they have always been, but its essence changes to the Body of Christ when the priest makes his dedication. Luther saw these philosophical terms as a papal conspiracy to enslave Christians to idolatry, the worship of bread. In fact, Luther's alternative doctrine—which denied that the priest's words brought about any change in substance, while asserting that the Body of Christ was present in the administration of the Sacrament—seemed to many to be equally abstract. Far more

important to most of his followers were two basic changes that he later sanctioned in the Mass: permitting the laity to partake of the wine as well as the bread, and substituting German for Latin as the language in which the service was conducted.

To the delight and profit of many printers, thousands of copies of these and other works of Luther's pen circulated freely in different parts of Germany. Censorship of the press existed but could be applied only locally. In England or Spain, ruled by relatively strong central governments, Luther's works reached a limited audience, but in Germany, a book suppressed in one area would soon appear in another, often a remote town where the printer happened to be on good terms with the magistrates. Month by month, Luther's reputation as a fearless and outspoken rebel increased.

Germany's low rate of literacy—possibly no more than five percent of the population in the 1520s could read, and these people mostly lived in the towns—proved no bar to the spread of Luther's ideas. Reading aloud to a group was a common activity, and many Germans encountered Luther through sermons or informal discussions in taverns and bathhouses or at their dinner tables. In addition, the art of printing pictures, perhaps with a few lines of text, all carved from the same wooden block, had reached its zenith by the early sixteenth century; and pictorial images, often based on traditional symbols and readily understood allusions, could reach a far wider audience than the printed book. A woodcut could yield up to 4,000 copies before starting to deteriorate, as compared with the average book edition of 1,000.

The woodcut, together with the printed book, enabled Luther and his followers to initiate a campaign of mass propaganda. Luther had a clear understanding of the possibilities of both media: Though familiar with the elite culture of the theologians and able to put over a sophisticated point in Latin, he also understood the German people, their language and idiom, and the earthy metaphors and illustrations that would appeal to them. In all, Luther was to publish more than 3,000 separate works.

One limitation of the woodcut was its simplicity: It was hardly possible to transmit a complex theological message using only crude pictures and brief captions. Woodcuts tended to reduce all argument to a straightforward confrontation between good and bad—between devils and saints, or ravening wolves and faithful sheep. But this characteristic was not unsuited to Luther's own cast of mind. He held a dualistic view of the universe as an arena of perpetual struggle between good and evil forces, with human souls as the prizes. By about 1520, he had come to believe that the pope was in fact the Antichrist, and in his denunciations of his opponents, he took delight in using all the violent or scatological imagery that his fertile mind could command.

The swelling tide of inflammatory tracts convinced Pope Leo that proceedings against Luther could be delayed no longer. In June 1520, he issued a bull of excommunication that listed Luther's heresies and gave him sixty days in which to recant. But the legates entrusted with the task of publishing the bull in various German cities met with considerable opposition. At Mainz, where Luther's books were to be burned in the main square by the public executioner, this official turned to the crowd before applying his torch and asked whether the books had been justly condemned. With one voice they roared back, "No!," whereupon he refused to act. In Wittenberg, Luther turned the tables on Rome and revealed his talent for drama by organizing the public burning of the bull itself, along with various works of scholastic theology.

After the expiry of the sixty days, another bull was issued. This enforced the excommunication, the final weapon of the Church, cutting off the guilty party from all Christian society. Luther probably had enough popular support to withstand this

German reformers, among them Martin Luther *(far left)* and Phillipp Melanchthon *(near left),* shelter behind the formidable bulk of John Frederick I, elector of Saxony, in a group portrait painted in the early 1540s by Lucas Cranach the Younger. The son of Frederick of Saxony, who had obstructed the attempts of both the pope and the Holy Roman emperor to silence Martin Luther, John Frederick took a personal interest in the reformers' efforts to improve standards among both clergy and laity through preaching, catechism, and scholarship. But in 1547, the year after Luther's death, he was defeated by Charles V, imprisoned, and deprived of his titles.

papal blast, but he now also had to defend himself against the Holy Roman emperor, Charles V, who announced that he would judge the dispute at a diet—an assembly of representatives from every part of the empire—to be held in the city of Worms on the Rhine River. Although the recently crowned Charles was interested in reform, he ruled Spain and much of Italy, the heartlands of the Catholic church; this fact made opposition to the pope unthinkable and his verdict inevitable. Any doubts on the issue were removed when Charles, while traveling through the Netherlands on his way to Germany, made Lutheran heresy a capital offense.

The only good news for Luther in this time of crisis came in the form of a letter sent by Erasmus to Frederick of Saxony, urging him to maintain his support. The case against Luther, Erasmus asserted, was evil, based upon "the hatred of letters and the desire for supremacy." Despite his reservations concerning what he saw as Luther's impetuous haste to impose reforms, Erasmus was adamant that right was on his side: "The world thirsts for the gospel truth, and it seems to be carried in this direction by a longing ordained, as it were, by fate."

The Church originally hoped that the diet would condemn Luther without a hearing, but Charles insisted that justice must be seen to be done. Accordingly, Luther was granted a safe passage to Worms, and in April 1521, he appeared before an assembly of about 150 princes, councilors, and delegates from all parts of the empire. It was an intimidating audience, but Luther was imbued with a deep confidence in his cause. The disparity in power between him, a miner's son, and Emperor Charles V, ruler of vaster domains than anyone since Charlemagne, was canceled out by his belief that they were both equal—because equally sinful—in God's eyes. Truth was not the property of any historical institution, be it papacy or empire.

In the city's great torchlit hall, Luther was confronted with all his books and was asked just two questions: Were these works his, and if so, was he prepared to abandon the views expressed in them? He asked permission to consider his reply overnight. The next morning he answered yes to the first question. To the second, after speaking about the nature of his books, he replied:

> *Since your serene Majesty and your lordships request a simple answer, I shall give it, with no strings and no catches. Unless I am convicted by the*

Christ preaches to ordinary people in the countryside (*above*) while the pope (*right*), identified here as the Antichrist, prepares to don a triple tiara for lavish entertainment at his court. A Protestant vision of the true Church set against images of the dissolute papacy, these woodcuts were included, at Luther's suggestion, in a sixteenth-century Protestant passional, a devotional work for meditation on the life of Christ.

## The Battle of the Books

To win the hearts and minds of the largely illiterate German people, Protestant propagandists coupled their war of words with an onslaught of satirical illustrations that depicted the Church of Rome and its leaders as thoroughly corrupt and, in many cases, even satanic or monstrous.

Thanks to the introduction of the movable-type printing press, books could be mass-produced quickly and cheaply. Reducing complex theological arguments to a straightforward battle between good and evil, the vivid woodcuts such books contained hammered home the revolutionary sentiments expressed in their texts.

*testimony of Scripture or plain reason (for I believe neither in pope nor councils alone, since it is agreed they have often erred and contradicted themselves), I am bound by the Scriptures I have quoted, and my conscience is captive to the Word of God. I neither can nor will revoke anything, for it is neither safe nor honest to act against one's conscience. Amen.*

The earliest printed version of his speech ended, "Here I stand, I can do no other." After such defiance, the verdict was certain. The Edict of Worms placed Luther under the ban of the empire, a sentence that denied him all civil and legal rights.

But before the edict could be published, Luther had gone into hiding. Although he had been granted a safe-conduct to return to Wittenberg, his protector Frederick of Saxony feared for his safety and, not willing to be seen to support him openly, arranged an ambush. In the middle of a forest, Luther and his companions were set upon by armed men and taken to the remote castle of Wartburg outside the town of Eisenach. Here he remained concealed for nearly a year. He grew his beard and hair, wore the clothes of a knight, and adopted a pseudonym. The letters he wrote during this period reveal that he suffered greatly at times from depression and also from constipation and piles, because of the unaccustomed rich diet. However, he put his

Human souls, crammed into a barrel by a mallet-wielding demon, are carted off to hell in a wagon fashioned from the body of the pope; bishops, cardinals, and monks make up the spokes of the wheels. This German or Dutch drawing gives garish form to the Protestant view of the papacy as a vehicle of the devil.

enforced inactivity to good use. He wrote a number of pamphlets and, in the final weeks of his stay, turned to what was perhaps the greatest achievement of his life, the translation of the Bible into German.

Luther's German version of the New Testament, rendered from the Greek, was published in 1522; the Old Testament took much longer, because of other demands on his time, but was completed in 1534. The dissemination of Luther's Bible was to make the Saxon dialect in which it was written the standard language for all Germany. For his New Testament translation he had few books on hand and no other scholars in the vicinity to consult, but he made every effort possible to employ a rich and accurate vocabulary. When researching the exact German words for the biblical names of parts of animals used in sacrifices, for example, he took the trouble to visit a slaughterhouse to learn the precise terms employed there.

Luther was fully aware that even to attempt to translate the Bible was to risk his life. The only version of the Scriptures recognized by the Church was the Latin Vulgate, translated by Saint Jerome in the fourth century, and many had met death for producing or even owning unauthorized editions. But Luther also knew that he was no longer alone. If, during the years following the publication of the Ninety-five Theses, the pope had been more determined in his opposition or Frederick of Saxony more hesitant in his support, Luther's voice could have quickly been silenced. But he had survived this critical period, and he spoke now as one of a whole chorus of reformers.

The timing of Luther's protest against indulgences had been crucial. His call for ecclesiastical reform had coincided with a number of grievances and aspirations that were rising to the surface of German society, and his message proved open to interpretations that differed widely in their emphasis. The educated urban clergy supported Luther's condemnation of corruption within the Church. German nationalists, seeking political independence from the empire, found common cause with Luther's challenge to the authority of both emperor and pope. Political dissidents of many kinds saw in Lutheran ideas a means to bring about a more just society based upon Christian ideals. And Luther's advocacy of the virtues of discipline, hard work, and thrift—qualities that were to be given even greater emphasis in the decades to come—chimed neatly with the interests of a rising class of wealthy merchants whose capitalistic enterprise was transforming the traditional economic practices of Europe.

As a result, it became increasingly difficult to separate the purely religious focus of Luther's message from political, social, and economic issues; and while Luther remained in hiding, his ideas were being developed in ways he had not foreseen.

In 1521, a former Franciscan preacher named Johann Eberlin published a series of pamphlets in which Luther's criticisms of the Roman church were developed into a wide-ranging list of prescriptions for life in an ideal society. Priests were to be elected by their congregations and were to be allowed to practice "all honorable trades and occupations." Stiff penalties were laid down for immoral conduct: Adulterers were to be executed, chronic drunks drowned, and blasphemers publicly beaten. Eberlin also described in detail the new places of worship where Christians should gather:

> Churches are to be built wide and strong and without extravagance. They are to contain no precious stones nor any silver or gold save for the Eucharistic cup. . . . They are to have no liturgical vessels beyond what is necessary for two priests. A common tablecloth may be used for the altar, although its color may be altered. Within churches one may read, sing, and teach only what is written in the books of the Bible.

In Switzerland—then a confederation of states that, though nominally part of the Holy Roman Empire, was largely autonomous—Huldrych Zwingli, a preacher based in Zurich, carried out reforms far more rigorous than anything Luther had advocated. Obeying to the letter the second commandment—"Thou shalt not make unto thee any graven image"—he rid the town's churches of crucifixes, statuary, chalices, censers, and other ritual objects. He enjoyed the full support of the local authorities; and the pope, fearing that interference would be counterproductive, left him alone.

In Wittenberg, Luther's followers were acting with similar vigor under the direction of another lecturer at the university named Andreas Karlstadt. They destroyed pictures

Carrying a banner emblazoned with the symbol of their uprising, an unlaced boot, German farmers surround a captured knight during the Peasants' War of 1524-1525. Angered by their landlords' rapacity, thousands of peasants—like Luther rejecting papal rule—sought to throw off their feudal shackles. The bloody suppression of their ill-equipped armies ended the possibility of the Reformation's becoming a militant movement; thereafter, its successes were won by argument, discipline, and peaceful application of pressure on local authorities.

and statues in churches, abolished the Latin Mass, and encouraged the clergy to marry. Karlstadt himself threw away his priest's robes, married a young woman of fifteen, and administered Communion in the clothes of an ordinary citizen. There had also appeared in the city certain bearded strangers who called themselves Heavenly Prophets; these visitors came from the town of Zwickau, and their pastor, Thomas Münzer, interpreted the authority of the Bible according to the "inner light" that he claimed was vouchsafed directly by God to his chosen people.

In 1522, Luther returned to Wittenberg. He considered that the immediate threat to his safety had abated, and besides, he was anxious to restrain his more radical colleagues. Luther, though approving their aims, sought to moderate their means: "Christian love should not employ harshness here." But he was powerless to rein in Münzer or to limit the appeal of his fiery message to the peasantry. Convinced that the end of the world was imminent, Münzer insisted that change would come through revolution by the common people, whom he saw as God's instrument. He was chased out of a number of Saxon towns by alarmed magistrates, but in 1524, an opportunity arose for Münzer to put his beliefs into practice.

The Holy Roman emperor, Charles V *(far left),* discusses with the elector of Saxony a point of dispute in the Confession of Augsburg, a statement of Protestant creed offered by the reformers in 1530 in a last attempt at reconciliation with the Church of Rome. This document stressed the common ground between Lutheranism and the Roman Catholicism on basic principles of faith, but important differences remained concerning the rites known as the sacraments—some of which, such as baptism, Communion, marriage, and penance, are depicted in the background of this painting. The result was stalemate, and toward the end of the year, a military alliance of German princes was formed to defend Protestant worship.

In the summer of that year, bands of peasants in the southern region of the Black Forest took up arms against their landlords. One of the first local rebellions was provoked by the demand of a countess that the workers on her estates in Stühlingen collect strawberries for her table and snail shells on which to wind her embroidery silks when they were busily engaged in gathering in the harvest from their fields. The uprisings were spontaneous and uncoordinated, but by 1525, castles and monasteries were being plundered across the whole of southern Germany and Thomas Münzer had taken command of a peasant army in Thuringia. Several manifestoes were published listing the peasants' demands: Along with the abolition of certain taxes and feudal obligations, these included the right to choose their own pastors and other reforms that echoed the ideas of Luther and his colleagues.

Luther himself was horrified. He feared that the present and potential achievements of the reform movement were being squandered in anarchy. Ecclesiastical and not political or social change had always been his goal: He believed that human life was so short, and eternity so long, that there was no point in wasting time on issues of social engineering and justice. If God had placed some people in authority and made others peasants, then such was his will, and to oppose it was to do the Devil's work. While peasants fought and died against the professional armies of the princes, Luther wrote one of his most uncompromising tracts, "Against the Murdering, Thieving Hordes of Peasants." In this work, he fully endorsed the slaughter of the masses that was taking place: "So let anyone who can, strike, kill, or stab, secretly or openly, recalling that nothing can be more venomous, damaging, or demonic than a rebel."

The princes whose territories were being ravaged needed no such encouragement. Against their disciplined troops, the ill-equipped peasant armies quickly fell apart; some 100,000 rebels were killed, and many more were left homeless. Captured after the battle of Frankenhausen in May 1525, Münzer was tortured and executed.

The failure of the Peasants' War was a turning point for the Reformation. Mass support for radical leaders had vanished, and the progress of reform was now dependent on the cooperation of more-moderate leaders, local town councils, and the princes. During the rest of the 1520s, the caution that this situation induced in Luther's followers proved beneficial to their cause. Rejecting the use of coercion, they paced their demands to suit the time and place. Lutheran evangelists entering towns and cities across Germany preached obedience to the law as well as ecclesiastical reform, and they won over a steadily increasing number of citizens. Magistrates and councilors, mediating between the conservative princes and emperor and the increasingly reform-minded citizens, found themselves compelled to accede to popular demands and so further the transformation of Luther's ideas into actual practices.

The evangelists were particularly successful in the imperial cities, which boasted the highest concentration of those people—including educated clergy and wealthy merchants—who had most to gain from religious and political reform. As early as the spring of 1525, the councilors of Nuremberg, bowing to popular pressure, took action to expel Catholic preachers, assume control of all ecclesiastical appointments, and establish a training college for new ministers whose curriculum was supervised by Philipp Melanchthon, a close colleague of Luther's. Strasbourg, Ansbach, Hamburg, and other cities soon followed Nuremberg's example; and although in certain towns it took a decade or longer for reforms to be formally instituted, more than two-thirds of the imperial cities in Germany eventually adopted Lutheranism. After the death of Frederick of Saxony in 1525, his successors continued to support Luther; and the

# THE GENEVA EXPERIMENT

Beginning in the 1540s, the most dynamic and influential leader of the Reformation was John Calvin, a French preacher who established in the independent city of Geneva a regime that channeled all the energies of its subjects into the service of God. From there, evangelists traveled across Europe, and they even converted many Lutherans in Germany to the stricter discipline of Calvinism.

Calvin's church was administered by a hierarchy of teachers and pastors—responsible for defining and preaching correct doctrine—and elders and deacons, who en-

forced discipline and oversaw charitable works in the community. All aspects of civil life came under their control: They closed taverns, banned dancing, and published a list of proscribed Christian names.

Calvin himself, a dour but charismatic leader of great intellectual power and prodigious energy, preached as many as five sermons a week, ceaselessly revised the treatises in which he expounded his theology, and demanded the highest standards of morality from his followers. Those who defied his edicts faced excommunication, banishment, or death. Geneva became known as the Protestant Rome, the focus of an authority even more uncompromising than that of the papacy it opposed.

A French painting of 1564 shows a congregation in Lyons listening to the sermon of a Calvinist preacher.

reform movement was strengthened by the recruitment in 1526 of Philip of Hesse, the ruler of a large state adjoining Saxony, and in 1528, of Albert of Hohenzollern, ruler of the duchy of Prussia.

By 1529, when Charles V sent word to a diet convening at Speyer that the traditional forms of Catholic worship should be restored, six princes and fourteen cities were sufficiently committed to Lutheranism to issue a protest against this demand. They became known as the Protesting Estates, and the word "Protestant" was subsequently applied to anyone who left the Roman church. Meeting in the following year in the small town of Schmalkalden on the borders of Saxony and Hesse, the Lutheran princes and delegates from the cities formed the Schmalkaldic League and pledged: "Wherever any one of us is attacked on account of the Word of God and the doctrine of the Gospel, the others will immediately come to his assistance."

This growing political strength could never have come about had not Charles V been distracted by many other problems. During much of the 1520s, Charles was preoccupied with establishing his authority in Spain; he also had to fight off French incursions into his territories in Italy and repeated invasions by the Ottoman Turks, who were intent on expanding their empire both in the Mediterranean and in central Europe. Each time Charles attempted to subdue the rebellious German princes, he was interrupted by a renewed French or Ottoman attack. In 1529, when the Ottomans advanced as far as Vienna, Charles was eventually compelled to grant temporary toleration to the Lutheran princes in return for their military support.

Continually frustrated in his attempts to impose religious unity and obedience to the Church of Rome in the empire, Charles was helpless to prevent the reform movement from consolidating during the next two decades. In any case, the Reformation was now becoming an international phenomenon, with active centers far beyond Charles's sphere of influence. In England, Henry VIII rejected the authority of the pope—who refused to allow him to divorce Catherine of Aragon when she failed to bear him an heir—and in 1534 established the Anglican church. Sweden and Finland had adopted Lutheranism in 1527 and 1528, and in 1536, a Lutheran national church was established in Denmark also.

In the same year, a French theologian named John Calvin arrived in Geneva, where he was to preach a rigorous brand of reform whose influence was to be even more extensive than Lutheranism. Believing that nothing less than a complete restructuring of both church and society was necessary, Calvin developed a coherent set of doctrines to deal with all aspects of civil and ecclesiastical life. These precepts were stamped with the imprint of Calvin's own austere personality, and they bore witness to the jealous God of the Old Testament rather than the merciful God of the New Testament. Participation in worldly pleasures such as singing, dancing, or drinking was severely curtailed. Church officials were given the right to inspect all households at least once a year to check on backsliders; they were empowered to order members of the congregation to account for their actions and, if necessary, to excommunicate them. Only God's chosen people, Calvin preached, were assured of salvation, and these elect were distinguished as much by their deportment and Christian code of conduct as by their profession of faith.

Convinced that their church would be strengthened through discipline, the citizens of the independent republic of Geneva submitted to Calvin's strict regime; and from Geneva, a new generation of evangelists set out to spread the Calvinist message throughout Europe. The doctrines they preached—more radical than Lutheranism in

# TO THE GLORY OF GOD AND ROME

The colossal wealth accumulated by the Church of Rome through the levying of taxes, the receipt of gifts, and the sale of pardons enabled a succession of sixteenth-century popes to fulfill one of the highest aspirations of the Italian Renaissance: to make Rome a city whose splendor would surpass even that of its ancient past. Italy's greatest architects were commissioned to fill the city with new churches and monuments of an unprecedented grandeur, and the finest artists of the age—including Michelangelo, Raphael, and Titian—memorialized the popes with statues and paintings.

It was Michelangelo who most unremittingly found himself at the Vatican's beck and call. Born near Arezzo in 1475 and trained in Florence, he quickly established a reputation as a consummate sculptor. In 1505, Pope Julius II called Michelangelo to Rome to design and sculpt his own tomb.

Julius and his successors were fickle and ungrateful taskmasters, and although the project occupied Michelangelo on and off for forty years, it was never completed. In the meantime, Michelangelo painted the vast ceiling of the Vatican's Sistine Chapel and drew up plans for one of Rome's greatest monuments, Saint Peter's Basilica. By the time of his death in 1564, his work for both papal and secular patrons had made the versatile artist a legend in his own time.

Sculpted for the tomb of Pope Julius II, this muscular statue of Moses was based by Michelangelo on a passage in the Latin Vulgate Bible that referred to horns emanating from the prophet's head—a mistranslation of the light beams described in the original Hebrew text. None of the other thirty-nine life-size figures originally commissioned for the tomb were completed.

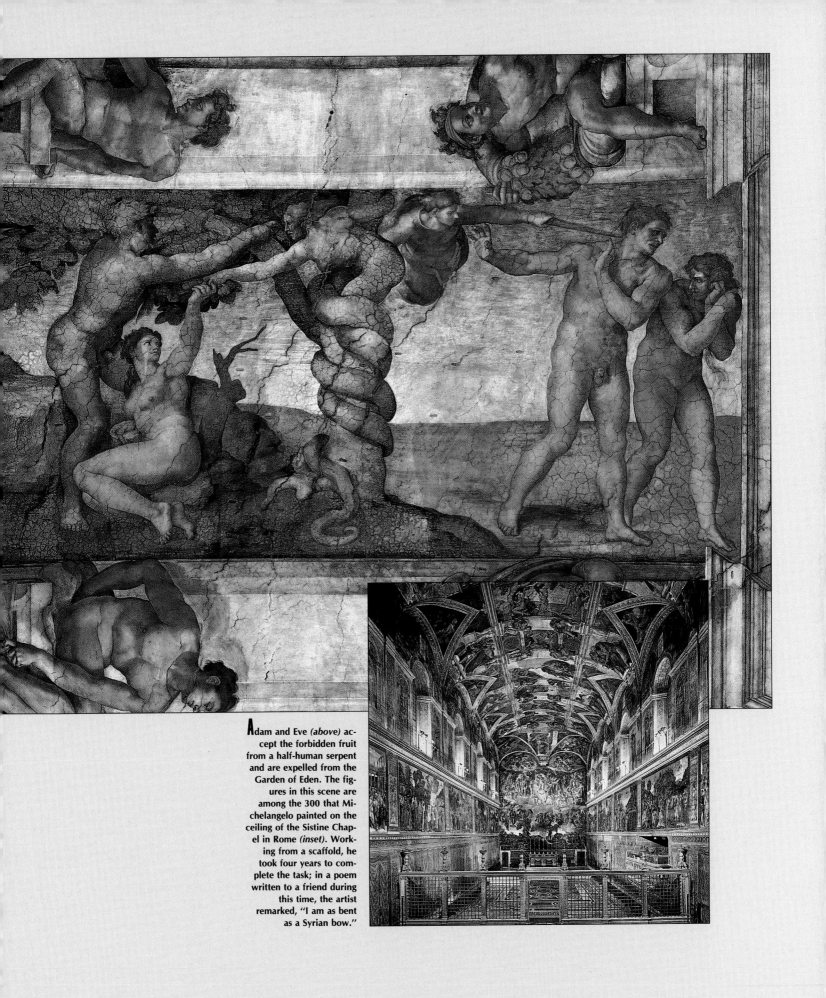

**A**dam and Eve *(above)* accept the forbidden fruit from a half-human serpent and are expelled from the Garden of Eden. The figures in this scene are among the 300 that Michelangelo painted on the ceiling of the Sistine Chapel in Rome *(inset)*. Working from a scaffold, he took four years to complete the task; in a poem written to a friend during this time, the artist remarked, "I am as bent as a Syrian bow."

their reordering of social as well as religious life, and less tied to nationalist political struggles—rapidly gained support in France, the Netherlands, and Scotland.

Luther, meanwhile, remained firmly at the helm of ecclesiastical reform in northern Germany and demonstrated in his own writings the increasingly authoritarian tendencies of the Reformation as it developed from a protest movement into an official religion. The violent rebellion of the German peasants in 1525 had seemed to Luther to show that ordinary people, left to themselves, could not be trusted to find their way to God. From that time onward, he put less emphasis on the need for all to read the

Bible and more on discipline and indoctrination—not least in his views on the family, which he regarded as central to Christian life.

Dismayed by a widespread ignorance of the most basic Christian doctrines, Luther composed catechisms to be used in homes and schools so that, through constant repetition, children might build a firm foundation in the faith. He urged fathers to instill in their children the habit of reciting the Ten Commandments, the Apostles' Creed, and the Lord's Prayer at mealtimes and upon rising and going to bed—"and unless they repeat them they should be given neither food nor drink." Only at an advanced stage could they then be allowed to study the Bible.

His attitude toward women was even more dogmatic, conditioned by a stern conviction that the duty of all women was to marry and bear children: "A woman does not have complete mastery over herself. God created her body that she should be with a man and bear and raise children." Nor was he sympathetic toward the dangers of pregnancy: "If women grow weary or even die while bearing children, that does no harm. Let them bear children to death, that's what they're there for." The general effect of Lutheran reforms was to narrow the choices that had previously been available to women: In states that adopted his creed, divorce became even harder for commoners to obtain than in Catholic principalities, and the suppression of nunneries denied the possibility of a celibate, religious vocation.

For all his strictures on women and children, however, Luther found great joy in his own marriage. He wed in 1525, the year marked by the mass slaughter of the rebellious peasant armies. His wife, Katharina von Bora, was one of nine nuns who had escaped from a convent. Luther had undertaken to find them husbands; when the last of the nine kept reminding him of his promise, Luther finally decided to marry her himself. She bore him six children, and in the two decades of their marriage, while the progress of the Reformation was being determined at the conference tables of Europe, Luther's domestic life became increasingly the center of his attention.

He continued to write, preach sermons, and teach new students at the University of Wittenberg. He continued especially to argue: not just with delegates of the Roman church but with allies or potential allies such as Erasmus and Zwingli. He exchanged angry letters with the former, and with the latter, he quarreled bitterly at a meeting arranged by Philip of Hesse in 1529 to affirm unity in the reform movement.

Two years later, Zwingli was killed in battle while defending Zurich against the forces of reaction in Switzerland. Erasmus died in 1536. Luther lived on into old age—a patriarchal figure in a household crowded with children, student lodgers, and visitors from abroad—an elder of a church that was still young. He was increasingly troubled by illness and by bouts of depression in which he wondered at his responsibility for the consequences of the movement he had initiated. He died of a heart attack on February 18, 1546.

Two months before Luther's death, a general council of the Roman church met at Trent, just north of the Italian border and within the Holy Roman Empire. Its purpose was to restore order and authority to the ministry, and its convocation was the culmination of an internal movement for reform that had been gathering pace since the end of the previous century, even before the outspoken criticisms of Luther.

The call for change had been especially strong in Spain—where in 1480, King Ferdinand and Queen Isabella had founded the Inquisition, a tribunal charged with rooting out heresy—and in Italy, where the accession of Pope Paul III in 1534 marked

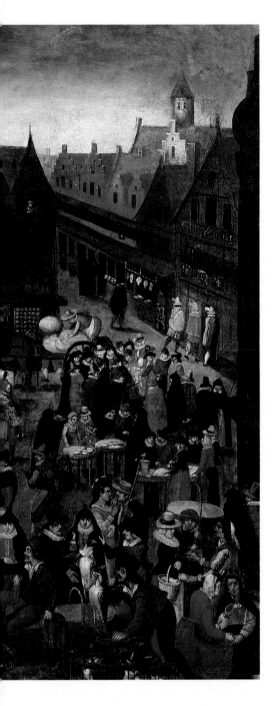

Bustling activity in the marketplace of Antwerp in the Netherlands reflects this port's emergence as the most important commercial center in Europe during the early sixteenth century. Profiting from new trade routes linking Spanish and Portuguese territories in the Americas to Europe, the city fathers adopted forward-looking and tolerant policies that opened up this cosmopolitan port to the most advanced intellectual as well as economic ideas of the age, allowing Lutheran evangelists to flourish side by side with capitalistic entrepreneurs.

In a detail from a Japanese screen, European merchants meet a party of Jesuit missionaries, Franciscan monks, and Japanese citizens. In the distance, a priest performs a Christian service for Japanese converts. The Society of Jesus was founded in 1540 by Ignatius Loyola, a Spanish soldier who, having been seriously injured in battle, transformed his military ardor into religious zeal. Together with ecclesiastical reforms initiated by the pope and his bishops, the Jesuit order helped bring about a grass-roots resurgence of the Roman church during the latter half of the sixteenth century. Jesuit missionaries, who received a rigorous and broad-based education, not only won converts in Asia, Africa, and the Americas but brought parts of Protestant Europe back within the fold of Roman Catholicism.

the beginning of vigorous new policies to combat the tide of the Reformation. In 1540, Pope Paul gave his blessing to the Society of Jesus, a militant group of priests dedicated to propagating the faith through education and missionary work. The bishops at Trent approached their task with similar determination, and between their first meeting and the final adjournment of the council in 1563, they succeeded in revitalizing the Roman church. They legislated against corruption, established training colleges for priests, and drew up an index of books forbidden to Catholics. And they reaffirmed almost every doctrine that Luther had attacked, reserving for the Church of Rome the exclusive right to interpret the Bible and command obedience.

In 1547, Emperor Charles V—briefly relieved of hostile pressure from both France and the Ottomans—roundly defeated the Protestant army of the Schmalkaldic League at Mühlberg in Saxony. But the victory came too late. By this stage, even those rulers

who had remained loyal to the Catholic church were unwilling to bow to the emperor's authority, and the Protestants rebuilt their military strength by making an alliance with the new king of France, Henry II. Renewed fighting forced Charles to accept the inevitable, and in 1555, he signed the Peace of Augsburg, which gave all secular German princes and independent cities the right to choose between Lutheranism and Catholicism. Subjects were to abide by their ruler's choice, although those who dissented were permitted to migrate to other territories.

Thus, where a prince so chose, his people could adopt Lutheranism without fear of reprisals. The Reformation in Germany had passed into law. However, in ending what they perceived to be the tyranny of Rome, the leaders of reform had found it necessary to impose a discipline that—in its restrictions on gambling, dancing, begging for alms, and other aspects of civil life—was even more enveloping. There were now two orthodoxies within Germany in place of one, a situation that inevitably gave rise to tensions between their respective followers.

In fact, the Peace of Augsburg was an expedient truce rather than a final settlement. The toleration it granted to Lutherans in Germany did not extend to Calvinists, Jews, or other minority groups. In the following decades, Calvinist gains and the success of the reformed Roman church in winning back many of its former adherents made the treaty increasingly out of date. Also, despite the growth of a national consciousness that had accompanied the Reformation, the treaty failed to resolve the disunity of the fragmented territories that made up the Holy Roman Empire; and early in the seventeenth century, renewed religious and political conflict was to lead to the Thirty Years' War, in which Germany was rent by both civil war and foreign invasions.

Outside Germany, the coexistence of Christian communities obedient to sharply opposed doctrines led to similar conflict. At the heart of most European states there was now a core of committed dissidents who placed loyalty to their church above loyalty to their country. Their demands were radical and nonnegotiable, for they did not seek toleration but a total religious change: They wished their faith to be the only one permitted in the land. To suppress these nonconformists, who were branded as heretics, governments resorted to extreme measures, including burnings at the stake.

In addition, the success of the Reformation altered the diplomatic balance. As some countries became Protestant and others remained Catholic, old alliances were broken and new bonds of common interest were forged between religious minorities and those adhering to the same faith in different countries. Until the passions unleashed by the Reformation began to die down in the late seventeenth century, every international conflict was, to some extent, also a religiously motivated civil war.

The conservative Luther would have been horrified by the subversion of the social order that followed in his wake. In Scotland, followers of the Calvinist preacher John Knox were to depose the Catholic Queen Mary so as to secure the triumph of the Presbyterian church. In the Netherlands, Protestant fervor combined with nationalist sentiment in a long and bloody revolt against the rule of Catholic Spain. In France, bitter feuds between Calvinist and Catholic political factions culminated in the Massacre of Saint Bartholomew's Day on August 24, 1572; on that day and in the following weeks, more than 10,000 Protestants were killed. This bloodshed left an enduring legacy of prejudice and suspicion. It is doubtful whether, when he wrote his theses against the sale of indulgences in 1517, the young Martin Luther realized how deeply his vision would touch the hearts of his fellow Christians. Certainly he could not have foreseen that the price of saving human souls would be so high.

# AN EMPEROR'S FADING DREAM

*"The name of king? o' God's name let it go.
I'll give my jewels for a set of beads,
My gorgeous palace for a hermitage."*

Spoken by the king in Shakespeare's play *Richard II*, first performed in 1595, these words echoed precisely the sentiments expressed by Charles V, Holy Roman emperor forty years earlier. In 1555 and 1556, he formally abdicated his title as ruler of domains in the Netherlands, Italy, and Spain and then retired to the remote monastery of Yuste among the wooded hills to the north of the Tagus valley in Spain.

Shakespeare's relentless examination of the nature of kingship throughout his history plays, and in particular his emphasis on the burdens placed upon a king's shoulders by the real and symbolic responsibilities associated with his status, reflected contemporary anxieties shared by rulers and subjects alike. In Europe in the sixteenth century, an array of religious, political, and economic problems placed new strains upon a system that focused all authority in the person of the king, the head of state. In his prime, Charles V ruled between one-half and one-third of Christian Europe, yet his struggles over forty years to impose order and unity on his extensive realm proved in the end to be utterly fruitless. The most prominent king in Europe, he was perhaps also the most severely tested, and his career demonstrated as clearly as any Shakespearean play the limitations of the supposedly absolute powers with which he was invested.

Charles's failure was all the more galling because, at the start of his career, no person had been better placed to succeed than he. He was born in 1500 in the Flemish city of Ghent into the family of the Hapsburgs, the Austrian sovereign dynasty that took its name from the castle, Habichtsburg (Hawk's Castle), built in 1020 on the Aare River in present-day Switzerland. His grandfather Maximilian was ruler of the Hapsburg hereditary lands on the fringes of

Germany and was also Holy Roman emperor, a position that gave its incumbent nominal authority over almost 1,000 semi-independent states in central Europe. To increase his family's holdings still more, Maximilian sought heiresses as wives for both himself and his son; thus, while still in his teens, Charles became ruler of the largest state in Europe. From his paternal grandmother he inherited part of Burgundy in eastern France and most of the Netherlands; from his maternal grandmother, Castile and Spanish territories in the Caribbean; from his maternal grandfather, Aragon, Sardinia, Sicily, and the southern half of Italy. The position of Holy Roman emperor was elective, not hereditary, and when Maximilian died in 1519, the most likely candidate to succeed him appeared to be Francis I of France. But Charles's ambitions were backed with a potent weapon—money. On the security of his royal revenues in Spain, Charles borrowed 800,000 florins, an enormous sum for the time, and with this money he simply bought the necessary votes. On October 23, 1520, he received the imperial crown.

As a result of bribery, the marriages engineered by his grandfather, and the opportune early deaths of rival claimants, Charles was now ruler of domains that stretched from Vienna to the Atlantic in a patchwork of kingdoms, counties, duchies, archbishoprics, electorates, and principalities. His lands, moreover, would soon include an expanding, gold-rich empire in the New World. In looks, personality, and training, he scarcely seemed equal to this awesome role. A small, spare youth, he had the jutting lower jaw that was characteristic of the Hapsburgs, and his habitually open mouth gave him a vacant expression. Educated in the company of selected nobles at the old-fashioned court of Ghent, he

Painted terra-cotta bust of Charles V at the age of seventeen

had always shown more interest in hunting and fencing than in book learning, and his gluttony and dislike of administrative duties were already well known. But in his arrogant belief in his right to rule, and his ambition to win glory and honor on the field of battle, Charles possessed the qualities that were most expected of a ruler in his time. In addition, he took to heart the words of one of his advisers: "Sire, God has granted you a most wonderful grace. . . . He has set you on the way toward a world monarchy, toward the gathering of all Christendom under a single shepherd."

This goal reflected the traditional status of the Holy Roman emperor as temporal ruler of the Christian nations of the Western world. The empire dated back to the eighth century, when Charlemagne, king of the Franks, had conquered most of the Christian lands of western Europe and had been invested by the pope with the imperial title. Since that time, despite a gradual loosening of the bonds of empire by the growth of local political interests, the concept of a united Christendom had survived as a compelling ideal; and in the early sixteenth century, its appeal was reinforced by the aggressive menace of the Ottoman Turks, who sought to advance their Muslim empire into the heart of Europe.

However, as Charles was about to discover, the idea of a commonwealth of nations linked by their adherence to a single cause no longer matched the actual constituency of the empire. Its many hundred separate political units varied widely in their interests and the degree of autonomy

they had gained. Equally, the several other parts of Europe that Charles ruled did not regard themselves, and could not be governed, as provinces of a single state. The very fact that Charles enjoyed many titles—duke of Burgundy, count of Flanders, archduke of Austria, king of Castile and Aragon, as well as a host of other appellations that took up several paragraphs in the prefaces to state documents, indicated that he was bound to observe the different customs and political traditions of his miscellaneous heritage.

The government of Charles's widespread domains was also complicated by basic administrative problems. Chief among these was money: There was no uniform system of taxation, and territories in one part of the empire became ever more reluctant to bear the financial burden for wars fought in another part. Also, vast distances separated the capital of Spain from the Netherlands and from Naples in southern Italy: During the two or three weeks taken by a mounted or ship-borne courier to deliver the emperor's commands, their relevance to events could easily be lost.

The one obligation recognized by all Charles's subject lands was their duty to defend their sovereign or his territory against direct attack. For this reason, Charles was bound to contend that all his wars were defensive actions against an external aggressor. In the case of his campaigns against successive Ottoman invasions of Europe and advances in the Mediterranean, this was indeed the case. But in Charles's other wars, the issues were

Hammered-steel shield of Charles V

not so clear-cut, nor was Charles's claim to be the champion of Western Christendom unchallenged. Francis I of France, surrounded on three sides by Hapsburg territories, found it expedient to argue that he, not Charles, was the foremost Christian ruler of Europe. And from the very beginning of Charles's reign, opposition to the authority of both himself and the Church of Rome was steadily increasing in the German lands of the Holy Roman Empire.

Faced with three implacable enemies—the Ottomans, the French, and the rebellious German princes who espoused the cause of the Protestant Reformation—Charles found himself committed to a cycle of warfare and diplomacy that lasted throughout his reign. His personal bravery in battle was never in doubt, and his energy and determination were evident in his ceaseless travels from one part of the empire to another and his fluent mastery of the German, French, Spanish, and Dutch languages. But whenever he appeared to be on the point of decisively overwhelming one of his foes, another would attack, and so allow the first to recover. For example, on one occasion, he was about to enforce obedience to the Roman church on the German princes when the French opened hostilities, and so, in his own words, Charles "rather did what he could than what he wished and had resolved to do."

Despite his respect for the sincerity of the criticisms of the Roman church voiced by Martin Luther and other leaders of the Reformation, Charles remained determined to preserve religious unity. But his relations with the papacy were troubled: In 1527, Rome was pillaged by German troops in Italy whose pay was in arrears, and Charles's various attempts to reach a theological compromise with the Protestants were not approved. When he proposed a general council of the Church to discuss such matters, he was informed that "the pope and the cardinals would sooner see this council in hell than on earth."

Throughout the 1530s and 1540s, the pattern of hasty alliances, a campaign, a brief peace, a fresh Ottoman advance, and renewed French threats was constantly repeated. At one point, Charles challenged the French king to personal combat, "without armor but with sword and dagger, on land or sea, on a bridge or an island, in private or with our two armies present." This gesture, spurned by Francis, typified Charles's chivalric attitudes; it probably also reflected his growing concern at the cost of endless warfare.

By the beginning of the 1550s, the resources of Charles's empire were seriously depleted. All of his states faced bankruptcy, and even the gold revenues from the Spanish territories in America were mortgaged for years to come. In 1552, the Ottomans struck at Spanish possessions in the Mediterranean, the French invaded Germany, and the German princes mobilized against their emperor yet again. Charles himself was becoming both physically and mentally incapable of governing. Besides frequently being confined to bed by recurrent attacks of gout, he may have been diabetic; he also suffered from acute depression, and a

Two-headed eagle of the Holy Roman emperor and arms of Charles V

Spanish diplomat reported that he was "constantly sunk in thought, and often he will weep so hard and with such copious shedding of tears, he resembles a child." The emperor briefly roused himself to counter the French, and he brought about a temporary peace in Germany by granting formal toleration to the Protestant princes; but then, with relief, he made over the Hapsburg domains in Spain, the Netherlands, and Italy to his son, Philip, and in 1555, he announced his abdication. "I realize," he explained, "that I can no longer undertake the tasks I ought to do both to satisfy my conscience and to secure the common good of my subjects and vassals."

Living as a pampered invalid in the monastery at Yuste, Charles spent much of his time attending church, fishing out of a window of his rooms into the pond beneath, and eating. Orders for melons, trout, potted fish, and other delicacies of the table were regularly dispatched, and Charles even obtained a dispensation from the pope that allowed him to enjoy breakfast before early communion. However, like Shakespeare's King Lear, who also sought to relinquish his sovereign responsibilities but not his authority, Charles remained actively in touch with the outside world: He retained the title of emperor, at least in part because the Germans did not want Philip as his successor, and he sent regular letters to his son on matters of state policy.

"Exterminate heresy lest it take root and overturn the state and social order" was Charles's most frequent advice; but by the time of his death from malaria on September 21, 1558, it was too late for such a policy to be effective. The chance of uniting all Europe under Hapsburg hegemony had passed, and there would never be another. The Hapsburg lands were ridden with debt and dissent, their stability now threatened as much by internal chaos as by foreign invasion. Moreover, even as an ideal, the concept of the Holy Roman Empire as a bulwark of Western Christendom no longer existed: Religious unity had been shattered by the Reformation, and political divisions had been aggravated rather than healed by the formal recognition of Protestant states alongside those still adhering to the Church of Rome.

Charles's abdication was perhaps an implicit acknowledgment of the impossibility of his role. The loss of authority suffered during his reign by both the Holy Roman Empire and the papacy, the chief political and religious institutions of Europe, was in fact caused more by the emergent strength of the forces ranged against them than by the failings of individual rulers. During this period, a mold cast in the Middle Ages was irretrievably broken.

In the course of the next century, the old order would be replaced by powerful national monarchies capable of controlling the problems they faced. These newly vigorous states would prove fertile seedbeds for scientific experiment and adventure, and for a spirit of endeavor that would extend European influence across the whole of the continent of North America. Although Charles was not to know it, far more would be gained than had been lost.

# THE CONQUEST OF THE NEW WORLD

2

The native populations of both Mexico and Peru possessed a legend concerning a wise god who had once ruled their land, who had vanished mysteriously, and who would return. Though similar in outline, the myths of the two peoples differed in detail. The Aztecs of Mexico, who divided their calendar into cycles of fifty-two years, believed that their god, Quetzalcoatl—portrayed as both a plumed serpent and a white-skinned, bearded man—would arrive from the east during the twelfth year of a cycle. Among the Incas of Peru it was prophesied that the deity Viracocha would come back from the west during the reign of their twelfth emperor, or Inca.

And in the early decades of the sixteenth century, the peoples of Mexico and Peru had good reason to believe that these prophecies were being fulfilled. In 1519, the twelfth year of an Aztec cycle, white-skinned men with beards landed on the eastern coast of Mexico. Twelve years later, during the reign of the twelfth Inca, seaborne strangers landed on the Pacific shores of Peru. But the visitors were no gods. They were Spanish adventurers known as conquistadors—literally, "conquerors"—and they had come not to lead the Aztecs and the Incas into a new golden age, but to take from them the precious metals in which their territories abounded. Within two years of each of these landings, the native emperors, the Aztec Montezuma and the Inca Atahualpa, whose densely populated dominions were capable of mustering tens of thousands of warriors, had been overthrown and captured by the Spanish commanders Hernán Cortés and Francisco Pizarro, who measured the strength of their own contingents in the hundreds.

In the years that followed, carracks sailed eastward laden with gold and silver for the treasury of the Spanish kingdom and returned with more conquerors. Some Spaniards settled, built cities, and mined precious metals in the lands they had taken from the Aztecs and Incas. Others, displaying reckless courage in the pursuit of wealth and glory, expanded their conquests in regions with less developed civilizations. The pioneers' endeavors made Spain the richest and most powerful nation in Europe for a century. In the process, the newcomers wrested control of the future of the North and South American continents.

Cortés and Pizarro, the founding fathers of Spain's American empire, came from the harsh pastureland of the Extremadura region of western Spain. They were both the sons of hidalgos—members of the minor gentry—although Pizarro was illegitimate. They grew up in a society that believed the only proper occupation for a gentleman, or indeed for any man who wanted to better himself, was war. Since the eighth century, generations of Spanish soldiers had fought against the Muslim Moors occupying the south of their country, and many of them had grown rich in the process. The Church had blessed them as crusaders, and the king, as long as he was given

The deathly stillness of this masklike face of Quetzalcoatl, legendary ancestor of the Aztec emperors of Mexico, presages the fate of the people who claimed him as their god. The Aztecs' belief that the leader of a Spanish invasion force in 1519 was a reincarnation of Quetzalcoatl sapped their will to resist; within two years, their armies were defeated and their culture in ruins. In the following decade, the Incas of Peru were overwhelmed as well; before the century was out, the enormous wealth of these American civilizations had been transferred to the Spanish treasury.

From their island bases in the Caribbean, colonized in the last decade of the fifteenth century, Spanish adventurers set sail to conquer an empire in Central and South America. Hernán Cortés—depicted here on a medal minted in 1529 *(inset, right)*—seized the Aztec capital of Tenochtitlán in 1521; in the 1530s, the Inca empire in Peru was subdued by Francisco Pizarro *(inset, below)*. The rule of Spanish viceroys over the territories of New Spain and New Castile determined the pattern of their development for centuries to come.

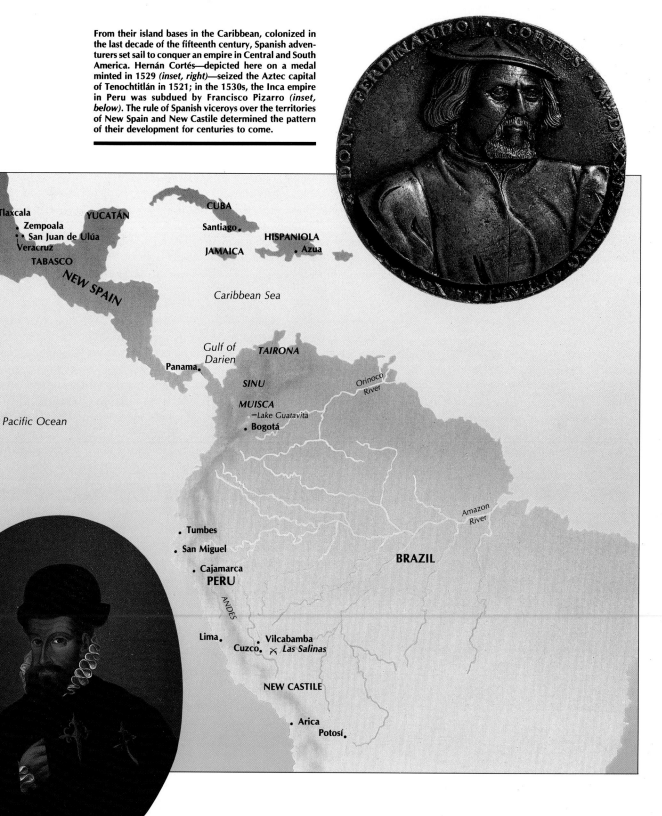

**38**

one-fifth of their booty, acknowledged their right to the rest. When they captured farms and villages, he divided the land into lots, known as *repartimientos,* and distributed them among the captors.

From the beginning of the fourteenth century, when the Moors had been driven from all of Spain except for the southern kingdom of Granada, Spanish soldiers served in north Africa or Italy, where the rewards were fewer. But in 1492, the same year in which Granada finally succumbed, the Genoese captain Christopher Columbus discovered the islands of the Caribbean and, by claiming them for the Spanish crown, made them the objective for a new generation of professional conquerors.

Pope Alexander VI, himself a Spaniard, sanctioned the conquest of the newly discovered lands on condition that the inhabitants be converted to the Catholic faith. Columbus returned to the Caribbean with shiploads of settlers to establish colonies on the island of Hispaniola (now divided into Haiti and the Dominican Republic); other settlers followed him, excited by the crude gold objects he had brought back from his first journey. From Hispaniola, they spread out to found colonies on the other islands and on the mainland in Panama. They conquered and settled in the name of God and in the service of Charles V, Holy Roman emperor as well as the king of Spain, but at the same time they realized that they were also acting in their own best interests. "The king's fifth" was a small price to pay for legitimate title to what they hoped would be fabulous wealth.

The repartimientos granted to settlers in the New World by the governors of the new territories included allocations of native Indians. The avowed purpose of this system was to provide the native peoples, who were officially regarded as Spanish subjects, with some form of feudal protection: In return for the Indians' labor, the settlers were responsible for their welfare and religious instruction. In practice, however, the Spanish masters generally used the Indians as forced labor.

Cortés and Pizarro were among those who sailed to Hispaniola at the beginning of the sixteenth century. Cortés was described by Bernal Díaz del Castillo, who was to serve with him in Mexico and write an account of the expedition, as tall and strong; Díaz added, perhaps alluding to the reputation Cortés had acquired as a womanizer, "had his face been longer he would have been handsomer, and his eyes had a somewhat loving glance yet grave withal." He sailed from Spain in 1504, and on his arrival in Hispaniola he was given a repartimiento of Indians. Seven years later, Cortés took part in the conquest and settlement of Cuba and built up a fortune in mines and ranches. He became one of the leading citizens of the capital—at that time Santiago de Baracoa—which twice elected him its mayor. But civic dignity did nothing to quell his adventurous spirit. He was twice arrested for breach of promise and twice managed to escape; and having compromised one of the few wellborn ladies on the island, he was left with no honorable choice but to marry her.

Then, in 1519, the thirty-four-year-old Cortés was appointed by the governor of Cuba, Diego Velázquez de Cuéllar, to lead an expedition to the part of the mainland known to the Spaniards as Mexico. Two earlier expeditions had returned from the Yucatán peninsula with ominous reports of organized armies and hideous human sacrifices; but they had also brought back sufficient quantities of gold ornaments to prove that there was more gold on the mainland than on any of the islands.

Velázquez provided only one ship, but Cortés mortgaged everything he owned to buy three additional vessels, and other captains provided him with more. When Velázquez saw the enthusiasm with which men rallied to Cortés's newly embroi-

The Aztecs' lack of coinage and a written language proved no bar to their development of a sophisticated and efficient administration. This page from an Aztec painted manuscript lists the tribute that subject cities—identified by the symbols on the left—were required to pay to Montezuma, the emperor, twice a year. The items specified by pictorial symbols include cotton blankets, warriors' costumes, shields, strings of jade beads, gold ornaments, and bunches of precious feathers.

The Spanish commentary accompanying the pictographs was inscribed by a priest who spoke Nahuatl, the Aztec language, on the instruction of Antonio de Mendoza, appointed in 1535 as the first viceroy of New Spain. The tribute roll was part of a manuscript commissioned by Mendoza to provide the king of Spain with information about his new subjects; also included were a copy of an ancient history of Aztec rulers and a description of the customs and daily life of the Aztec people. But at the time this culture was so meticulously recorded, it was already doomed. The Aztec political institutions were destroyed by the Spanish conquest, and the population rapidly declined. Mendoza himself established a mint to introduce metal currency and imported printing presses and paper from Spain.

# AN AZTEC ENCYCLOPEDIA

dered standard, he began to fear that his commander was too independent a spirit to remain loyal. By the time he took action to bring his subordinate to heel, however, it was too late. The lieutenant who was ordered to arrest Cortés reported that he had too many soldiers to be challenged. On February 10, 1519, Cortés set sail with eleven ships. Apart from their crews, a few African slaves, and about 200 Indians, some of whom were women, he had seven small cannon, sixteen horses, and 508 soldiers. Thirty-two of these were armed with crossbows and thirteen with harquebuses; the rest had only their swords.

The little army landed near the mouth of the Tabasco River on March 13, only to be opposed by thousands of warriors carrying wicker shields and armed with slings, bows, javelins, and large stone-bladed swords. It was an awesome sight, but by the end of the day the field was littered with the bodies of native troops, at the cost of just two Spanish lives, and the Spaniards had learned an encouraging lesson. The wooden tips of the arrows fired by the Tabascans and their stone blades were no match for steel tips, swords, and armor. On open ground, the tight-packed ranks of Tabascan warriors were horrifyingly vulnerable to the impact of shot from the Spanish cannon and charges from the tiny troop of cavalry. Despite their courage, each group of Tabascans fell back as soon as its leader was killed or wounded; and also, surprisingly, they seemed to be more interested in capturing their opponents than killing them. It was only later that the Spaniards discovered why: The cult of human sacrifice practiced by the native peoples in their religious ceremonies had created an insatiable demand for living victims.

Cortés followed up his victory with an offer of reconciliation. Using as his interpreter a Spanish man named Aguilar, a survivor from an earlier expedition who had learned to speak the local language, he invited the Tabascan chiefs to assemble outside his tent. To demonstrate his strength, he ordered a cannon to be fired: "It went off with such a thunderclap as was wanted," reported Díaz, "and the ball went buzzing over the hills, and as it was midday and very still it made a great noise, and the Indians were terrified on hearing it." He also placed a stallion in front of the Tabascans and, unknown to them, a mare behind them: "The horse began to paw the ground and neigh and become wild with excitement," Díaz continued, "looking all the time toward the Indians and the place whence the scent of the mare had reached him, and the Indians thought he was roaring at them." Cortés then told the Tabascans that they were now subjects of the king of Spain, and ordered them to aban-

A statuette carved from jadeite represents one of the several hundred Aztec rabbit gods, which were associated with luck, fertility, and drunkenness. These minor deities belonged to a complex pantheon that included the gods of peoples conquered by the Aztecs during their rise to preeminence in Mexico.

don their religion. The next day, after an exposition of Christianity, the priests who accompanied the expedition celebrated Mass in the middle of the Tabascan town. In return, as tokens of their submission, the Tabascans presented the Spaniards with food, gold ornaments, and twenty young women. Since the conquistadors had sworn not to cohabit with heathens, the women were baptized before being distributed among the captains.

One of the women was an Aztec of noble birth who had been sold into slavery by her mother as a child. Apart from Tabascan, she spoke Nahuatl, the language of the Aztecs, and she was to become one of the most valuable members of Cortés's entourage. She was described by Díaz as "good-looking and intelligent and without embarrassment." Respected by the Spaniards as Doña Marina, she became Cortés's mistress and one of his closest advisers, and after a while she bore him a son.

From Tabasco, Cortés sailed for four days along the coast to a place later known as San Juan de Ulúa. He had now entered the empire of the Aztecs, who little more than 100 years earlier had established a fortified base on an island in Lake Texcoco, from where they had spread their dominion over almost all the peoples between the oceans. Absorbing the cultures of earlier civilizations, they had evolved complex legal and administrative systems, and had developed outstanding skills as architects, stonemasons, and craftsmen. But although their island capital, Tenochtitlán, was supported by a flourishing agriculture, the Aztecs had remained essentially a military people. Warfare was regarded as a sacred ritual, the earthly equivalent of the constant heavenly struggle between the sun and the moon and stars, and the source of the human blood that sustained the sun god. Every day in the Aztec temples, prisoners

A manuscript illustration shows Cortés returning to the Aztec capital after forcing the surrender of an expedition sent from Cuba in 1520 to arrest him. The baggage of the helmeted conquistadors is carried by porters recruited from subject peoples of the Aztecs, now allies of the Spaniards. Near the front of the column, behind Cortés and his Aztec mistress, Doña Marina, marches a black African slave; in the years that followed, the smallpox virus said to have been introduced to Mexico by this slave was to kill off a large proportion of the Aztec population.

of war and young men and women from vassal peoples were sacrificed to ensure that the sun would rise again.

Cortés learned about the Aztec empire from ambassadors dispatched to San Juan de Ulúa by the Aztec ruler Montezuma, and he also learned by implication that the emperor was apprehensive. The ambassadors brought with them extravagant gifts—gold and silver crests with feathered plumes, beautifully wrought golden animals, an embossed golden sun the size of a cartwheel—but they also passed on Montezuma's instruction that Cortés should not visit his capital.

In fact, the news of Cortés's arrival in Aztec territory had plunged Montezuma into a severe personal crisis. An Aztec text recorded that at this time the emperor "enjoyed no sleep, no food, not one spoke more to him. Whatsoever he did, it was as if he were in torment." The timing of the Spaniards' arrival and their very appearance seemed to signify that their leader was the god Quetzalcoatl returned to claim his land. On the other hand, Montezuma was a highly intelligent and pragmatic ruler who remained unconvinced that a band of unkempt soldiers could really be the retinue of a god. The presents he sent to their leader were designed to cover all eventualities. They included the insignia worn by the Aztec high priest when he impersonated Quetzalcoatl at religious ceremonies—trappings that might compel Cortés to reveal his divine identity, if such it was. The gifts of gold were intended to buy the strangers off, if they were mortals.

Montezuma's strategy failed. When the flow of gifts came to an abrupt end, Cortés moved on up the coast to a sheltered anchorage in the mouth of a river. Here the conquistadors founded their first settlement, Veracruz, and a town council was elected with Cortés as captain and chief justice. As a properly constituted munici-

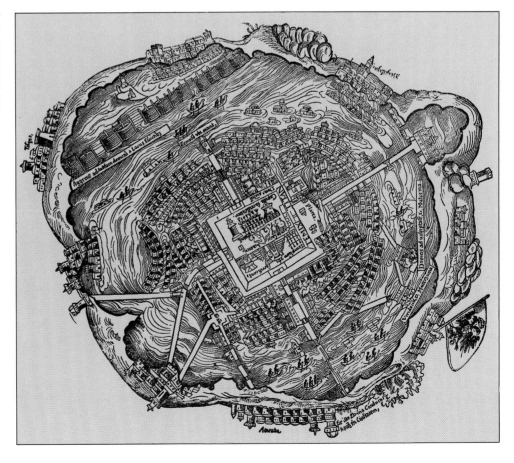

This map of Tenochtitlán, the Aztec capital, was based on a plan given to Cortés by Montezuma. Built on an island in Lake Texcoco and linked to the mainland by broad wooden causeways, the city housed some 200,000 inhabitants. Four major roads divided the city into quarters and led to a central plaza. Here, towering 130 feet above the surrounding single-story houses, stood the massive temple pyramids on which Aztec priests performed rites of human sacrifice.

pality, Veracruz owed its allegiance directly to the king of Spain and not to any of his officers; Cortés was now the leader of an independent community and no longer responsible to the lieutenant governor of Cuba.

Cortés knew that he could not hope to conquer the Aztecs without winning the support of their unwilling subjects, and while the town of Veracruz was being constructed, he made an alliance with their vassals the Totomacs, who lived nearby in the stone city of Zempoala. He also persuaded them to arrest five Aztec tax collectors, an open act of defiance against their overlords. When Montezuma sent two of his nephews to protest that the visitors were encouraging rebellion, Cortés answered that the Totomacs were now subjects of the king of Spain and announced his intention to visit Tenochtitlán.

Before he set out, Cortés made sure that there would be no turning back. He destroyed all of his ships but one, which he loaded with the treasure that had been taken so far and sent to Spain with a declaration of loyalty from the citizens of Veracruz to their king. On August 16, he charged 150 of his men with garrisoning the settlement. Then Cortés and the rest of the conquistadors, together with contingents of Totomacs, set their faces toward the Aztec capital.

The 250-mile route led over harsh terrain whose inhabitants were no less inhospitable. From the hot, dry coastal plain, the Spaniards climbed steep paths of steps cut into the rock of mountains, made their way through narrow passes 10,000 feet above sea level, and stumbled over stones and lava dust into a cold, gray, desolate plateau. Beyond the plateau they marched through salt marshes into the foothills of more mountains, where sandstorms gave way to hail and rain. At last their path led them high among volcanic peaks into the land of the Tlaxcalans, whose warlike spirit and mountain strongholds made them the only people in the area to have remained independent of the Aztecs.

Fiercely defending their homeland, the Tlaxcalans fell back in a series of mountain skirmishes and drew up their huge army on open ground. Sheer numbers of troops, however, could not prevail against cavalry and cannon. After two terrible defeats, the Tlaxcalans tried cunning. They sent spies into the Spaniards' camp posing as ambassadors, but Cortés saw through their deceit and sent them back with their hands cut off. Then they tried a night attack, but the Spaniards were waiting for them. Eventually, after the Spaniards had retaliated with two successful night attacks of their own, the Tlaxcalans agreed to make peace. The sworn enemies of the Aztecs became the most loyal allies of the invaders, and Cortés led his men without hindrance into their capital, Tlaxcala.

Adding a Tlaxcalan contingent to his army, Cortés marched on to Cholula, the last great city before the Aztec capital itself, which the Spaniards called Mexico. The citizens of Cholula had received orders from Montezuma to welcome the Spaniards and then ambush them, but Marina heard about the plan from a Cholulan woman and warned Cortés. The Spaniards and their allies struck first, killing about 6,000 Indians; and once again, awed by the guns and horses of the white-skinned conquistadors, a subject people of the Aztecs changed their allegiance.

With the Totomacs, Tlaxcalans, and Cholulans behind him, Cortés was now capable of fielding a formidable army. Montezuma had good reason to be cautious. He sent gifts and another ambassador, pleading unconvincingly that he had no responsibility for the planned ambush. He then he sat back and waited for the inevitable. The Spaniards gained their first sight of his capital when three conquistadors ascend-

Bound into this gold-studded headdress, a gift from Montezuma to the king of Spain, the long green quills of the quetzal bird were deemed by the Aztecs the most precious of all exotic feathers. Skilled Aztec artisans *(inset, left)* fashioned such plumes into ceremonial costumes, cloaks, banners, and shields, many of which were decorated with detailed pictures made by gluing small feathers to stiffened cloth or fig-bark paper.

These illustrations from an account of Spanish atrocities in Mexico by Bartolomé de Las Casas, a Spanish bishop, show native Indians being tortured, burned, and having their hands cut off. Following Las Casas's exposure of the conquistadors' brutality, laws were enacted to protect the native population; in theory, the Indians enjoyed the same rights as all subjects of the king of Spain, but in reality, they had little recourse against the oppression of their new masters.

ed the volcanic peak of Popocatépetl, from whose summit could be seen "the great city of Mexico, and the whole of the lake, and all the towns that were built in it."

On November 8, 1519, Cortés's men marched out over five miles of wooden causeway and drawbridges through villages built on water to the stone city of Tenochtitlán, which was in the middle of Lake Texcoco. The causeway was so wide that there was enough room for eight men to ride abreast, and 1,000 of the leading citizens escorted the conquistadors along it. Montezuma was waiting in the center of his capital, borne in a litter "beneath a marvelously rich canopy of green-colored feathers with much gold and silver embroidery." According to Díaz, he was "about forty years old, of good height and well proportioned, slender, and spare of flesh. He did not wear his hair long, but so as just to cover his ears; his scanty black beard was well shaped and thin. His face," Díaz continued, "was somewhat long, but cheerful, and he had good eyes and showed in his appearance and manner both tenderness and, when necessary, gravity."

By now, Montezuma was almost certainly convinced that the Spaniards were men of flesh and blood, no more divine than he. Nevertheless, he had become fatalistically resigned to what he saw as his inevitable fate, and he greeted Cortés as the representative of the god Quetzalcoatl, publicly attributing the Spaniards' success to powers beyond human control.

The conquistadors were housed in a palace next to Montezuma's and treated with meticulous courtesy. There followed almost a week of diplomatic stalemate, each side waiting for the other to make the next move. The only break in the routine came on the sixth day, when the Spaniards inadvertently discovered the extent of the fortune within their grasp. In one of the rooms in their quarters they noticed the outline of a door beneath the plaster. On breaking it down, they found a horde of golden objects that, they subsequently learned, was the treasure of Axayacatl, Montezuma's father. It was enough to make every one of the conquistadors rich beyond his dreams.

On the seventh day, two Tlaxcalans arrived with the news that one of the Aztec provincial governors had attacked a group of Spaniards on the coast and killed several. To Cortés, this intelligence was sufficient pretext for a bold but scarcely honorable move. Accompanied by his interpreters and five captains, he marched into

Montezuma's apartments and seized the Aztec emperor. This was an easy feat to perform, for according to Díaz, the Spaniards always remained armed in Montezuma's presence; their only mark of respect was to take off their helmets. The ruler suspected nothing until it was too late. He was charged with treachery, and when Marina warned him that he would be killed if he refused, he agreed to accompany Cortés to the Spaniards' quarters, where he was held under guard. When the offending governor answered Montezuma's summons, Cortés burned him to death in public while Montezuma watched in chains.

From that moment on, Montezuma became a puppet ruler. His courtiers and captains, fearful for his safety and accustomed to unquestioning obedience, carried out every order that he gave under Cortés's instructions. But the Spaniards also were in effect prisoners, knowing that, if Montezuma were to command his subjects to rebel, they would be doomed.

This stalemate was broken by the unexpected news that Spanish soldiers had landed on the coast, sent from Cuba by Governor Velázquez to arrest Cortés. Leaving the impetuous Pedro de Alvarado in command in Mexico, Cortés hurried eastward with 250 men and made a night attack on the newcomers' lodgings in Zempoala. They were taken completely by surprise. Within an hour they had surrendered. Their leader was imprisoned in Veracruz, and the rest of them, willing or not, were conscripted into Cortés's army.

Cortés now commanded an additional 600 foot soldiers, 80 cavalry, and more than a dozen cannon. They had arrived just in time. In Tenochtitlán, the nervous Alvarado—believing that the long-expected uprising against the Spaniards was imminent—had attacked and killed almost 1,000 Aztec citizens who were attending a religious ceremony. The citizens had risen in response, and the Spaniards and their allies were now besieged in their quarters.

Cortés arrived in the capital during a lull in the fighting. Leading his reinforcements through empty, silent streets, he joined Alvarado in the beleaguered palace. There was no time for recrimination. The next day, the Aztecs renewed their attack, fighting from dawn till sunset. The Spaniards repaired their defenses overnight, and the following day, Cortés took Montezuma to the roof. At the sight of him the Aztecs fell silent, but as soon as he started to plead for peace, they answered with a shower of missiles. A stone struck Montezuma on the head, mortally wounding him. Resigned to his fate, Montezuma refused treatment, and three days later, he died. The new Aztec emperor was Montezuma's brother, Cuitlahuac, who had been the commander of the relentless attack.

The Aztecs were too numerous to be conquered by a small force in the narrow confines of a city, and the Spaniards and their allies had too little food to be able to withstand a long siege. Their only hope was to fight their way out. Carrying a mobile bridge to use at drawbridges or gaps in the causeway, they crept out of their palace under cover of darkness and pouring rain. When their vanguard reached the edge of the causeway, Aztec watchmen raised the alarm. From there on, Cortés's forces hacked their way to the mainland at a terrible cost in casualties. "To one who saw the hosts of warriors who fell on us that night and the canoes full of them coming along to carry off our soldiers, it was terrifying," wrote Díaz. In what was to be remembered as La Noche Triste—the Night of Grief—Cortés lost more than 2,000 Tlaxcalans and about 600 Spaniards, most of whom were new recruits. In their desperate struggle to reach safety, the Spaniards were forced to abandon all their cannon and supplies and most of Axayacatl's treasure, which fell from the causeway and sank to the bottom of the lake.

Cuitlahuac followed the retreating allies, and on July 7, 1520, he massed his warriors to annihilate them. But he was now fighting in open country, and although Cortés had lost all his guns, he still had twenty-two horses. At the end of a long day's fighting, the battle of Otumba was won by cavalry, cold steel, and courage.

Cortés was now committed to total war, and he withdrew to Tlaxcala to rebuild his own army. He received timely assistance from expeditions dispatched by the governors of both Cuba and Jamaica, the former to reinforce his earlier expedition and the latter to found a new colony. Cortés had no difficulty in persuading them to join forces with his own army instead, and he also made use of their ships, sending one to Jamaica to buy horses and another to Spain to find new recruits and plead his case before the king. Months later, when the Spanish reinforcements finally arrived, they brought with them the welcome news that His Majesty favored the claims of Cortés over those of Velázquez.

But Cortés's most fortuitous new ally—if that is how it may be described—was smallpox. An African slave who landed with the expedition from Cuba had been suffering from this disease. "It was owing to him," recounted Díaz, "that the whole country was stricken and filled with it, from which there was great mortality, for according to what the Indians said they had never had such a disease . . . and on that account a great number of them died." The epidemic spread to the Aztec capital, where it claimed Cuitlahuac among its many victims. As well as causing widespread loss of life, the smallpox dealt a devastating psychological blow: Observing their own people dying by the thousand while the Spaniards remained almost completely unaffected, the Aztecs could not but conclude that the god of their enemies was stronger than their own divinities.

Around Christmas of 1520, Cortés moved down to the shores of Lake Texcoco to prepare for his final assault on the Aztec capital. Timber and tackle were brought in from the hills and the coast, and carpenters built boats on which guns were mounted, so that the assault over the causeway could be supported by fire from the water. By the beginning of May 1521, Cortés had under his command a dozen boats that had been fitted with guns, approximately 600 Spaniards—including more than 70 horsemen—and, by his own estimate, more than 75,000 native auxiliary troops.

For nearly three months the Aztecs defended their capital with reckless courage. Several times the Spaniards were driven back, and a number of them were captured, including Cortés's page Orteguilla, who was seized while helping his unhorsed master to remount. Those who came closest to the center of the city watched in horror as their companions, Orteguilla among them, were forced up the steps of the pyramid to the altar. There, they were held down by black-robed priests while their chests were cut open with a stone blade and their pounding hearts torn out. The hearts were burned before images of the Aztec gods; the bodies were flung to the bottom of the steps, where the torsos were fed to wild animals and the limbs were roasted and then eaten by priests.

The end came when the Aztecs, reduced to eating the roots of herbs and the bark of trees, could resist no longer. Toward the middle of August 1521, amid piles of rotting corpses, many of them the victims of smallpox, the Spaniards and their allies took the last corner of the Aztec capital, slaughtering some 15,000 Indians. As the new king, Montezuma's son-in-law, tried to escape in a canoe, he was captured by the crew of a Spanish boat. The surviving citizens were allowed to leave unhindered: "During three days and nights they never ceased streaming out," reported Díaz, "and

# PORTUGAL'S WESTERN EMPIRE

By the Treaty of Tordesillas in 1494, Spain and Portugal agreed to divide the New World between them along a line of longitude 370 leagues west of the Cape Verde Islands. Accordingly, when the Portuguese navigator Pedro Álvars Cabral sighted land in South America to the east of this line in 1500, he claimed the territory in the name of the king of Portugal.

Portuguese ships were soon sailing regularly to collect the precious red dyewood, brazil, that gave the new colony its name. But because no gold was discovered there, another thirty years passed before settlements were founded. An administrative capital, Bahia, was established on the coast in 1549, and the Portuguese began to export sugarcane to Europe. To work the labor-intensive sugar plantations, slaves were imported from western Africa. Many thousands of native Indians were also enslaved, despite the protection afforded them by Jesuit missionaries and by legislation designed to protect their rights; others fled beyond the regions controlled by settlers. The 1542 chart shown at right, with the conventional north-south axis reversed, shows Indian laborers building a stockade on the east coast; the area depicted is outlined on the inset map.

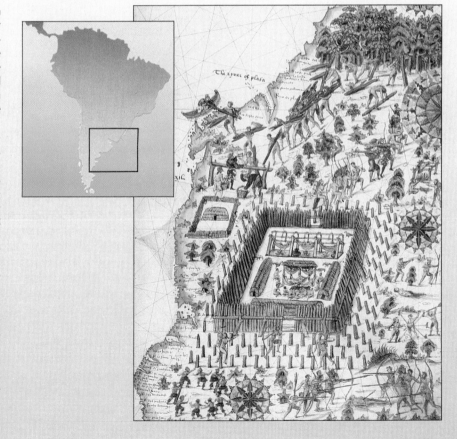

The first meeting between Francisco Pizarro and Atahualpa—the Inca, or "ruler"—is depicted on the title page of an eyewitness account of the conquest of Peru by Francisco de Xerez. Borne on a litter, Atahualpa listens to the speech of a Dominican friar, who presented him with a breviary; moments later, the Inca dashed the book to the ground, and Spanish soldiers rushed forward to seize him.

the causeways were crowded with men, women, and children, so thin, yellow, dirty, and stinking that it was pitiful to see them.'' Cortés had made himself master of the Aztec empire.

In the following year, when building had already begun on the new Spanish city of Mexico, Cortés received letters from the king appointing him governor and captain-general of New Spain. The news of his success brought fresh encouragement to other settlements of the New World, and it reached Panama at the same time as reports from the south of another rich Indian empire. To two citizens of the isthmus, Francisco Pizarro and Diego de Almagro, both of whom were more than fifty years old and illiterate, this new goal offered what was probably their last chance to make a fortune.

Pizarro had accompanied Vasco Núñez de Balboa on an expedition that had discovered the Pacific Ocean. Since then he had served as a magistrate and lived as a settler on land adjoining that of Almagro, a popular but boastful man who had left Spain in a hurry after a stabbing incident. But he still had grand ambitions, and in late 1526 he acquired ships for an expedition and set sail south from Panama. He had first bound himself to a contract with Almagro and a priest, Hernando de Luque, by which it was agreed that they would share all gains equally and that Pizarro and Almagro were to be joint commanders.

Off the swampy coast of Ecuador, many of the expedition's 160 men succumbed to disease and hunger. However, Pizarro himself, a tough and single-minded leader, was determined not to give up, and when a ship was sent to bring back the survivors, he risked a gesture as dramatic as Cortés's destruction of his ships. Drawing a line on the sand with his sword, he challenged those who were willing to continue to step over and stand beside him. Only thirteen men crossed the line, but they were enough to keep the expedition going. Pizarro sailed south of the equator and landed at the city of Tumbes, where to his surprise and delight, he was amicably received and shown a temple whose walls were lined with gold and silver.

Tumbes was governed by the Incas who, like the Aztecs, were a military people who had conquered their empire in the previous century and had absorbed the culture of earlier civilizations. From their capital at Cuzco in present-day Peru, they ruled over an area that stretched more than 2,000 miles from north to south through the Andes. Their public buildings were made of stones cut with great skill, some laid in neat horizontal courses and others huge blocks interlocking with uncanny precision. They built canals, hillside terraces for farming, and a network of roads and rope bridges along which armies and messengers could move quickly on foot from one end of the empire to the other. Subject peoples were organized into agricultural collectives on the arid coastal plain and the rain-soaked hills, where they cultivated the corn and potatoes that, together with domesticated llamas and guinea pigs, formed the basis of the national diet. They were converted to the Inca religion and taught to worship the sun, although human sacrifice was seldom demanded.

Pizarro returned to Panama with gold and silver ornaments, emeralds, embroidered cloth, llamas, and young Inca boys, who were to be trained as interpreters. But to raise enough money for a full-scale expedition, he had to sail to Spain to plead his case before the king. Having recently been visited by Hernán Cortés, the king greeted the prospect of conquering another rich empire with unqualified enthusiasm, and he appointed Pizarro governor and captain-general of the new colonies, which were to be known as New Castile; Almagro was designated commandant of Tumbes, and Luque became protector of the Indians.

Although the appointment of a single commander was in keeping with Spanish policy, it contradicted the terms of the partnership agreement. Almagro was resentful, and he was further offended by the haughtiness of Hernando Pizarro, one of four half brothers whom Francisco Pizarro brought back among more than 100 recruits from Spain. Almagro was prevented from dissolving the partnership only by being promised the governorship of all the lands that lay beyond those of his partner.

Eventually, at the end of 1530, Pizarro set sail from Panama in three ships with 180 men, twenty-seven horses, and a few cannon, expecting Almagro to follow with reinforcements as soon as possible. After thirteen days, when headwinds forced him to put in to the coast, he decided to continue the journey by land. Disease and skirmishes with bands of Indians imposed additional delays, and when he finally reached Tumbes, more than a year later, he found it deserted and in ruins.

The apparent disaster was in fact the outcome of a great piece of good fortune for Pizarro. From the inhabitants of the surrounding countryside he learned that on the death of the Inca Huayna Capac, the empire had been devastated by a civil war between two of his sons, Atahualpa and Huáscar. Far away in the south, one of Atahualpa's victorious armies had just captured Huáscar outside the capital, Cuzco. Pizarro could not have come at a better time: Atahualpa and his soldiers were still distracted by the war, and there was a chance that Pizarro might be able to follow Cortés's example and exploit the divisions among the Indians. In addition, the smallpox epidemic that had ravaged the Aztecs had reached the Incas through indigenous contacts around 1525, with consequences no less drastic than in Mexico.

During the next few months Pizarro was joined by two small groups of reinforcements, one of which was led by Hernando de Soto, who was later to explore North America. Pizarro also founded his first settlement, San Miguel, on the coast south of Tumbes. From there he set out in search of Atahualpa, who was rumored to be only twelve days' march away. On the way, the Spaniards met with an ambassador from Atahualpa, who invited them to come to his camp. With 168 soldiers, 62 of them mounted, Pizarro followed the ambassador up into the thin air of the Andes, and on November 15, 1532, he looked down into a flat valley at the town of Cajamarca and, outside it, the massed tents of Atahualpa's army.

Pizarro led his men into the town, which had been evacuated, and sent his brother Hernando and Hernando de Soto to pay his respects to Atahualpa. The Inca received them sitting on a stool in a stone bathhouse built around a natural hot spring. Pizarro's secretary, Francisco de Xerez, later described Atahualpa as "a man of thirty years of age, of good appearance and manner, though somewhat thickset. He had a large face, handsome and fierce, his eyes reddened with blood." After declining an invitation to dine with Atahualpa, the two emissaries returned to report that Atahualpa intended to visit Pizarro the next day.

The apprehensive conquistadors spent the evening debating their predicament.

The regal pose of Atahualpa in this Spanish portrait belies the fragility of his authority. A civil war for control of the Inca empire had divided the loyalties of his people, a situation the Spanish invaders were quick to exploit. Less than a year after defeating his brother's army, Atahualpa was killed by his Spanish captors.

There were at least 40,000 warriors in the Inca camp, and unlike the Aztecs, they had weapons with copper tips and blades. In the end it was decided that the best plan would be to seize Atahualpa when he came to visit them.

On the following day, Atahualpa kept the Spaniards waiting until the sun had begun to sink before he made his ceremonial entrance, accompanied by 6,000 unarmed warriors and carried by 80 blue-liveried nobles on a silver-plated litter lined with parrot feathers. He halted in the center of the town square and listened impassively while a priest and an interpreter delivered an exposition of Christianity. Then Pizarro gave the signal. Cannon fired and armed Spaniards sprang out from their hiding places around the square. Atahualpa was seized and his troops, shocked by the loss of their emperor and the desperate fury of the Spaniards, panicked. After just two hours of fighting, 2,000 lay dead in the square alone and thousands more on the plain beyond the town. When the Spaniards asked Atahualpa later why he had fallen for such an obvious trap, he smiled wryly. He had come intending to make a prisoner of Pizarro; his ambassador had told him that the Spaniards were not fighting men.

Like Montezuma in Mexico, Atahualpa became a puppet ruler. His soldiers, who regarded him as the descendant of the sun, obeyed without question when he ordered them to disperse; and when he saw the eagerness with which the Spaniards plundered precious metals in the empty camp, he offered to pay Pizarro a ransom. In return for his freedom, he would fill one of the halls in Cajamarca with gold and fill a nearby room twice over with silver. Pizarro did not believe that this was possible—the hall was roughly twenty feet long and sixteen feet wide—but the offer was too good to refuse. Drawing a line on the walls about seven feet from the floor, he gave Atahualpa two months to fill the hall to the level of the line.

A few weeks later, the first installments of the ransom arrived. The Incas failed to meet the deadline, but the treasure kept flowing in; after more than five months, when the pile of finely worked golden objects was just short of the line, Pizarro set up forges, melted them down, and turned them into ingots, so that it would be easier to divide the gold fairly and transport the king's fifth to Spain. By then Almagro had arrived with enough men to double Pizarro's strength; when the spoils were distributed, they too were given a modest share.

But Pizarro did not release Atahualpa, even though it seemed as dangerous to keep him as to let him go. There were rumors that an army was on its way to rescue him, and many of the Spaniards believed that it was acting on Atahualpa's orders. He had already managed to send secret instructions to his soldiers to murder Huáscar, in order to prevent Pizarro from enthroning his estranged brother in his place. When Almagro's men argued that the only way to prevent an attack was to kill Atahualpa, de Soto was sent out on a reconnaissance to see if there really was an approaching army. In his absence, hysteria in the Spanish ranks came close to mutiny. After an Indian reported that he had seen an army not far away, Pizarro reluctantly gave in to his men's demands. Atahualpa was condemned without a trial. By accepting baptism, he avoided death by burning, which according to the Inca religion would have denied him reincarnation; instead, on July 26, 1533, he was tied to a chair and garroted. Soon afterward de Soto returned; he had seen no sign of an army.

From Cajamarca the Spaniards set out on the long journey to the Inca capital of Cuzco, about 750 miles to the south. Their route led over high mountain passes between peaks rising more than 21,000 feet above sea level. Three times Pizarro's men had to fight off attacks from Inca armies loyal to the dead Atahualpa. But the harshness of their passage was in part alleviated by the paved roads and steps that had been laid across the Andes by the Incas, and they also enjoyed the goodwill of the local people who had supported Huáscar. In November, Pizarro finally reached Cuzco, where he installed another of Huayna Capac's sons, Manco, as his puppet Inca. By emulating Cortés's daring, Pizarro had established himself as the master of an even richer empire.

But Cortés possessed political skills that Pizarro lacked, and in the following years, the stability of Spanish rule over the Inca empire was continually threatened by rebellion and bitter personal feuds. In Mexico, Cortés had made the former Aztec capital his own, which enabled him to take over its administrative system and maintain continuity, and he had kept a tight control over his subordinates. In Peru, Pizarro decided that the city of Cuzco was too remote to be his capital; in January 1535, he founded a new one at Lima on the coast, from where it proved difficult to control the highlands; he was also unable to restrain the greed and cruelty of his soldiers, which drove the native population to desperate rebellion.

Discovered in 1545, the silver-veined mountain of Potosí in present-day Bolivia yielded more than 18,000 tons of silver ore before the mines were exhausted in the following century. Mined by Indian forced labor and carried down the slopes by llamas, the ore was crushed to a powder by hammers and then mixed with mercury to extract the metal. The wheel that powered the hammers—seen in the foreground of this drawing—was driven by water from an overhead pipe fed by melted snow and rain from reservoirs.

The puppet ruler Manco escaped from Spanish custody, rallied an army reputed to number more than 100,000 warriors, and laid siege to Cuzco, which was garrisoned by only 190 men under the command of Pizarro's brother Hernando. Incas loyal to Manco destroyed several expeditons sent from Lima to relieve Cuzco, and they even attacked Lima itself. Manco abandoned the siege after only six months when his supplies ran out, but he was preparing for another assault in 1537 when Almagro suddenly appeared on his flank with more than 500 Spaniards. Returning from a profitless exploration of the territories to the south, Almagro had come to take advantage of the Pizarros' misfortune. After failing to make an alliance with Manco, he seized Cuzco for himself and imprisoned its lieutenant governor, claiming that the city was so far south that it was in his territory and not Pizarro's.

Franciso Pizarro opened negotiations, and Almagro released his brother. But the Pizarros were only buying time. On April 26, 1538, Hernando Pizarro defeated Almagro's army at the battle of Las Salinas, and ten weeks later he ordered the garroting of its sixty-three-year-old commander.

Retribution was not long in coming. Almagro's supporters appealed for help to their friends at the Spanish court, and nine months later, when Hernando Pizarro visited Spain, he was arrested and imprisoned for twenty years. On Sunday, June 26, 1541,

# THE GOLD OF EL DORADO

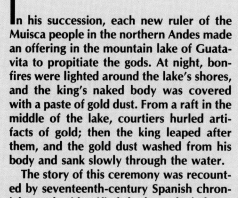

In his succession, each new ruler of the Muisca people in the northern Andes made an offering in the mountain lake of Guatavita to propitiate the gods. At night, bonfires were lighted around the lake's shores, and the king's naked body was covered with a paste of gold dust. From a raft in the middle of the lake, courtiers hurled artifacts of gold; then the king leaped after them, and the gold dust washed from his body and sank slowly through the water.

The story of this ceremony was recounted by seventeenth-century Spanish chroniclers, who identified the legend of El Dorado—or the "Golden Man," ruler of a kingdom of untold riches—with the Muisca. In fact, the legend was born in Quito in present-day Ecuador in 1541, several years after the Muisca had been conquered by a Spanish adventurer named Gonzalo Jiménez de Quesada, and the supposed location of this elusive realm altered over the following decades as successive expeditions failed to discover it. By 1595, when the English explorer Sir Walter Raleigh sailed up the Orinoco River, the legendary kingdom was believed to be in what was then southern Guiana.

The enigma of the Golden Man was never solved. But the gold artifacts fashioned by the Muisca and other peoples living in what is now Colombia were worthy of being associated with the legend. The works shown here were among those that escaped the attention of the Spanish conquerors, who melted down every object they seized.

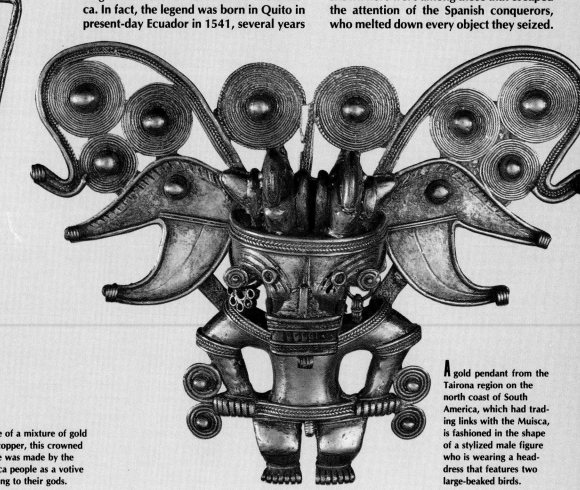

Made of a mixture of gold and copper, this crowned figure was made by the Muisca people as a votive offering to their gods.

A gold pendant from the Tairona region on the north coast of South America, which had trading links with the Muisca, is fashioned in the shape of a stylized male figure who is wearing a headdress that features two large-beaked birds.

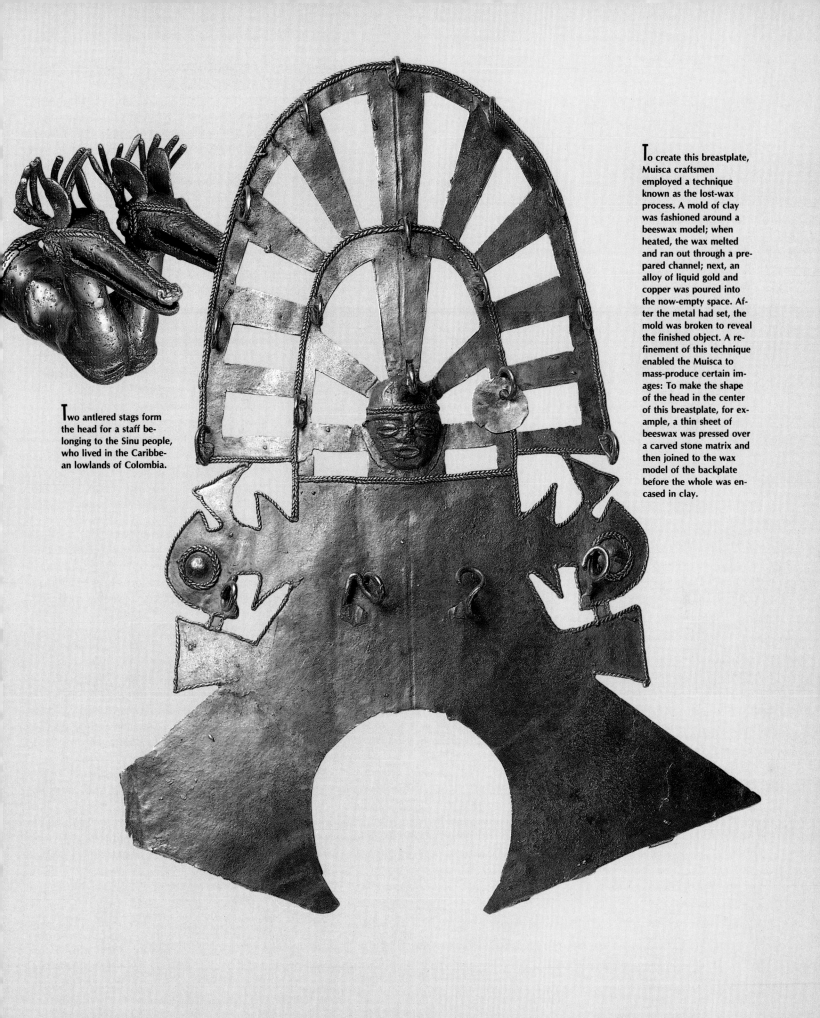

To create this breastplate, Muisca craftsmen employed a technique known as the lost-wax process. A mold of clay was fashioned around a beeswax model; when heated, the wax melted and ran out through a prepared channel; next, an alloy of liquid gold and copper was poured into the now-empty space. After the metal had set, the mold was broken to reveal the finished object. A refinement of this technique enabled the Muisca to mass-produce certain images: To make the shape of the head in the center of this breastplate, for example, a thin sheet of beeswax was pressed over a carved stone matrix and then joined to the wax model of the backplate before the whole was encased in clay.

Two antlered stags form the head for a staff belonging to the Sinu people, who lived in the Caribbean lowlands of Colombia.

Francisco Pizarro was dining in the undefended governor's palace in Lima when twenty assassins broke in. Pizarro defended himself stoutly while his guests fled into the palace gardens, but he was quickly surrounded and killed.

A year after Pizarro's death, the arrival of a viceroy in Peru brought an end to the short-lived era of the conquistadors. Spain had been prepared to let its new empire be conquered by entrepreneurs, but it was not going to let them run it. The machinery of royal authority had already reached Mexico several years earlier when Cortés was removed from the office of governor and replaced by a viceroy in 1535. For a while he stayed in New Spain and led a few expeditions, including one to Baja California, but in the end he returned to his native country. On December 2, 1547, the greatest of all the conquistadors died on his estate near Seville, rich but disillusioned and embittered.

As far as possible, the Spanish colonies on the continent of America were henceforward administered as though they were provinces of the kingdom itself. A new supreme authority was established, the Council of the Indies, and under its supervision the colonies received not only viceroys and new governors but judges, tax collectors, and other officials.

The economy received an enormous boost from three huge silver strikes, two in New Spain and another in the part of New Castile that is now Bolivia. The prospect of easy riches attracted new settlers, and as fleets sailed eastward laden with silver, others sailed westward with wave after wave of immigrants. By the middle of the century, around 100,000 Europeans had established themselves in Spanish America.

In principle, the native peoples of America were regarded as free subjects of Spain, and the repartimiento system was adapted to release them from all obligations to the Spanish settlers except to pay tribute in the form of local produce and precious metals. The church also set about its business of conversion with high ideals. The early missionaries, most of whom were Franciscan, Dominican, and Augustinian friars, believed that among the Aztecs and the Incas they would be able to establish a church as pure and simple as the one that first followed Christ. But good intentions

**Gold from the New World cascades in tiers of statuary behind the altar of the cathedral in Seville. The influx of gold and silver into Seville, home port of the Spanish treasure fleets, financed the campaigns of Charles V, Holy Roman emperor and king of Spain, for three decades and made Spain the richest country in Europe. Filtered through expanding networks of trade, some of this wealth reached as far as the court of Mogul India.**

and new laws were not easy to put into effect in a tough young society more than 3,000 miles distant from the mother country. Most of the Spanish settlers were convinced of their racial superiority, and accordingly had few qualms about maltreating the Indians assigned to their custody. And the missionaries began to realize that the number of their conversions was not necessarily a measure of success: Many of the local peoples kept up the practices of their earlier religions in secret, and few were convinced of the virtue of monogomy.

Neither church nor state could protect their charges from the most damaging consequences of thousands of years of isolation. Lacking immunity to smallpox and other diseases such as measles and influenza, which were the common experience of childhood in Europe and Africa, the people of Mexico and Peru succumbed by the hundreds of thousands. Between the landings of the conquistadors and 1570, the population of what is now Mexico may have fallen from around 25 million to 2.65 million, and the population of Peru from an estimated 9 million to 1.3 million. The transfer of infection was not all one way, however. The local women gave the Spanish men syphilis, a disease that was unknown in the Old World until 1493. By the latter part of the sixteenth century, there were parts of Europe where it had spread to epidemic proportions.

While new colonial societies were evolving in Mexico and Peru, the extent of the Spanish empire steadily grew. In some regions, the fighting between Spaniards and the native populations went on for decades, and the last Inca stronghold at Vilcabamba in Peru did not fall until 1572. By the end of the century, however, the American territories under Spanish control included—in addition to the Caribbean islands, Mexico, and Peru—all of Central America, the northwestern and central regions of South America, and Florida. The Philippines were occupied around 1570, and when Spain became linked to Portugal in 1580, it also gained control over the Portuguese settlements in Brazil, east and west Africa, the East Indies, the Persian Gulf, and on the west coast of India. This was the first empire on which the sun never set. Much of it survived until the beginning of the nineteenth century, when independence movements in Central and South America gathered momentum after Spain had been subjugated by Napoleon Bonaparte.

The reasons for the remarkable military success of the Spanish forces were many, not least being the vulnerability of the Indians to imported diseases and the superiority of Spanish weapons. The conquistadors themselves used to say, "After God we owe victory to the horses." In addition, the native legends concerning the return of their ancient gods worked to the Spaniards' favor: The ingrained beliefs of the American peoples that all events had a supernatural cause, and that the arrival of the invaders was divinely ordained, induced a fatalism and resignation that sapped their will to resist. But all such advantages might have gone for nothing were it not for the desperate courage of men who, marooned in an alien continent and facing seemingly impossible odds, had nothing to lose but their lives and everything—but one thing above all—to gain. "My companions and I," said Cortés, "suffer from a sickness of the soul that can be cured only with gold."

# ELIZABETH'S ENGLAND

In every parish of England, the church bells pealed. On the rolling downs of the southern counties, in the high northern dales and the damp flatlands of the eastern fens, the sounds of celebration rang out across the realm. In the great market towns of the Midlands, oxen and venison roasted on spits in preparation for public feasts; companies of players and musicians entertained the crowds in the glow of bonfires that blazed all night. At Cambridge, the doctors of the university donned scarlet gowns and marched in procession from their colleges to hear sermons and orations in honor of their sovereign. And far from home, in the remotest reaches of the western ocean, the sailors on English ships fired volleys from their vessels' guns and split the sky with a burst of fireworks.

In the year 1576, when the anniversary of Queen Elizabeth's accession to the English throne was first declared a public holiday, the occasion became marked by general rejoicing. The pageantry of medieval chivalry was revived by the nobility, who challenged one another to ritual combat in honor of their queen and offered up solemn or comic verses full of allusions to life at court and enlivened with elaborate props and theatrical machinery. Those who took part in the tournaments knew that they were participating in an age no less colorful or glorious than that of the knights and heroes they imitated.

On November 17, 1558, the young daughter of Henry VIII had taken into her hands the troubled island kingdom that she would rule for nearly half a century. Her long reign would see political perils, economic crises, and natural disasters, real or suspected subversion at home, and foreign enemies massing for attack. But it would also be an era when genius flowered and wealth increased, when adventurers found new worlds to conquer and even the most isolated farmer felt the stirrings of national pride. Hungry vagabonds still roamed the highways, and fortunes were lost as well as won. For those who shared in its successes, however, the reign of Elizabeth was England's golden age.

The queen's predecessors had not been blessed with such good fortune. The latter part of her father's reign, and the eleven years that followed—when the crown had passed first to Elizabeth's adolescent half brother, Edward, then to her doomed half sister, Mary—had been dangerous days. England was surrounded by enemies: Scotland, linked to France by marriage, brooded on old hatreds and dispatched marauding armies; on the Continent, France glowered and Spain, supposedly an ally, sent spies and bided its time. At home, the population endured a long run of bad harvests, devastating epidemics, and an ever-mounting escalation of prices.

These material difficulties were compounded by religious upheavals. In England, as elsewhere in northern Europe, the thousand-year hegemony of the Roman Catholic church had begun to crumble. The pious no longer looked solely to Rome as the fountainhead of spiritual truth but studied the radical Protestant teachings coming out of Martin Luther's Germany and John Calvin's Geneva. In 1525, the reformer William Tyndale translated and distributed the first English edition of the Scriptures; he was subsequently martyred for his pains. Members of the gentry, doctors of divinity, and the merchants who imported not only goods but new ideas from their Continental counterparts now disputed the moral and theological authority of the papal hierarchy and went on to formulate hard questions about the very nature of the social order.

Whatever his theological opinions, Henry VIII had private reasons for encouraging

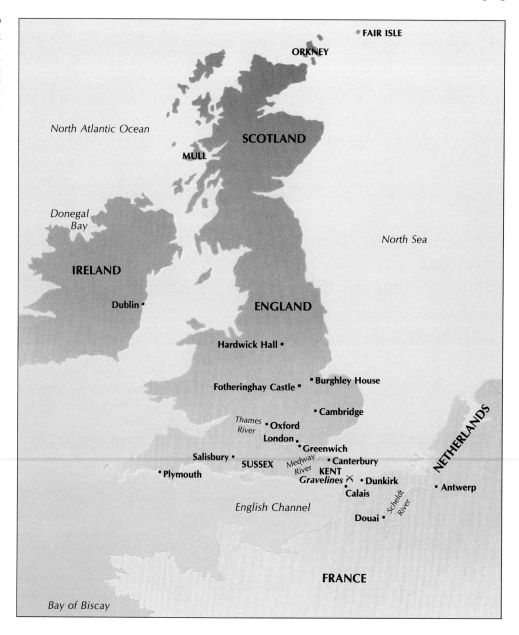

Beset not only by Scotland and France, longstanding enemies of England, but also by Spain, a rising menace, Elizabeth sought to keep England out of foreign wars. She concentrated instead on resolving her kingdom's internal problems. Eventually, however, this isolationist policy proved impracticable. By the end of her reign, English troops were fighting in the Netherlands and Ireland, and they engaged in a long war with Spain that followed the defeat of the Spanish Armada in 1588.

a breach from Rome. For years, he had been desperate to rid himself of his Spanish wife, Catherine of Aragon. The alliance with Spain, which had made the match politically desirable, was disintegrating, and—far worse—the lady had failed to produce a male heir who survived. Henry had petitioned the pope for an annulment of his marriage, but he wearied of waiting while Rome prevaricated under pressure from Spain. In January 1533, Henry secretly wed his mistress, Anne Boleyn, and in May, the archbishop of Canterbury, Thomas Cranmer, took it upon himself to dissolve Henry's marriage to Catherine of Aragon.

These acts led to total schism. Henry declared that he, not the pope, was the head of the English church, with sole authority over its clergy. In 1536, the king began to dissolve the monasteries and annex their vast landholdings to the Crown. He next sold these properties, at bargain prices, to nobles, gentlemen, rich yeoman farmers, and merchants. As well as filling the royal coffers, the sale was a shrewd political move on Henry's part: The landed classes now had their own stake in his ecclesiastical reformation.

Henry's fledgling church proved more successful in the long run than his efforts to ensure a male succession. Intrigues among rival factions at court led to Anne Boleyn's undoing, and her execution for treason. By the time of his death in 1547, Henry had married no fewer than six wives, producing only three surviving children: Catherine of Aragon's daughter, Mary, Elizabeth by the ill-fated Anne, and—at last—a son. By his own decree, his throne was to pass first to Edward the son, then—if the son had no heirs—to Mary, and then to Elizabeth.

Just nine years old when he inherited his father's crown, Edward VI, the son of Jane Seymour, reigned in name only while powerful Protestant nobles ruled the state on his behalf. He was succeeded after his death from tuberculosis in 1553 by Mary, who had remained loyal to the Catholic faith of her unhappy mother and who sought to bring England back into the Roman fold by decree and by union with a Catholic country. The times were hard for her Protestant subjects. Some 500 of their leaders opted for temporary exile on the Continent; approximately 280 others, ranging from clergymen to cloth weavers, were burned as heretics; the majority, to avoid either exile or the stake, officially recanted, but offered only a minimal show of religious conformity. In 1554, when Mary agreed to marry her cousin, the heir to the Catholic throne of Spain, a revolt erupted, and 4,000 rebels marched on London. The uprising was quashed, but resentment simmered. When Mary died, childless, in the sixth year of her reign, to be succeeded by the Protestant Elizabeth, many of the new queen's subjects felt their prayers had been answered.

Elizabeth's early years had been singularly bleak and might have crushed a less sturdy character. Shunted from one drafty royal palace to another, unvisited by either parent, she was granted only the scantiest of funds from the royal purse after the execution of her mother. But there was no comparable stinting on the princess's education. Her principal tutor was the distinguished Cambridge scholar Roger Ascham, whose teaching was based—in striking contrast to the rote learning, enforced by the cane, that was typical of the time—upon kindness, patience, and respect for his pupil. The results were impressive indeed: Elizabeth proved to be a brilliant student, with a particular gift for learning languages. She could converse as freely in Latin as if it were her mother tongue, and could read, write, and translate from both Latin and Greek with ease. She was fluent in Italian, and possibly in French as well, despite the disparaging remarks one Gallic envoy would later make about her accent.

During Mary's reign, Elizabeth acquired a political acumen that would stand her in good stead for the rest of her life. Because the queen suspected, not without reason, that her half sister would make an ideal rallying point for rebellious Protestants, she had Elizabeth locked in the Tower of London when the revolt of 1554 broke out and kept her under close surveillance thereafter. An injudicious word or gesture on Elizabeth's part might have sent her to the block, in a grisly repetition of her mother's fate. Her courage and shrewdness during these years impressed her contemporaries, not least the Venetian ambassador, who reported back to his government in 1557 that Elizabeth "is a young woman whose mind is considered no less excellent than her person, although her face is comely rather than handsome, but she is tall and well formed, with a good skin. . . . She has fine eyes, and above all a beautiful hand of which she makes a display; and her intellect and understanding are wonderful, as she

# THE SIX WIVES OF HENRY VIII

Kings in the sixteenth century married not for love but for dynastic reasons—to sire a male heir or to forge a foreign alliance that would further their strategic aims. The pressing weight of these obligations so disrupted the private life of Henry VIII—shown opposite in a portrait painted by Hans Holbein the Younger around 1538—that during the last fourteen years of his reign, he ran through a roll call of six wives. His first marriage, to the Spanish princess Catherine of Aragon, lasted twenty-four years but produced only a daughter, Mary; Henry's defiance of the pope in ending this marriage led England to break with Rome and establish the Anglican church. Anne Boleyn bore him a second daughter, Elizabeth, but was executed in 1536 after being convicted of adultery. In 1537, Henry fathered a son, Edward, by Jane Seymour, but his new queen died just twelve days after the prince's birth. Henry's diplomatic marriage to Anne of Cleves from the Protestant Rhineland was never consummated, and was quickly annulled. Catherine Howard, her successor, went to the block for adultery after only eighteen months. Overweight and ill, Henry finally achieved domestic contentment with Catherine Parr, who outlived him.

Catherine of Aragon

Anne Boleyn

Jane Seymour

Anne of Cleves

Catherine Howard

Catherine Parr

showed very plainly by her conduct when in danger and under suspicion."

Elizabeth was two months past her twenty-fifth birthday when she became queen in 1558. She was to need all the talent, perspicacity, and wisdom she could command in the difficult years that followed. The state of the nation on her accession, according to one courtier, left much to be desired:

*The queen poor, the realm exhausted, the nobility poor and decayed. Want of good captains and soldiers. The people out of order. Justice not executed. All things dear. Excess in meat, drink, and apparel. Divisions among ourselves. Wars with France and Scotland. The French king bestriding our realm, having one foot in Calais and the other in Scotland. Steadfast enmity but no steadfast friendship abroad.*

Despite these difficulties, the machinery of government, controlled by able administrators, remained intact. Elizabeth built on these foundations by choosing gifted councilors who were distinguished more by their intelligence and talent than by noble blood or exalted birth. A wealthy financier, Sir Thomas Gresham, was drafted to help sort out the muddled finances of the realm. As her secretary of state, Elizabeth named Sir William Cecil, a veteran administrator well versed in legal matters and diplomacy, who quickly established himself as the queen's closest colleague, a position he would hold for forty years. Every message and letter that entered and left the court passed through his hands; he controlled the vast network of government servants at work in England and abroad, and was privy to all state secrets. Like his sovereign, he was an intellectual, of scholarly tastes and conservative inclinations. The queen knew she could rely on his obedience to her will, if not always on his approval of her opinions.

Working closely together, Elizabeth and Cecil set to work to restore the decayed fortunes of the realm. As a first step, the Privy Council, the innermost circle of government, was reduced from thirty-nine to nineteen members. The chosen few who remained included veteran statesmen who had served under Edward and Mary as well as new men who brought fresh perspectives to the many problems facing the Crown. The council met in long and increasingly frequent sessions; if Elizabeth was absent from a meeting, she demanded detailed briefings. She made it plain to her advisers that she, not they, would steer the ship of state, declaring: "I will have here but one mistress and no master."

One of Elizabeth's first priorities was to set the storm-tossed Church of England on a firm foundation. Elizabeth was conservative in her religious views and disliked the recent reform that permitted the clergy to marry, but she was stoutly opposed to the authority of the pope. The Act of Supremacy, passed by Parliament in 1559, broke anew the link with Rome and confirmed the queen as the head of the Church, while the accompanying Act of Uniformity set out its approved forms of worship, introduced a new English prayer book to replace the Latin one, and made attendance at services compulsory. Devout Roman Catholics were not—at this stage—to be punished for practicing their faith in private. Maintaining that "consciences are not to be forced," the queen of England asked only for outward conformity to the laws of the land and for loyalty to the sovereign.

Nursing this legislation through Parliament was no easy task. The House of Commons was sympathetic, but a number of conservative clerics in the House of Lords (which included the aristocracy of both church and state) baulked at changes in ecclesiastical government and at the establishment of a layman—indeed, a laywoman—as supreme governor of the Church. Elizabeth expedited the matter by arresting two bishops and ensuring that their most powerful supporters were prevented from attending the chamber while the subject was debated. The pro-Roman bishops that Mary had appointed to the Church were removed from office and replaced by Protestant divines, including some who had fled to the Continent during the persecutions of the previous reign.

A large part of the population outside London and the counties immediately around it took little interest in theological debate, but other measures taken by the new queen and her councilors touched such people's lives more directly. They reformed the currency by removing the debased coins that had been in circulation since the reign of Henry VIII. To enlarge the agricultural labor force, they decreed that all able-bodied men not specifically permitted to engage in other trades should work the land. And, most important for those who fought in wars, or lived near vulnerable coasts and borders, the Crown negotiated treaties that ended hostilities with France and its partner, Scotland. The failure of an English attempt to aid the French Protestants by

seizing the port of Le Havre in 1562 convinced Elizabeth that England should stay out of Continental entanglements. Besides, Europe's balance of power was changing: England continued to walk warily with the French, but Spain, though still nominally an ally, began to seem the greater threat.

In the early years of her reign, one of Elizabeth's most powerful diplomatic tools was the prospect of her hand in marriage, for he who controlled the queen controlled England. During the reign of Mary, Elizabeth had turned away a succession of foreign princes, announcing that she could imagine no happier state than spinsterhood. But still, and especially after her coronation, the suitors came. Philip II of Spain, Mary's widower, made a lukewarm proposal, for form's sake, and was apparently relieved to be turned down. Scions of the European nobility offered themselves as bridegrooms: the sons of the German emperor, the duke of Savoy, the Scottish earl of Arran, and the French dukes of Anjou and Alençon, the last of whom was affectionately referred to by Elizabeth as "our frog." Elizabeth entertained their envoys courteously, considered their proposals, and played for time.

English Protestants were alarmed at the prospect of their sovereign's falling prey to the blandishments of a foreign Catholic. A pamphleteer named John Stubbs lashed out in print against the duke of Alençon, calling him "the old serpent himself in the form of a man come a second time to seduce the English Eve and to ruin the English paradise." Stubbs was arrested and had one hand chopped off for his presumption, but many of his compatriots privately shared his misgivings.

**This royal pavilion was probably designed for the fortnight-long extravaganza of jousting and feasting staged in northern France in 1520 to seal a short-lived treaty of friendship between Henry VIII and Francis I. So lavish were the gilded decorations adorning the tents in which the two sides were encamped—the English contingent alone numbered around 4,000—that the occasion became known as the Field of Cloth of Gold.**

Homegrown admirers fared little better than their alien counterparts, although several enjoyed their moments in the sun. The courtier who held the highest place in Elizabeth's regard was Lord Robert Dudley, to whom she eventually gave the title earl of Leicester. Inside the court and abroad, rumors circulated about the extent of their intimacy; foreign monarchs amused themselves with the gossip that the queen of England was about to wed her master of horse.

To a delegation of noblemen who requested Elizabeth to marry in 1562, so that an heir might be born to succeed her, she replied: "At my own time I shall turn my mind to marriage if it be for the public good." At other times she expressed herself more forcefully: "I would rather be a beggar and single than a queen and married." It is possible that the matrimonial disasters of her father, and the unhappy marriage of her half sister, Mary, had deeply affected Elizabeth's attitude toward wedlock, and over time, it became clear that the queen's only marriage would be to her people. Prayers for the sovereign's long life and good health were more than mere ritual formula: The problem of the succession would exercise Parliament, court, and country until the end of her long reign.

In the meanwhile, Elizabeth set out to dazzle her subjects on stately processions in London, or during her royal progresses through southern England and the Midlands, when she traveled with her entire court to visit her nobles and councilors in their rural seats. The lavish, jewel-encrusted costumes of the queen and her attendants, and their magnificent carriages and horses, made a lasting impression of royal dignity and power. But, with a superb sense of timing, she could drop the mask of regal aloofness, command her servants to draw her carriage close to the crowds, and thank her people for their loyalty in a pretty speech.

For the nobles upon whom she bestowed the honor of entertaining her, a royal visit was an expensive mark of favor. Feeding 300 guests, who might stay for a week or more, with their servants encamped in tents, could strip the surrounding countryside of its game and livestock, and drain it dry of ale and wine. The wealthiest men provided theatrical entertainments, armies of musicians, and fantastic landscapes devised by clever artificers for their sovereign's amusement. On one of these occasions, culminating in a fireworks display, a stray spark ignited the thatched roof of a nearby peasant's cottage. Appalled that celebrations in her honor should cause distress to a poor subject, Elizabeth insisted on paying for the reconstruction of the ruined house out of her own purse.

Such openhandedness would have surprised her servants at court. She was not thought of as a generous employer, and those who worked for her often felt it necessary to subsidize their low wages by accepting bribes from outsiders wanting access to, or favors from, the queen. The court was indeed the fountainhead of all power and privilege. The queen had innumerable benefits in her gift: tax exemptions, land grants, appointments to high office, and the rights to collect customs dues on all manner of imports and manufactures. As a consequence, she was pursued, endlessly, by the seekers of these plums, and she complained to her ladies-in-waiting about the rapacity of those around her.

Elizabeth habitually worked far into the night on state papers and rose late: "I am not a morning woman," she confessed. But court life also provided a wealth of entertainments and amusements for diversion, and time was made for hunting expeditions, daily gallops on horseback, tennis matches, archery, and dancing—Elizabeth was an energetic dancer, adept in the high leaps and complicated figures

Painted from life in about 1592, this portrait of the aging Elizabeth by Isaac Oliver was kept in the artist's studio as a pattern for more-finished—and more-flattering—pictures. In the last decade of the reign, while the succession remained unresolved, it was considered politically unwise to depict the queen as old. All accurate representations were therefore destroyed by the Privy Council, and painters were encouraged to represent the queen as eternally young and nubile. Thus the public image of England's monarch became known as the Mask of Youth.

of pavanes, lavoltas, and galliards. Her master of the revels organized masques on allegorical themes and brought in companies of professional actors and musicians.

Full of traps and temptations, the court could be a place of danger as well as pleasure. The courtier who was indiscreet, overambitious, or injudicious in his choice of friends faced ruin; even Sir Walter Raleigh, one of the most gifted men of the age, was not immune from Elizabeth's wrath, and was imprisoned in the Tower of London when it was discovered that he had secretly married one of the queen's ladies-in-waiting. Once angered, the queen was implacable. A jaded veteran, Sir Walter Mildmay, warned his son:

*Know the court, but spend not thy life there, for court is a very changeable place. I would rather wish thee to spend the greatest part of thy life in the country than to live in this glittering misery.*

The countryside might be remote from the excitements of court, but it was, politically and economically, the heart of the realm. The lord lieutenants and deputies of the counties, the justices of the peace, the members of Parliament for country districts, and even Elizabeth's professional administrators—numbering in all no more than 2,500 men—were drawn primarily from the ranks of the rural gentry. As a group, these men tended to be better educated than the members of the high nobility, sending their sons to the universities of Oxford or Cambridge or to the London law schools, the Inns of Court, to prepare them for careers in government, law, or the Church. Impressed by their collective abilities and enterprise, Queen Elizabeth very often favored this class over the nobility when she conferred rights to collect a particular tax, or to hold the monopoly on the manufacture or importation of a staple product such as salt or wine.

England was essentially a rural, agrarian society, with most of its wealth derived from the products of its fields and pastures, and during Elizabeth's reign, the land-owning class climbed to new heights of prestige and prosperity. Wool and the textiles made from it were the backbone of England's economy and supplied its principal exports. In addition to providing year-round employment for skilled spinners and weavers, the cloth industry was a part-time source of livelihood for agricultural laborers of both sexes.

As the population grew and food prices inflated—they would climb by some 600 percent between 1550 and 1650—land values rose accordingly. Gentlemen farmers found that the property they had acquired at bargain rates after the dissolution of the monasteries was now worth vastly more than they had paid for it. Their tenants prospered considerably from the increased prices they received at market, making it possible for landlords to raise rents without causing hardship. And estates could be exploited in other ways: by selling off woodland to meet the mounting demand for building materials, or by developing the mineral rights under the soil.

The formidable Bess of Hardwick, the daughter of an obscure country squire in the Midlands, was one of many landowners who amassed a huge fortune during Eliza-

beth's reign. She married a wealthy but short-lived neighbor, and by shrewd use of her inheritance, she transformed a single estate into a vast property empire, acted as a banker and mortgage holder for much of Derbyshire, developed lead mines and ironworks, and built country houses that outshone most royal palaces in gaudy magnificence. While thus engaged, she also found and outlived a brace of even richer husbands, provided dazzling dynastic marriages for her children, and acquired the title of countess of Shrewsbury.

The imposing edifice that the countess built at Hardwick in Derbyshire, with its glittering tiers of glass windows, was part of a massive Elizabethan building boom. Sharing in the growing prosperity, the nobility and gentry, and the well-to-do merchants of the towns, replaced their timber houses with handsome new ones of brick or stone. Yeomen and the more prosperous peasants built new farmhouses or rebuilt old ones, making them warmer, sounder, and infinitely more comfortable, and filling them with a growing number of worldly goods.

William Harrison, the author of the comprehensive *Description of England,* published in 1577, remarked that even the primitive smoke holes of humble cottages had been replaced by proper chimneys. Windows, once covered with sheets of thick horn or with wooden lattices, now, increasingly, were glazed. People who had previously slept on straw pallets or coarse mats, covered only with a rough sheet, now enjoyed the comforts of proper beds, bed linen, blankets, and bolsters. Their heads rested on pillows, an indulgence previously reserved for women in childbed. They ate their meals on pewter plates instead of rough wooden platters and replaced their old wooden spoons with utensils of tin or, if they were rich, of silver.

As well as adding to their domestic comforts, prosperous Elizabethans loved to surround themselves with color. "If you look into our gardens," Harrison marveled, "how wonderfully is their beauty increased, not only with flowers, but also with rare and medicinable herbs . . . so that in comparison of this present, the ancient gardens were but dunghills." Indoors, walls were hung with elaborate tapestries or painted cloths, decorated with scenes from ancient myths and legends, imaginary landscapes, fantastic beasts, clusters of fruit, and floral garlands. Less flamboyant households paneled their rooms with English oak or in wainscoting imported from the Baltic. Money was not a problem, and the merchants who dealt in foreign luxuries waxed fat as their customers demanded French wines, Oriental spices, fragrant oils and dried fruit from the sunny coasts of the Mediterranean, gold and ivories from Africa, dyestuffs from the Levant.

But trade could not flow in one direction only, and England now faced difficulties in selling its wares abroad. War was the problem in the Low Countries, where Dutch Protestants were in rebellion against Spanish rule, and the blockade of the Scheldt River below Antwerp after 1572 impeded the export of wool and textiles. And during most of the reign, mounting tensions between England and Spain augured badly for the free movement of English merchant vessels anywhere between the North Sea and the Strait of Gibraltar.

The merchants and mariners of England therefore looked outward in search of new markets. A few forays had been made in earlier reigns. These included the voyage

Accompanied by richly attired courtiers and ladies-in-waiting, Elizabeth is borne in a canopied chair through the streets of London in this painting executed in 1600. Second from the left is the bearded figure of Lord Howard of Effingham, who commanded the English fleet against the Spanish Armada. Such processions, and also the queen's summer progresses through the countryside, were calculated propaganda exercises: The opulence of her dress, the dignity of her bearing, even the words she exchanged with onlookers, were all designed to bind her subjects' loyalty to the Crown.

of John Cabot to Newfoundland and Nova Scotia in 1497, and that of William Hawkins to Africa and Brazil during 1539 and 1540. English ships had also sailed around Europe's northern coasts to Russia, and the Muscovy Company was founded in 1555 to develop trade with the formidable empire of Czar Ivan the Terrible. But these were episodic ventures, and under Elizabeth, a more comprehensive effort was made to extend English influence overseas. The first years of her reign saw new trading ventures along the coasts of Africa and fresh attempts to find shortcuts, eastward and westward, to the Orient. Other expeditions crossed the equator, in search of the legendary southern continent, the *terra australis incognita*.

The Spanish resented these incursions into their territory and were particularly alarmed by the activities of the seafaring entrepreneur John Hawkins, son of William. Spanish settlements in the West Indies depended on slave labor; their merchant ships could hardly keep up with the demand for captives from West Africa, the usual source of supply. Hawkins, as untroubled as any of his contemporaries by the evils of the slave trade, saw a commercial opportunity. Sailing first to Guinea, he purchased a cargo of 300 prisoners from local traders, then crossed the Atlantic to the Caribbean, where he found a ready market.

On his third transatlantic journey, in 1568, Hawkins's luck ran out. After disposing profitably of his human cargo, he turned toward home, only to have one of his largest vessels battered almost beyond repair by sudden gales. The fleet limped into the nearest harbor, which was the Mexican port of San Juan de Ulúa. While crewmen and carpenters struggled to mend the damage that had been done to the ship, a

This 1588 panorama of London, the largest city in northern Europe, shows its densely packed houses sprawling westward around the bend of the Thames River to Westminster, the seat of Parliament and the court, and eastward beyond the Tower of London. The single bridge spanning the river led into Southwark, a district noted for its market gardens and places of public entertainment. Many of the streets were named after their flourishing markets of fresh produce *(inset)*; despite congestion caused by a continuous influx of new inhabitants, the countryside was close at hand, and most householders had their own backyards in which they could grow vegetables or herbs and keep a pig.

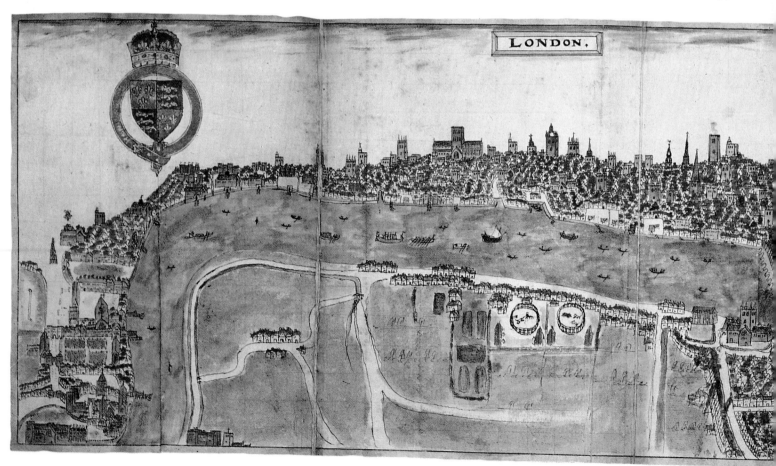

Spanish flotilla arrived, bringing Philip II's new viceroy of Mexico to take up his post.

Sailing alongside the English vessels, the viceroy ordered his men to board and capture Hawkins's ships. In the mayhem that followed, many of the English sailors were slaughtered. About 200 survivors crowded aboard the nearest ship. Working frantically, they managed to ready the vessel and sail it out of firing range, but they had no time to take on food or water. Some sailors asked to be put ashore, seeing no other hope of survival; the colonists treated them charitably, but the authorities brought them to trial as heretics, sentenced some to toil as galley slaves, and burned others at the stake. Those who stayed on board the ship endured a nightmarish journey. Out of the 400 men who had set out from England at the start of the expedition, only 70 returned in January 1569.

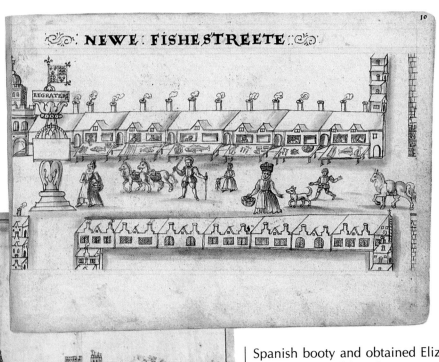

Whatever vestiges may have remained of Anglo-Spanish friendship were now destroyed, although it would be nearly twenty years before the two nations engaged in full-scale war. In the meantime, England was building more ships than ever before, and its new generation of talented and ambitious sailors did not intend to let their rivals dominate the seas.

The most celebrated of these adventurers was Francis Drake, who was a cousin of John Hawkins's and had been present at San Juan de Ulúa. In an effort to recoup some of their losses on that ill-fated voyage, the Hawkins family sent Drake to plunder Spanish colonies in the Caribbean. This he did with a vengeance, raiding towns, attacking treasure fleets bound for the homeland, and terrorizing the coasts. Spain reviled him as a pirate; Elizabeth officially disavowed him, to mollify the Spanish ambassador, but privately she smiled upon his activities.

Drake had wider ambitions than seizing Spanish booty and obtained Elizabeth's support for a voyage around the world on which he would seek out opportunities for trade and territories ripe for English settlement. He set out from Plymouth in November 1577 with five vessels and a company of 164. Drake traveled in considerable comfort: He ate off gilt-edged silver dishes marked with his coat of arms, and he had the air of his cabin sweetened with perfumed waters.

After sailing across the Atlantic and down the coast of South America, all of Drake's ships except his own, the *Golden Hind,* were forced to turn back by the dangerous currents and winds around the Strait of Magellan. Undeterred, Drake pressed on alone, launching surprise attacks on Spanish settlements along the coasts of Chile and Peru, and ransacking the treasure ships that were anchored there. He then crossed the Pacific—he was the first Englishman to do so—and, after visiting various islands in the East Indies, followed the route pioneered by Portuguese navigators across the Indian Ocean. He rounded the Cape of Good Hope without mishap, then sailed up the west coast of Africa and back to England, where he arrived in November 1580, just three years after he had left it.

The spectacular success of this voyage proved beyond a doubt that England's mariners were now as skilled and as daring as those of any other nation. In April 1581, Francis Drake was knighted by his proud and grateful sovereign.

The activities of Drake and his fellow seafarers were not the only reasons for the deterioration in Anglo-Spanish relations. Religious tensions also played a part. After an unsuccessful rebellion by Catholic nobles in the north of England, Pope Pius V issued a papal bull in 1570 that excommunicated the queen and enjoined all good Catholics to work toward her downfall. Philip II of Spain could now justify his opposition to Elizabeth as a crusade against a heretic, and in the following years, he helped subsidize various plots to depose her in favor of her Catholic cousin, Mary Stuart, queen of the Scots, who had a claim to the throne because of her descent from the sister of Henry VIII.

The Scottish queen had been forced to take refuge in England in 1568, after her own subjects rose up against her and accused her of murdering her husband. English Protestants feared that Mary—whom Elizabeth kept imprisoned in various castles—might become the figurehead for additional Catholic uprisings. In fact, most Catholics in England were content to live as a minority, practicing their faith in private, but a number of conspiracies against Elizabeth were uncovered; and in the last of these, Mary was strongly implicated. It is possible that a letter from Mary to the leader of the

An illustration from a moral treatise published in 1569 shows alms being distributed to the needy by government-appointed officials. After Henry VIII's dissolution of the monasteries in the 1530s, the poor had depended solely on private charity; during Elizabeth's reign, the number of paupers and vagrants increased steeply, and laws were enacted to raise public money for their welfare.

plot, expressing her approval of the planned uprising, may have been forged, but the scheme bore all the hallmarks of secret Spanish intervention, and Elizabeth's Parliament bayed for blood. The queen, apparently with reluctance, signed her cousin's death warrant, and Mary was beheaded at Fotheringhay Castle in the county of Northamptonshire in 1587.

Elizabeth had always favored a policy of tolerance, protesting that she did not wish to "make windows into men's hearts," but many of her subjects were less accommodating. Their unease was fueled by a stream of Jesuit missionaries who filtered into England from a seminary at Douai, in the Spanish-controlled Netherlands. The Jesuits' goal was to undo the Reformation by returning England to the faith of Rome, and if necessary, they were prepared to endure martyrdom for their cause. Parliament obliged them by making it a capital offense for Catholic priests to enter England. Between 1580 and the end of Elizabeth's reign, 180 Catholics were executed for treason. They went to the scaffold and the stake convinced that they suffered for their faith; the official view was that they died because they favored England's enemies.

In 1585, Philip II had told the pope that he intended to invade England. The Vatican did not trouble to keep his promise secret, and a network of English spies sent home frequent reports on Spanish plans. But even without this intelligence, it was apparent that England faced the prospect of a western Europe entirely under Spanish domination. In 1580, Philip had inherited the Portuguese empire, together with its substantial fleet. In France, Spain was supporting a militant faction that was determined to exclude the Protestant heir to the throne from the succession. Farther north, Spanish forces were fighting to retain control of the Netherlands; and when England sent funds and fighting men to support the Dutch rebels, Philip interpreted this action as a declaration of war against Spain. In fact, Elizabeth would have preferred to avoid war at all costs, deeming it a shameful waste of human and financial resources, but circumstances now forced her to consider it.

As an island kingdom, with nowhere more than seventy-five miles from a coast, England inevitably depended on the sea as a first line of defense. Henry VIII, breaking with the old practice of using only conscripted merchant ships for war, had established a royal navy, with vessels built specifically for war and two royal dockyards to service them. Queen Elizabeth added new ships and ordered the upgrading of old ones, without relieving the merchant fleet of its obligation to come to her country's aid in times of crisis.

In an effort to buy time, Elizabeth sent Sir Francis Drake on a preemptive strike. In April 1587, he launched a surprise attack on the harbor of Cadiz in southwestern Spain, where part of Philip's fleet was anchored. The operation, which was nicknamed "the singeing of the king of Spain's beard," destroyed twenty-four ships that had been prepared for an invasion of England and wiped out a substantial part of the Spanish forces' supplies. As the smoke cleared, Drake sailed out toward the Azores, where he hoped to seize some of the ships known to be heading home to Spain laden with spices from India and silver from the Americas. The warships attached to the Spanish fleets managed to fight off Drake's attack, and he succeeded in capturing

Horse-drawn coaches and covered wagons—such as the one shown here in a manuscript illustration—were introduced into England around the middle of the sixteenth century, at about the same time that local parishes were made responsible for the upkeep of roads within their boundaries. Outside the immediate environs of London, however, coaches were rarely used: Highways were rutted and overgrown, the vehicles were unsprung, and a journey of just thirty miles could take longer than twelve hours.

Built in 1599, London's Globe Theatre *(far right)* was home to Lord Chamberlain's Men—the theatrical company for which Shakespeare *(right)* wrote nearly half of his thirty-nine plays. The Globe, commissioned by the theater company and constructed on the south bank of the Thames River, could accommodate an audience of 3,000. On every day of the week except Sunday, playgoers from every level of society—laborers, students, merchants, and courtiers—assembled to participate in the heady mixture of topical satire, bawdy comedy, and sublime tragedy encompassed by the newly mature English drama.

The well-off sat on benches in the timber-framed galleries sheltered by a thatched roof; the poor stood in the central pit open to the sky. Both could purchase food and drink throughout the performances, which generally started around 2 p.m. and concluded with a song-and-dance act some three hours later. The raised stage backed toward the afternoon sun, so that the actors performed in the shade.

Thirty-five in the year the Globe was built, Shakespeare was then at the peak of his profession and enjoying its rewards: In 1597, he purchased the second-largest house in Stratford-on-Avon, his birthplace in Warwickshire. But as an actor and shareholder in his company, as well as a playwright, he had little time for relaxation. Companies comprised about twenty male actors, including the young apprentices who performed female roles, and they put on a different play every day. Leading actors had to memorize a number of major roles, and others played several parts in each production.

Working with minimal scenery and props—some hanging curtains, a throne, a bed, a few stools or benches—actors relied heavily on the quality and delivery of their lines to win the boisterous audience's approval. Shouting and clapping, or hissing and a barrage of apple cores, soon told them whether they had succeeded.

# A STAGE FOR ALL THE WORLD

only one ship. Nevertheless, the Spanish suffered heavy losses of men and munitions, and were further battered by storms before they reached safe harbor.

Early in 1588, the queen began to mobilize for war. The navy would be the first line of defense, but land forces also had to be organized. England had no standing army; instead, the fittest men of each community were formed into local companies, given weapons and equipment, and instructed in their use. The lord lieutenants of every county were instructed to muster these companies and drill them into readiness; the nobles were called upon to supply their horses and retainers for the cavalry. In a spirit of patriotic fervor, the members of the gentry volunteered their services and donated funds, horses, muskets, and such men as they could spare from their estates. Some 50,000 foot soldiers and 10,000 horses were assembled; 29,000 men from London and the south of England formed the queen's personal defense force.

At the mouths of the Thames and Medway estuaries, leading into the North Sea, pontoon barriers were erected. Should Spanish vessels penetrate these defenses, every strategic bend in the Thames River concealed an artillery platform to deter the invaders with a barrage of gunfire. One thousand beacons were mounted on tall iron

poles along the southern coast and upon every commanding hilltop in Sussex and Kent. At the first sight of a Spanish sail, these baskets of pitch and tar would be set alight, one after another, sending the alarm to London in twenty minutes or less.

As England waited, Spain assembled a seemingly invincible invasion force in the port of Lisbon. Never before in Europe had so many vessels, fighting men, arms, and provisions been gathered together in one place, to set sail simultaneously and travel such a distance to the battleground. Following the death of the elderly marquis of Santa Cruz in early 1588, command of the Armada was entrusted to the duke of Medina-Sidonia. Although he lacked experience in naval warfare, and was at first highly critical of the whole enterprise, Medina-Sidonia was a skilled and tactful leader who was respected by all his captains.

The Spanish fleet of 130 great ships left Lisbon at the end of May 1588 and, after struggling against strong headwinds, set sail again from the northern port of Corunna in late July. The strategy that Philip had finally settled upon, with little reference to his professional commanders, called for Medina-Sidonia's Armada to rendezvous in the English Channel with a fleet of small transport vessels and barges carrying an army from the Spanish Netherlands, led by the duke of Parma. But the message that Medina-Sidonia sent to Parma, announcing his arrival in the Channel, did not get there in time. Instead of meeting with Parma's support fleet, he found the combined forces of Elizabeth's Royal Navy and her merchant ships, ready to pound the Spanish vessels with artillery fire.

Although the combatants were equally matched in terms of ships and guns, the Spaniards were not adequately prepared for the battle that ensued. Their soldiers, armed with pikes and muskets, waited on the decks for their opponents to approach and confront them according to the traditional rules of war. Instead, the English artillery began to bombard their ships from a distance. Thanks to constant practice and the efficient design of their guns, the English were able to fire about ten rounds to the Spaniards' one. In addition, the Spanish gunners were constantly impeded by the large number of soldiers on board their ships.

At Gravelines, off the Flanders coast between Calais and Dunkirk, the English moved in closer for the kill. During the night of August 7, eight fire ships—unmanned vessels packed with explosives and with loaded guns that would fire when the heat reached them—were directed toward the Spanish formation. Panic-stricken Spanish captains ordered their anchors to be cut, causing their ships to run aground or drift helplessly away from the rest of the fleet. The next day, in a nine-hour battle, the English gunners crippled more Spanish ships and blasted others full of holes as they struggled to escape.

What the English cannon started, the weather finished. Fierce storms drove the remnants of the invasion force northward, up and around the coast of Scotland and down toward Ireland in the west. Warships sank in Tobermory Bay, off the Hebridean isle of Mull, and off the Irish coast at Donegal; one, driven far north of the rest, went down in the frigid waters off Fair Isle, between Orkney and Shetland. Crews were forced to abandon ships beyond repair and take their chances on hostile shores. Medina-Sidonia's own flagship, its ruptured timbers lashed together with rope, took a month to struggle home to Spain.

Philip's great crusade against the heretic queen, his much-vaunted Enterprise of England, ended in disaster. Sir Walter Raleigh, offering a professional soldier's view of Philip's failure, said that "to invade by sea upon a perilous coast, being neither in

Cut off from the influence of Italian Renaissance art after Henry VIII's breach with the Church of Rome, Tudor artists developed a genre unique to England—the miniature portrait, often less than three inches tall. Initially, these exquisite objects were almost exclusively a royal prerogative, and their bestowal by the queen was deemed a mark of signal favor. But by the end of the century, they were widely commissioned by the wealthy classes. Producing a miniature was a laborious process. Requiring three sittings of several hours apiece, each painting was progressively worked up with fine squirrel-hair brushes to a jewel-like finish; the results were treasured by their owners in ornately carved ivory boxes or worn discreetly as lockets.

The most celebrated exponent of the style was the painter Nicholas Hilliard, son of an Exeter goldsmith, who became Elizabeth's foremost portraitist. Reproduced here, slightly larger than actual size, is a full-length miniature by Hilliard that probably depicts Elizabeth's last favorite, Robert Devereux, second earl of Essex. Dressed in the queen's colors of black and white, the lovesick youth displays the melancholy mien that became fashionable in Elizabeth's twilight years.

# THE MIRROR OF AN AGE

possession of any port, nor succored by any party, may better fit a prince presuming on his fortune than enriched with understanding." The undeclared war between the two kingdoms would continue until the end of Elizabeth's reign, but the once indomitable foe was cut down to size. English ships, and English sailors, had proved their worth, and their homeland now took its place among Europe's principal powers.

Never had England's self-confidence been greater, and no symbol of the realm's new glory was more potent than Elizabeth herself. The old pagan goddesses had been driven underground by one thousand years of Christianity, and the English Reformation had done its best to suppress the Roman Catholic cult of the Virgin Mary. In place of these all-powerful female deities of the past, England now had its Virgin Queen. Poets compared her to chaste Diana, moon goddess and huntress, or, even more aptly, to Astraea, a many-faceted figure from classical mythology who was at once virgin and fertility goddess, bringer of justice and cornerstone of empire, the harbinger of a new golden age. Painters depicted Elizabeth in robes of near-impossible magnificence; in her hands they placed rainbows, white ermines, and other objects expressing peace, virtue, majesty, and truth in the intricate, allusive language of Renaissance signs and symbols.

In 1590, the poet Edmund Spenser presented to Elizabeth the first part of his allegorical poem, *The Faerie Queene*. By this title, the author explained, "I mean glory in my general intention, but in my particular, I conceive the most excellent and glorious person of our sovereign." Spenser's verse represented the epitome of the learned, allusive style that was favored in court circles, where the writing of poetry was considered as important an accomplishment as fencing or horsemanship. It drew upon a knowledge of the literatures of ancient Greece and Rome that had been brought to northern Europe earlier in the century by scholars such as Erasmus and Sir Thomas More. But the benefits of this scholarship were not limited to the court or the universities, and it was out of the creative mix of new learning, popular culture, and the vigorously expanding English language that the chief literary masterpieces of the Elizabethan age were born.

Of all the arts, it was the theater that was most open to innovation. In breaking the unity of the Catholic church throughout Europe, the Protestant Reformation had loosened the bonds that for centuries had made drama an instrument of the Church, its purpose being to illustrate the themes and moral precepts of Christianity. In addition, since the rate of literacy was low and popular culture was oral rather than written, the theater had by far the largest potential audience. Londoners flocked to attend the comedies, tragedies, and historical dramas of a gifted generation of playwrights: Ben Jonson, dissector of his fellow Londoners' foibles in a string of satires; Christopher Marlowe, creator of *Dr. Faustus* and *Tamburlaine the Great,* who made outrageous atheistic statements, declared that "he who loves not tobacco and boys is a fool," and surprised no one when he came to a bad end in a tavern brawl; and above all, William Shakespeare, whose fusion of popular appeal with profound human and intellectual qualities made him a writer, in the words of Ben Jonson, "not of an age, but for all time."

The playwrights drew their inspiration from Greek and Roman histories, bawdy Italian romances, the chronicles of English kings and warriors, street ballads, and pamphlets and folk traditions with which their audience was closely familiar. Their language was rich and racy, studded with foreign words and flourishes, reflecting

England's newly opened windows on the outside world. Many of them began their careers in the theater as actors, and as veteran showmen, they knew how to work a crowd: Passages that flowed like music, startling insights into the human heart, were interspersed with sword fights, battles, murder, and mayhem, to keep ditchdiggers and philosophers entertained in equal measure.

The theater's ability to impart ideas and to amuse was one reason it acquired powerful enemies as well as friends. Many Puritans, who represented the most radical strand of Protestant thought, opposed all such secular recreations as dangerous deviations from the path of Christian virtue. In periods of real or threatened epidemic, the authorities may have had cause to close crowded theaters as possible breeding grounds for infection; when no such excuses presented themselves, they tried to close them anyway, and in the 1590s, they frequently succeeded. At such times, playwrights and other writers had special need of the wealthy and powerful patrons they attracted. With the right to style themselves "the Lord Chamberlain's" or "the Lord Admiral's" men, theatrical companies found it easier to keep their licenses for public performances, or to mount their productions for the private entertainment of the nobility and the queen.

Other arts besides the theater flourished in these years. John Dowland's *First Booke of Songes or Ayres,* published in 1597, was one of many such compilations issued by accomplished musicians. Nicholas Hilliard's miniature portraits of the queen and her courtiers introduced a new and distinctive school of English painting. Commissions from wealthy landowners for imposing new houses gave work to architects and landscape gardeners. And in London, booksellers and printers as well as actors and playwrights profited from the enormous popularity of the playhouses. In the environs of Saint Paul's churchyard, where the industry was centered, printed editions of current plays sold for the equivalent of half a day-laborer's wages. Also on sale were broadsheets, pamphlets, travelers' tales, collected sermons, lurid accounts of recent murders and executions, works of theology and history, translations of Continental literature, dictionaries and grammars of the English and foreign languages, even a

# THE MARITIME ADVENTURERS

"Whosoever commands the sea commands the trade; whosoever commands the trade of the world commands the riches of the world, and consequently the world itself." Convinced by the logic of the courtier and adventurer Walter Raleigh, English mariners in the second half of the sixteenth century contested the long-held monopoly of Spain and Portugal over trade routes to the New World. The slave trading of John Hawkins in the Caribbean and Francis Drake's attacks on treasure fleets brought England into direct conflict with Spain, but other voyages were undertaken to fulfill long-term goals. In 1576, Martin Frobisher explored Canada's northern coasts in search of a northwest passage to Asia; between 1577 and 1580, Drake circumnavigated the globe to seek out new trading opportunities; Humphrey Gilbert took possession of Newfoundland in 1583, establishing the first English colony in America. Raleigh himself attempted to found colonies in North America, and he led an expedition to South America in 1595. By 1600, the navigational skills and improved ship designs of the English had given them ascendancy over their rivals; in the following decades, they would proceed to establish their own colonial empire.

guide to thieves' English and an account of the trade secrets of the criminal fraternity. This variety of printed matter testified to the expanding tastes of an increasingly literate population, and to the breadth and vigor of the English Renaissance.

The capital city of London was the center of the Elizabethan universe, the fountainhead of wealth and power, attracting the ambitious and the desperate alike. Although its streets were crammed with thousands of shops, workshops, market stalls, and small factories, during the latter years of Elizabeth's reign, poverty was rising in most of the realm. As the 1590s progressed, the gulf between rich and poor became greater than ever before. There were too many people for the land to feed, and food prices continued the upward spiral begun earlier in the reign.

The poor, as preachers never ceased to observe, had always been present, but a new kind of pauper now appeared in the countryside. The traditional underclass had consisted mainly of those unfit to earn their own livings: the disabled, the sick, the orphaned, and the old. But the number of those who struggled to survive on society's margins increasingly included those who were capable of work but could find none: landless farm laborers, textile workers whose skills were superfluous when trade was slack, soldiers and sailors wounded in action. The highways were full of male and female vagrants, drifting or driven from one village to the next. Many women took to the road to conceal out-of-wedlock pregnancies and sought shelter in barns and haystacks when their time came; parish records duly noted the burials of nameless female travelers and their newborn infants. In many parts of rural England, afflicted by a run of disastrous harvests, starvation was a common cause of death.

Between 1572 and 1601, legislation was enacted and amended to raise funds for the support of paupers and to control the growing number of vagrants on the roads. These laws established a compulsory poor rate to be levied on the householders of each parish for the support of local pau-

A sixteenth-century chart shows the protected port of Plymouth in southwest England, a point of embarkation for many seafarers, including Walter Raleigh (far left) and Francis Drake (above).

pers, and they ordered the return of vagrants to their native parishes. Parishes were told to furnish ''a competent store of wool, hemp, flax, iron, or other stuff'' to provide work for the able-bodied unemployed. Overseers of the poor were appointed to assess and gather the poor rate, and to distribute the income to the needy.

Begging was banned, except under license. Those permitted to beg included paupers resident in districts with insufficient funds for poor relief, unfortunates who had lost their worldly goods, and disabled veterans from the wars—for example, an amputee might be granted a temporary license to beg until he had raised the fee to pay the surgeon. Cases deemed by the authorities to be less deserving were treated harshly. Unlicensed beggars were flogged or pierced through the ear with a hot iron. Their children were taken away, to be bound over to the custody of some upright householder, who would give them shelter and improve their morals in exchange for an indefinite period of unpaid servitude.

Poor laws, whether humane or Draconian, could provide only temporary and partial solutions to the problem of an overcrowded kingdom. Elizabethans looked

In this Dutch picture painted around 1600, the ships of the Spanish Armada, sent to invade England in the summer of 1588, retreat in disarray under cannon fire from the English fleet. The Battle of Gravelines, fought off the coast of France, commenced after the Spanish formation had been broken up by unmanned English fire ships, seen here in the middle background. Following the engagement, strong winds drove the surviving Spanish vessels northward, and many of them foundered on the rocky coasts of Scotland and Ireland.

speculatively toward the New World and laid plans to establish colonies in North America. In 1587, a company of 133 men and 17 women was sent to settle a part of the territory that in 1584 had been named Virginia—in tribute to the queen—by Sir Walter Raleigh. Four years later, these settlers were found to have vanished without a trace. Successful settlements would come, but Elizabeth would not live to see them.

Other Englishmen saw prospects for expansion nearer home, on the troubled island across the Irish Sea. The English had been active in Ireland since the twelfth century, and in 1541, Henry VIII had begun to style himself king of Ireland, although only a small area—in and around the old Viking settlement of Dublin—lay under English domination. The rest of the country was divided between Anglo-Irish earldoms, controlled by the descendants of medieval English adventurers, and the territories ruled by native Gaelic chieftains.

The English regarded the indigenous population as savages. The Irish, who had been Christians long before the English and had never swerved from their loyalty to Rome, saw the invaders as oppressors, intent on filling the country with their own people and forcing the native peoples to abandon the Catholic faith. Resistance mounted, and by the 1590s, the whole island was in revolt. Spanish gold provided fuel for the risings, and a powerful leader—Hugh O'Neill, earl of Tyrone—succeeded in uniting the Gaelic clans in a full-scale war.

The queen complained that she grew tired of reading the Irish dispatches, and that the conflict was bleeding her exchequer dry. Withdrawal, however, was unthinkable, and in 1599, she sent Robert Devereux, earl of Essex—her current favorite, and the stepson of her beloved Leicester, now deceased—to crush the rebels. The task might have been impossible even for a competent leader, but Essex's regime was a disaster. He ignored or disobeyed virtually every order the queen gave him, and his own alternative tactics led only to defeats and humiliations. In 1600, on hearing from his personal network of spies that a faction within the court was plotting against him, he hurried back to London.

Essex was placed under house arrest for his disobedience, and a committee of judges determined that he should be officially censured for his mishandling of Irish affairs. As an additional mortification, the queen threatened to withdraw the earl's main source of income—the right to collect duties on all sweet wines coming into the realm, which she had granted him years before as a mark of her particular favor. Brooding over these miseries, Essex sought redress in conspiracy. He gathered together a group of aristocratic malcontents, backed by a force of armed retainers and veteran soldiers. Essex and his supporters then prepared—or so rumor had it—to launch a revolt in the streets of London.

Messengers dispatched by the queen were taken prisoner by the rebels, but after a skirmish in the streets, Essex was arrested and charged with treason. Because of his rank, he escaped the slow and grisly death that was the usual fate of those convicted of the crime: to be hanged, taken down alive, disemboweled, and hacked to pieces. On February 25, 1601, he was beheaded at the Tower of London. Elizabeth did not attend the execution.

The queen's long reign was by then approaching its end. She was ailing and grew melancholic as she outlived a succession of old friends and close advisers. As her strength ebbed, she saw the triumphs of earlier years overshadowed by present troubles. A contemporary chronicler noted that, on one occasion when she was addressing Parliament, she nearly fainted; another sharp-eyed observer recorded that the queen was now painting her face, neck, and bosom with thick layers of cosmetics to disguise her sickly color.

Financially, the kingdom was no healthier than the queen, and Elizabeth was forced to appeal to Parliament to levy new taxes. The defeat of the Armada in 1588 had saved England from invasion, but other hostilities were steadily impoverishing the treasury. At sea, English ships continued to clash with rival fleets. On the Continent, English troops were committed to aiding the Protestants in both the Low Countries and France against Spanish armies. In Ireland, several thousand Spanish soldiers arrived in 1601 to help their coreligionists in their own war of liberation; it took months of hard fighting to drive them out again.

Aware of her subjects' economic hardships, Elizabeth agreed to one radical reform, allowing Parliament to repeal many of the monopolies she had granted over the years as a mark of privilege. No longer would the prices of staple goods be jacked ever higher by the need to pay some favored individual a tax for their import or sale. It was a popular move. When members of the House of Commons visited the queen to express their gratitude, she replied in kind:

> Though God hath raised me high, yet this I count the glory of my Crown, that I have reigned with your loves . . . I do not so much rejoice that God hath made me to be a queen, as to be queen over so thankful a people.

On both sides, the sentiments were sincere. Elizabeth's subjects at home were enjoying an uninterrupted period of peace and had good reason to be grateful. Abroad, England was embroiled in unresolved wars—but this very conflict testified to Elizabeth's achievement in transforming a backward, inward-looking land on the western periphery of Europe into a formidable international power, challenging its rivals for domination of the seas, trading with the emperors of the Orient, and claiming vast tracts of the New World in the name of its queen.

One final task remained: the naming of a successor. Elizabeth's cousin and privy councilor, George Carey, recorded in his diary for March 1603, that after much persuasion, the dying queen had taken to her bed, and that "there is now no hope of her recovery because she refuseth all remedies." Prompted by her chief ministers to announce her chosen heir to the throne, "she replied that . . . a king should succeed her; and who, quoth she, should that be but our cousin of Scotland. They asked her whether that were her absolute resolution. Whereunto she answered, I pray you trouble me no more; I'll have none but him."

Two days later, in the early hours of March 24, 1603, the queen died. Two noblemen, racing to be the first to deliver the momentous news, mounted their horses and rode hard for the Scottish border to tell the son of Mary Stuart, James VI of Scotland, that he was king in the land of his ancestral enemies, which his cousin Elizabeth had brought to greatness.

# THE GUNPOWDER REVOLUTION

Against the explosive power of cannon and muskets, no weapons that relied on muscle and marksmanship for their deadliness could prevail. During the sixteenth century, when gunpowder was exploited with increasing efficiency, small armies became able to defeat forces many times their size, and the survival of whole nations was often determined by whether their armies possessed the new technology of war.

Cannon were first used in Europe during the wars between England and France in the fourteenth century, but it was not until Charles VIII of France launched an invasion of Italy in 1494 that the potential of this weapon became widely recognized. The French horse-drawn guns—depicted on the right in a sixteenth-century manuscript illustration—enabled France to dominate Italy for thirty years. In the Middle and Far East as well as in Europe, other countries absorbed the lesson and hastily acquired artillery of their own.

To counter the new siege weaponry, military defenses were improved. The Italians showed the way by designing thicker, more substantial fortifications with elaborate fields of fire to break up an advancing enemy. The high cost of these defenses was accepted as the necessary price of security, both at home and abroad: To safeguard their overseas possessions, the Europeans built castles as well as citadels along the shores of the Americas, Africa, and Asia. So effective were these defenses that sieges could last months or even years, and the decisive encounter in wars was often fought between the besieging army and a

force sent to relieve the beleaguered city.

In field battles, the issue was increasingly decided by hand-held firearms—first the unwieldy harquebus, later the more efficient musket, invented in Spain. Although these weapons weighed about twenty pounds each and at best could fire just one round every two minutes, their shot was discharged with enough force to penetrate armor and stop a cavalry charge, and by 1600, tactics had been devised that minimized their handicaps.

These developments in land warfare were mirrored by similar changes at sea. Oared galleys gave way to sailing ships equipped with numerous cannon, and new battle formations were adopted that allowed the ships to take full advantage of their deadly firepower.

In this Indian miniature, the Mogul emperor Akbar—dressed in white, at the top of the hill—observes his cannon in action during the siege of a Rajput fort in 1568. Below the emperor, a team of oxen drags another heavy gun into position.

Led by Ivan the Terrible, Russian troops besiege the Tatar city of Kazan in 1552 with artillery and muskets. Mines, exploded in tunnels that had been dug under the walls, cut off the city's water supply, while above ground its defenses were bombarded by cannon mounted on wooden towers.

An army that lacked gunpowder could capture a fortified stronghold only by direct assault—which incurred heavy losses—or by the lengthy procedure of starving the inhabitants into surrender. Heavy artillery mounted on wheels dramatically transformed this situation, giving the besiegers a decisive advantage. The cannon that the Ottoman Turks brought with them from Constantinople (known to the Turks as Istanbul) made possible the capture of Belgrade and other cities in southeastern Europe in campaigns limited to a few months each year. In 1529, the Ottomans failed to take Vienna only because their artillery was delayed by bad weather and poor roads.

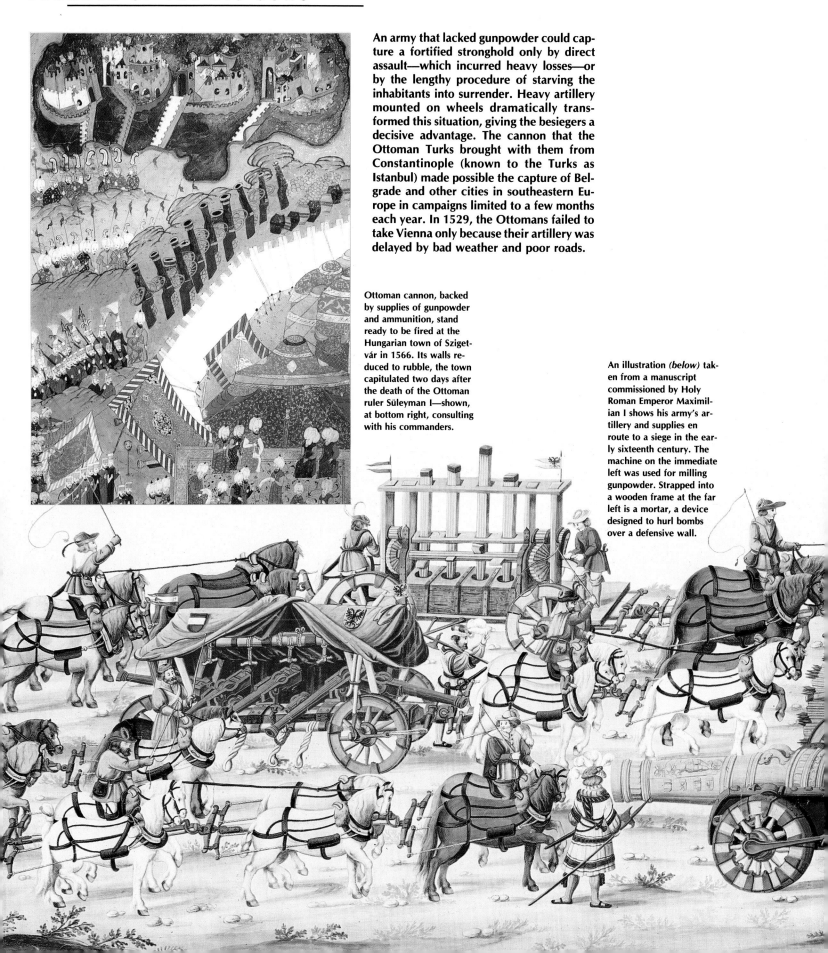

Ottoman cannon, backed by supplies of gunpowder and ammunition, stand ready to be fired at the Hungarian town of Szigetvár in 1566. Its walls reduced to rubble, the town capitulated two days after the death of the Ottoman ruler Süleyman I—shown, at bottom right, consulting with his commanders.

An illustration (below) taken from a manuscript commissioned by Holy Roman Emperor Maximilian I shows his army's artillery and supplies en route to a siege in the early sixteenth century. The machine on the immediate left was used for milling gunpowder. Strapped into a wooden frame at the far left is a mortar, a device designed to hurl bombs over a defensive wall.

# STRENGTHENING THE DEFENSES

To meet the challenge presented by siege artillery, military engineers designed defenses of increasing sophistication. Walls were built thicker and lower, and wide ditches kept enemy guns at a distance. In the early sixteenth century, Italian architects devised a system of projecting bastions linked by short curtain walls; built at an obtuse angle to render them less vulnerable to enemy bombardment, the walls of the bastions afforded many lines of fire to the guns they concealed, leaving no dead ground into which besiegers could advance unscathed. Despite the enormous cost of these fortifications, they were adopted by most European countries—with the result that sieges often were stalemated.

The star-shaped fortifications of the Italian town of Palmanova *(above right)*, built in the 1590s, ensure all-around protection. Artillery sheltered in each projecting bastion could fire both directly at an oncoming enemy and across the face of adjacent bastions *(right)*.

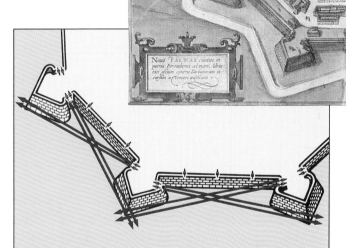

The massive stone foundation of Matsumoto Castle *(right)* in Japan proved an invincible barrier to besiegers. Replacing earlier wooden stockades that the advent of firearms had rendered obsolete, about sixty such castles were built in Japan between 1580 and 1640.

An illustration from a 1573 German manual on warfare shows attackers digging a tunnel to undermine a city's ramparts. In the sixteenth century, the use of gunpowder mines that could be exploded in the tunnels gave a new twist to this traditional siege tactic.

Designed around 1565 by an Italian engineer, the fortified Spanish settlement of Saint Augustine in Florida contained enough arms and ammunition to withstand a long siege. Such fortifications were essential to the security of European colonies in the Americas.

A detail from a painting of the battle of Pavia, fought in Italy in 1525, shows a massed squadron of harquebusiers, the troops who were chiefly responsible for Holy Roman Emperor Charles V's victory over Francis I of France. The French possessed fewer firearms and suffered more than eight times the number of casualties of the imperial army.

On the panels of a Japanese screen *(right)*, musketeers fire in unison at the battle of Nagashino in 1575, a decisive conflict in Japan's century-long civil war. The Japanese concern with long-range accuracy rather than close-range volley fire is evident in an illustration taken from a sixteenth-century training manual *(below)*.

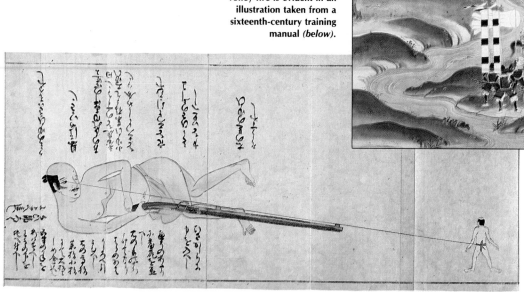

The introduction of firearms revolution-ized infantry tactics in the sixteenth centu-ry. Massed formations gave way to long, thin lines, and by the 1590s, the Dutch had developed the technique of continuous vol-leying—one rank of soldiers retiring to re-load while another took aim and fired. In addition, new drill movements were re-quired so that troops could fire in unison and maneuver quickly to protect their flanks. The growing reliance on firearms meant that the proportion of musketeers to pikemen gradually increased, as did the im-portance of infantry in relation to caval-ry—who could now be shot down before they were able to engage the enemy.

An African bronze depicts a Portuguese soldier firing a matchlock musket. From the beginning of the six-teenth century, guns were sold by the Portuguese to the kings of Benin on Afri-ca's west coast in return for gold, ivory, and slaves.

Featured in a detail from a tapestry of the Spanish Armada of 1588, this galleass *(near right)*—a cross between a galley and a sailing ship—carried some fifty guns and 300 rowers as well as several hundred crew and soldiers. The galleass's value was proven at Lepanto in 1571, when six of the vessels were said to have destroyed seventy Ottoman galleys.

The *Mary Rose,* shown below in a picture from a 1546 catalog of Henry VIII's English navy, was designed to accommodate more than ninety heavy cannon. The ship sank in 1545 when water flooded into the open gunports on the lower decks.

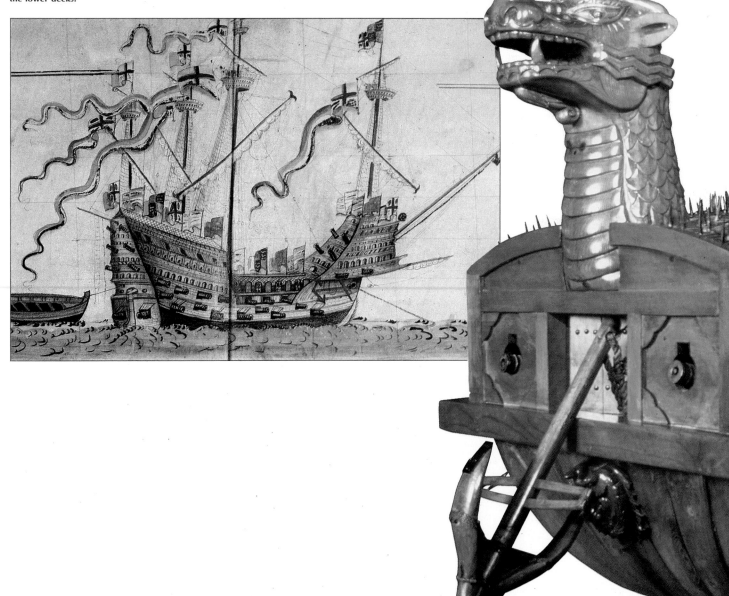

The use of cannon in naval warfare led to dramatic changes both in the design of ships and in battle tactics. The new vessels, armed with rows of cannon on several decks, resembled floating fortresses; by 1600, warships were larger than ever, and many countries' navy yards had become their most ambitious industrial enterprise. Although ramming, boarding, and hand-to-hand fighting were still prominent features of most engagements, broadsides fired from a distance became increasingly important. Accordingly, fleets prepared for battle by sailing in extended lines in order to bring the maximum possible firepower to bear upon the enemy.

A reconstruction of a Korean turtleship (left) shows cannon protruding from its gunports; its name derived from the spiked metal plates that prevented its being boarded. With these ships—shown also in the painting behind the model—the Koreans defeated a much larger Japanese invasion fleet in the 1590s.

# RUSSIA'S RUTHLESS CZAR

"To show his sovereignty over the lives of his subjects, the late emperor Ivan Vasilevich, in his walks or progresses, if he misliked the face or person of any man whom he met by the way, or that looked upon him, would command his head to be struck off. Which was presently done, and the head cast before him." The author of this report, an English envoy named Giles Fletcher, probably considered himself fortunate that he arrived in Russia four years after this tyrant had died in 1584. But the effects of Ivan's rule were still apparent, not least in the sullen discontent of the Russian people: "The desperate state of things at home maketh the people for the most part to wish for some foreign invasion, which they suppose to be the only means to rid them of the heavy yoke of this tyrannous government."

As Czar Ivan IV, Ivan Vasilyevich had ruled an expanding Russian state of more than six million people for almost half a century. The early years were auspicious: An energetic program of legal reforms promised to eradicate corrupt official practices, and a spectacularly successful campaign against the Tatars to the east greatly expanded the borders of the young state. Ivan was described at this time by Sir Jerome Horsey, another English envoy resident for many years in Russia, as a young man "comely of person, imbued with great wit, excellent gifts and graces, fit for government of so great a monarchy." But in the latter half of his reign, Ivan increasingly revealed a terrifying dual nature, the inspired statesman competing with a paranoid tyrant whose principal policy was terror. He became known as Ivan Groznyi, a word signifying that Ivan inspired great awe and fear among his people; it was commonly translated as "the Terrible." The cruelty of his autocratic rule was to cast a lasting shadow over the future of the Russian state.

The people over whom Ivan reigned were eastern Slavs united by a common language and by Orthodox Christianity, but until the fifteenth century, they had had no single sovereign ruler. A prosperous Russian state based upon the city of Kiev, sited close to the Dnieper River, which flows into the Black Sea, had flourished in the eleventh century but had later fragmented into independent principalities. These and neighboring territories had been overrun in the thirteenth century by Mongol armies sweeping westward across Asia. And for 150 years, their rulers remained vassals of the Golden Horde, a Mongol empire with its capital at Sarai on the lower Volga, north of the Caspian Sea. The Mongols approved the appointment of princes, conscripted soldiers for their armies, and exacted crippling taxes. The merest hint of rebellion from a Russian city brought upon it a merciless attack by "the accursed infidels," as early Russian chroniclers described their Muslim overlords.

By the end of the fourteenth century, however, Mongol power was waning, and Moscow—first mentioned in the chronicles in 1147 as a fortress on the Moskva, a

A detail from a sixteenth-century icon captures the lined and brooding face of Czar Ivan IV. Intelligent, devout, and domineering, Ivan stamped his absolute authority on the newly unified Russian state; but in the latter half of his reign, his suspicions of all around him verged on paranoia, and the fear he inspired in his subjects won him the appellation of Ivan the Terrible.

tributary of the Oka River—had become the political, spiritual, and military center of the oppressed Russian people. At Kulikovo, south of Moscow, a Muscovite army routed the Mongols in 1380 and lifted the spirits of Russian patriots. Fifteen years later, the Mongol capital of Sarai was sacked by the armies of Tamerlane, the founder of a new but short-lived Mongol empire; Tamerlane's heirs continued to exact tribute for another few decades, but the yoke of foreign rule was finally beginning to slip from Russia's shoulders.

Moscow owed its prominence to its strategic position at the heart of a network of rivers between the densely forested lands to the north and the bare steppes to the

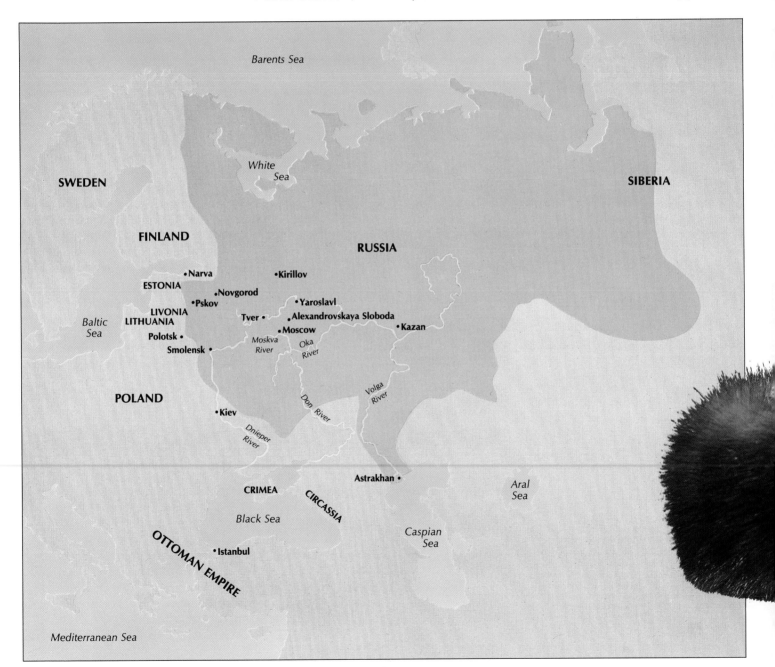

south. It profited from the trade in furs south to the Crimea, and it also benefited from a succession of shrewd rulers who had made it the seat of the Orthodox church and who now took advantage of the Mongol decline to expand and establish a new Russian state. Ivan III, who came to power in 1462 and later became known as Ivan the Great, subjugated the rival principalities of Tver, Yaroslavl, and Novgorod and acquired additional territory in wars against Lithuania and against Livonia on the Baltic Sea. He strove continually to enhance the status of Moscow in the eyes of the world: He married the niece of Constantine XI, the last Byzantine emperor, awarded himself the title of "czar of all Russia," and claimed that the rulers of Moscow were direct descendants of the Roman emperor Augustus. The word "czar," meaning independent ruler, was a Slavic contraction of "caesar."

When Ivan the Great died in 1505, his austere and ruthless son, Vasily III, inherited the uncontested leadership of a strong, expanding state. "Perceive, Czar, how all the Christian realms have converged into ours alone," wrote the monk Filofei to Vasily. "Two Romes have fallen, and the third stands," he continued, implying that Moscow was the successor to the imperial cities of Rome and Byzantium, "and a fourth there shall not be." But Russia was never at peace during Vasily's rule. In a bitter conflict along the disputed western borders, Vasily wrested the city of Smolensk from Lithuania. He also overwhelmed the independent city-state of Pskov to the northwest. To the east and south, the khanates of Kazan and Crimea—founded in the mid-fifteenth century by successors of the Mongol invaders who were known as Tatars—forced Vasily to keep his armies in constant readiness along the frontiers.

Under Ivan the Great and his son Vasily, the size of the Russian state increased from some 250,000 square miles to more than 1.5 million, and the Kremlin—the thirteenth-century wooden citadel in Moscow—was transformed with the aid of Italian architects and stonemasons into a showpiece of Renaissance art. Outside the Kremlin's crenelated brick walls sprawled an unfortified city of approximately 100,000 inhabitants. Its broad, unpaved streets were often deep in mud. Its timber houses burned like kindling when dry winds chased flames across the wood-shingled roofs; they were rebuilt nearly as rapidly. Vibrant, violent, and ever expanding, Moscow was a microcosm of the new Russian state.

On August 25, 1530, thunder rolled over the entire kingdom and—out of a cloudless sky—lightning struck the Kremlin. In distant Kazan, the Tatar capital to the east of Russian territory, the wife of the khan interpreted this phenomenon with chilling foresight. "A czar is born among you," she announced to visiting Russian dignitaries. "Two teeth has he. He will devour us with one and you with the other." Such were the legends that accumulated around the birth of Vasily's first son, Ivan. After a childless first marriage lasting twenty-five years, Vasily had been provided with a successor to the throne by his second wife, a beautiful young Lithuanian named Elena Glinskaya.

Vasily became a father none too soon. Three years later, he unexpectedly sickened and died. On his deathbed, he appointed seven of the principal boyars—Russia's hereditary noblemen—to serve on a regency council until young Ivan should come of age. The dying czar was fully cognizant of the chaos and bloodshed that now threatened. Since losing their political independence under Ivan the Great, many of Russia's regional princes had crowded into Moscow, where they jostled for status with the local aristocracy. More than thirty "royal" families were now clustered around the vacant throne, and only a woman and a three-year-old boy stood in the way of their ambitions.

The czarina did not gracefully step aside at the death of her husband as anticipated. She took as an ally and lover Prince Obolensky, a young military hero who, according to rumor, was Prince Ivan's real father. Together they reduced the regency council to the role of mere spectator and threw its leader into prison, where he died of starvation. Elena became regent herself and ruled for five discordant years, while the boyars chafed at the indignity of deferring to this foreign woman and her consort. She died in agony when Ivan was seven years old. Later in life he accused the boyars, who had rejoiced when she died, of poisoning her.

After the czarina's death, the boyars seized control of the administration. Their only united act, however, was to throw the detested Prince Obolensky into prison, where he died. A battle for power then raged between two of Russia's noblest families, who fell upon each other in a bloody and fruitless struggle.

In the midst of this maelstrom of violence and intrigue, young Ivan lived a lonely and stifled existence. His younger brother, Yuri, who was born deaf, offered scant

Wearing embroidered caftans and fur-trimmed hats, Russian boyars and wealthy merchants bear sable furs and other gifts to the court of the Holy Roman emperor in 1576. The boyars, the aristocracy of Russia, were pressed into imperial service during the reigns of Ivan's predecessors, being granted land and privileges in return for their administrative and military support. Ivan himself, whose childhood was spent in the shadow of boyar intrigues, sought to reduce their powers, and many of those who survived his purges lost their lands or were sent into exile.

companionship, and when not attending tedious court ceremonies in his role as official head of state, Ivan diverted himself with solitary and often cruel pastimes. He tore the feathers from living birds and hurled cats and dogs from the walls and towers of the Kremlin, delighting in their terrified cries and agonizing deaths.

The brutality of such pursuits echoed Ivan's experience of adult behavior. His beloved nurse, Agrafena, the only close friend of his childhood, was literally torn from his grasp and exiled to a distant nunnery from which she never returned. Her only crime was to have been the sister of Prince Obolensky. On another occasion, soldiers burst into Ivan's bedroom in pursuit of Metropolitan Ioasaf, head of the Orthodox church, who was dragged screaming from the room while the terrified boy looked on helplessly.

But the boyars were not able to treat their juvenile charge with indifference for long. When he was thirteen, Ivan saw Fyodor Vorontsov, a boyar with whom he had formed a friendship, beaten and dragged from the council chamber by Prince Andrei Shuisky and his supporters. A few months later, Ivan asserted his authority with the sudden violence that was to typify his reign. He ordered his soldiers to seize Prince Andrei and throw him to the huntsmen and their dogs. The prince's naked, half-eaten corpse lay on the street for two hours before anyone dared remove it.

Claiming his freedom from boyar supervision, Ivan embarked upon an unruly,

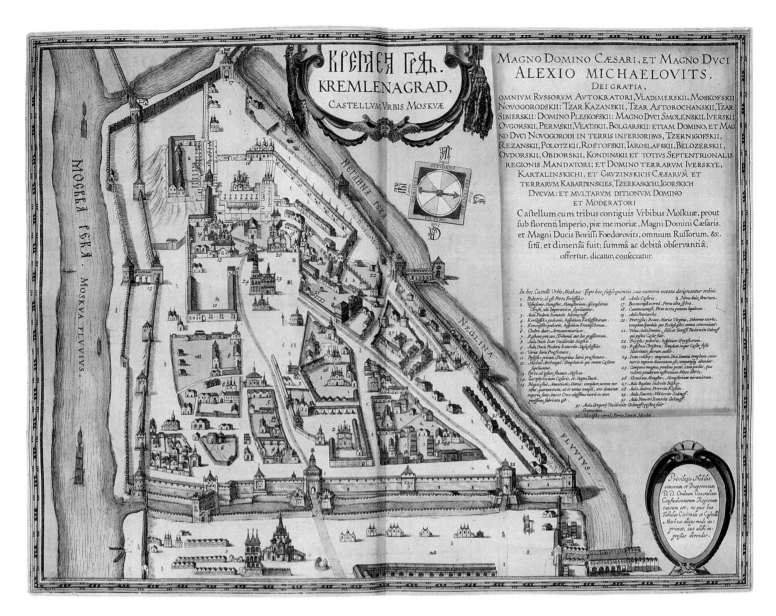

violent adolescence. With a gang of hell-raising young noblemen, he rode recklessly through the city streets, trampling pedestrians in the crowded marketplaces, and on his savage hunting expeditions, he took as much pleasure in robbing and beating the terrified peasants as in slaughtering animals.

The principal restraint to Ivan's dissolute life was Metropolitan Macarius, a cautious and learned churchman who remained a steadying influence on the young czar for many years. Under Macarius, Ivan learned to revere knowledge and to love books. In an age when a prince had no particular reason to be literate, Ivan became an exceptional scholar. He also became strongly attracted to the ritual observances of the Orthodox church, whose devout followers spent hours each week in church and prostrated themselves before the icons—painted representations of Christ or the saints—that adorned the walls of private houses and churches alike. Ivan's own observance of Orthodox practice took an extreme form: By knocking his head on the ground in front of icons, it is said that he developed a callus on his forehead while he was still a boy.

Throughout these formative years, Ivan gave little thought to the business of governing his people, and he was unable to curb the bitter feuds that raged between competing boyar factions. However, none of these animosities were evident during the ceremonial coronation of Ivan in the Cathedral of the Dormition on January 16, 1547. Before the assembled boyars and the magnificent ranks of archbishops and bishops, Metropolitan Macarius placed upon Ivan's head a fur-trimmed crown that was reputed to have belonged to the Byzantine emperor Constantine IX Monomachus. "Bring all the barbarian peoples under his power," prayed the metropolitan. "Let him look with mercy upon those who obey him; maintain his faith uncorrupted." At the end of this imposing ceremony, the entire assembly prostrated themselves before the sixteen-year-old boy, now Czar Ivan IV.

Within months of this extravagant ceremony, Ivan was made aware of the discontent of his subjects. The trouble started in the cities of Novgorod and Pskov in the northwest, relatively recently annexed to the new Russian state. Angered by corruption among the ruling boyars, the citizens attempted to petition their new czar with a list of grievances. Ivan grew angry and fearful at their impudent approaches, for although he had trampled down the common people while on horseback, he had never actually spoken to them. When a delegation from Pskov arrived on one of his country estates, Ivan reacted in panic, ordering his soldiers to strip them naked, singe off their beards, and scald them in boiling wine. At this point, a breathless messenger informed Ivan that the great bell of the Kremlin had inexplicably fallen, and the superstitious czar hastened back to Moscow.

The disturbances were spreading to the capital. A series of fires had destroyed a large portion of the city, and the citizens were seeking revenge on their incompetent rulers. Intimidated by his subjects, Czar Ivan was forced to begin governing the country in his own right.

No doubt sobered by this violent uprising, Ivan began his rule with liberal intentions and considerable common sense. A possible influence on his newfound maturity was his czarina, Anastasiya Romanovna Zakharina, whom he had married shortly after his coronation. "He being young and riotous," commented Sir Jerome Horsey, "she ruled him with affability and wisdom." A devout and unassuming woman, Anastasiya remained a loyal supporter to the czar throughout their thirteen years of marriage, dutifully conforming to the background role that was generally expected of Russian women.

In public, however, a Russian man—including the czar—took advice only from men. Chief among these in Czar Ivan's first few years of office was a priest named Silvester. This zealous, ascetic cleric became Ivan's spiritual, and then political, adviser. Ivan later complained that he was allowed no freedom by Silvester and his other domestic taskmasters. "How to put on shoes, how to sleep," he wrote, "all was done at the instance of my mentors, while I was like a child."

Also influential was an able young bureaucrat called Alexei Adashev, whom Ivan promoted from outside the circle of noble families that had traditionally dominated official positions. Adashev was, by all accounts, a remarkable man. Incorruptible and hardworking at his chancery office in the Kremlin, he was a paradigm of devotion at

This aerial view of the Kremlin during the reign of Boris Godunov, who became czar in 1598, displays the Moscow citadel's triangular shape and its protective river boundaries. Constructed by Italian architects and stonemasons during the reign of Ivan the Terrible's grandfather, its palaces, cathedrals, and towers—the administrative center of the new Russian state—survived repeated attacks and fires that reduced most of Moscow's wooden buildings to ashes.

Following the fall of Constantinople in 1453, the Orthodox church in Russia became independent of its Greek counterpart but entered into an uneasy alliance with the country's political rulers. The Church, anxious to retain its great wealth, had long seen fit to endorse the princes of Moscow as God's chosen rulers, with sovereignty over all Christian Russia. The czars knew that for as long as Moscow remained the seat of the Orthodox church, its status as capital city was guaranteed.

Ivan the Terrible maintained this partnership based upon mutual self-interest; he did, however, curtail the Church's independence. He appointed its leaders and censored their pronouncements, and lay down rules governing what subjects were suitable for religious art.

An icon depicting Christ's entry into Jerusalem *(above)* and a sumptuously bound Book of Gospels *(right)*, both produced in Ivan the Terrible's Kremlin workshops, exemplify the rich tradition of ornament that was an integral feature of the Russian Orthodox church.

home, where he tended the sick and sheltered pilgrims and impoverished holy men. In a century of extreme violence and cruelty, the period of Adashev's influence over the czar was a time of relative peace and prosperity.

The principal problem confronting Ivan and Adashev was how to create a bureaucracy capable of managing the huge state that Russia had recently become. The boyars, who bitterly resented the promotion of men such as Adashev, were a major obstacle. Their own system of determining who should hold office in the councils that advised the czar was based not on ability but on historical precedent, one boyar's seniority over another being determined by the relative importance of his ancestors. In disputed cases, a boyar who suspected that he was serving below his rightful station petitioned the czar to redeem his honor. This antiquated system had the effect of preventing the czar from bringing new blood into the administration—and Ivan, whose distrust of the boyars extended back to the early years of his childhood, was determined to destroy it.

While the boyars clung to their feudal privileges and hereditary estates, a new social class was increasing in size and influence. Known as servicemen, the members of this middle-ranking group were granted landholdings in exchange for their pledge to fight for the czar; if they refused to perform military service, their property would revert to the state upon their death. Ivan was quick to recognize the value of this system to himself and to encourage its growth: With an army of loyal and experienced servicemen, the state would no longer be forced to rely upon the cooperation of the boyars. Many of the servicemen were given land on the sparsely populated eastern and southern frontiers; others were granted estates on the lands of troublesome boyars whom Ivan forcibly relocated.

At the bottom of the social pyramid labored the peasantry, who constituted the bulk of the population. Peasants enjoyed few luxuries, and their welfare was rarely considered by even the most high-minded reformers in Moscow. Throughout the vast Russian state—which would expand by another 70 percent before the end of the century—severe climatic conditions limited the growing season, and peasant farmers possessed only the simplest wooden tools with which to work the land. Nevertheless, many peasants would later remember the early years of Ivan's rule as an age of freedom, peace, and plenty. Richard Chancellor, an English visitor to Russia in the 1550s, reported that "the ground is well stored with corn, which they carry to the city of Moscow in such abundance that it is wonder to see it." Above all, no matter how oppressive the landlord, a peasant could always move on. Every year after harvest, for a week on either side of Saint George's Day in November, a man and his family could seek employment on another estate or chance a new life on the edge of the Wild Field, as the lawless southern frontier was called.

Under the liberal influence of Adashev and the spiritual guidance of Silvester, Ivan vigorously attacked corruption and inefficiency. He railed against the wealthy, idle boyars, many of whom performed no military service at all, and he threatened a radical redistribution of property that would affect even the Church. When the land available to be granted as estates to the service gentry became scarce, Ivan had recourse to a solution that had been successfully initiated by his grandfather: Troublesome boyars were relocated and their estates divided up among the acquisitive new class of servicemen.

In 1550, Ivan and his closest advisers drafted a new law code that was aimed particularly at legal abuses in the provinces. Boyar officials had regularly grown rich on bribery and the almost limitless pickings to be had from the districts or cities they administered. Now government officers were to be paid according to their status every three or four years, and a procedure was instituted for lodging complaints against a corrupt official.

Adashev and his reform party next turned their attention to the army. Traditionally there had been no relationship between a man's wealth and his obligation to the state. Now boyars and servicemen were put on a more equal footing: Every landlord had to provide fully armed and mounted soldiers—with extra horses for distant campaigns—according to the amount of arable land that he owned.

The ordinary Russian cavalryman was armed with a bow and a sword; some might carry a javelin as well. He wore little armor, usually no more than a plain helmet and a shirt of mail. His strength lay in his speed and agility. From a galloping horse he could turn and shoot an arrow over his shoulder with deadly accuracy. A soldier also

had to have formidable stamina: On a meager diet, perhaps only a paste of flour and water and some bacon or dried fish, he was expected to survive long campaigns in the harshest of conditions.

Ivan had need of a strong, reliable army throughout his reign. Seeking to expand and secure his territory to the east, he led a campaign against the remnants of the Mongol presence when he had been on the throne just a year. After two unsuccessful expeditions against the Tatar capital of Kazan, which lay on the Volga River about 400 miles east of Moscow, his troops built a fortress of their own on the opposite bank of the river. From there, in the autumn of 1552, they launched a determined attack. They dug tunnels in which mines were exploded to destroy the pipes carrying water into the city. Then they stormed the main gates and fought the demoralized Tatars hand to hand in the streets.

Throughout the savage final hours of this battle, Ivan remained in his tent at prayer. Twice his generals urged him to bring his detachment of soldiers into the city, but he

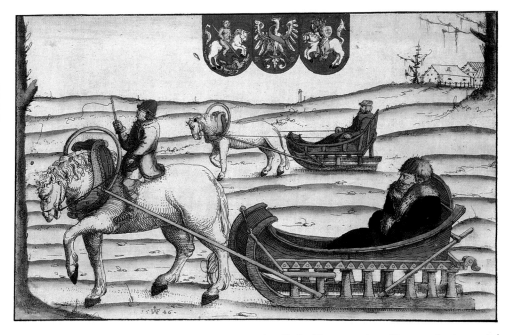

appeared not to hear them. When the czar finally led his men into Kazan, the imperial flag was flying over the ruins of the city. Still in an unworldly mood, he forgave the Tatar khan, who begged for mercy at his feet. "Unhappy man," he said, "you did not know the power of Russia."

The conquest of Kazan was Ivan's greatest military triumph. Four years later, with far less loss of life, he also annexed the khanate of Astrakhan to the southeast, thus gaining control of the entire length of the Volga and opening up a trade route to the Caspian Sea. But such glory was to prove short-lived, and the joyous acclamation that greeted Ivan on his return to Moscow after his victory against the Kazan Tatars was never to be repeated.

From the mid-1550s, Ivan's reign was increasingly stamped with the imprint of his own willful, quick-tempered personality. In the early years, he had been willing to take advice; shortly after his capture of Kazan, however, there occurred an event that confirmed his suspicions of the boyars' disloyalty, and from then on he determined that he, not his advisers, should decide state policy.

In the spring of 1553, Ivan fell gravely ill. As he lay near death, he summoned the leading boyars and instructed them to pledge their loyalty to his infant son, Dmitry. Many of the boyars, however, remembering the violent regency period during Ivan's own boyhood less than ten years earlier, were hesitant to acknowledge Dmitry's succession. Another candidate came forward: Prince Vladimir Andreyevich Staritsky, Ivan's first cousin. Why crown a helpless child, his supporters argued, when an adult of the royal blood was available? There was much fearful speculation and angry debate among the boyars before they reluctantly took the oath of loyalty to Dmitry.

Then, as if he had been playing a macabre practical joke, Ivan returned to health. Unavoidably he learned of the boyars' delay in obeying his command. On this occasion, to the surprise and relief of the dissidents, the czar took no action against the mutineers; but his confidence had been betrayed, and his hatred of the boyars grew even stronger.

Shortly after Ivan's recovery, the baby Dmitry died while the czar and his family were returning from a retreat at the northern monastery of Kirillov. There, a monk is reputed to have given him ominous advice: "If you keep near you men wiser than yourself, then perforce you will be subject to them." In light of his recent experiences, this statement expressed precisely the sort of wisdom that Ivan was prepared to absorb. "Even if my father had been alive, he would not have given me such useful advice," he gratefully replied.

Nowhere was Ivan's deepening mistrust of his advisers more apparent than in his conduct of a series of wars that began against Livonia in 1558 and continued sporadically for twenty-five years. Ivan was determined to gain access to the Baltic Sea in spite of opposition from Silvester, Adashev, and Metropolitan Macarius, whose combined influence had once been unquestioned. They urged him to concentrate his efforts against the Crimean khanate, in order to gain control of the Black Sea and a trade route to the Mediterranean. The czar would not listen. Instead he embarked upon a war that became a fruitless personal crusade.

By 1562, Livonia, which occupied a strategic location on the Baltic, had become a fief of the combined state of Lithuania and Poland. Other territories in the Baltic region were ruled by Sweden and Denmark, and Ivan soon found himself at war with the allied forces of all these states. Early Russian successes included the capture of the Baltic port of Narva and the independent city of Polotsk, but the momentum of these gains never led to complete victory. Meanwhile, the Crimean khanate siezed the opportunity to threaten Russia from the south, dangerously extending the country's military resources. This period of continual warfare contributed to the devastation of the land and the collapse of the economy.

Anastasiya Romanovna, Ivan's pious and unassuming wife, died in the summer of 1560. Deprived of her stabilizing influence, Ivan was overwhelmed by grief—and then by rage. The nearest were the first to suffer. Alexei Adashev, who had already fallen from favor because of his opposition to the Livonia campaign, was convicted for mishandling the war. He died in prison soon afterward, victim of a mysterious illness. The priest Silvester, who had strenuously defended his former colleague, retired to the Kirillov monastery; he was then banished by Ivan to a monastery on the White Sea, from which he never returned.

Adashev and Silvester, Ivan later claimed, had manipulated him for their own self-seeking purposes. "I was the slave on the throne," he wrote. "Will I ever be able to describe all that I suffered during those days of pain and humiliation?" Furthermore, Ivan was convinced that they had killed the czarina by witchcraft. In the purges that followed, anyone sympathetic to or closely associated with either man was executed or driven into exile.

From that time on, Ivan's domestic policy was determined chiefly by his hatred of the boyars. New legislation aimed at breaking the power of wealthy landowners made it illegal for a prince to leave his estate to a nephew or brother without government consent. Widows of servicemen were not to inherit their husband's property, but only an amount determined by the state. These laws both deprived the boyars of their principal source of wealth and gave the government much-needed land with which to reward the increasingly significant class of servicemen.

Although flight from Russia was a crime, many boyars escaped to Lithuania, where they took up arms against their mother country. The servicemen whom Ivan promoted in their place were derided by one disaffected prince as "the sons of priests or common people." Prominent among the czar's new favorites was his close adviser Maliuta Shkuratov, a name that was to become synonymous with terror.

Ivan remarried a year after Anastasiya's death, but Maria Temiukovna, a Circassian princess, exercised none of his first wife's restraining influence. And with the death of Metropolitan Macarius in 1563, Russia lost another voice of moderation. Ivan replaced him with his own personal confessor: Metropolitan Afanasii, he was convinced, would not preach to him about morality.

Ivan's personal sense of insecurity was aggravated by renewed onslaughts on the Russian state by both Crimea and Lithuania. Responding to this crisis, Ivan contrived a brilliant *coup de théâtre*. In early December 1564, he and his family, along with his closest advisers, left Moscow for a secret destination. A vast caravan of sleds, guarded by mounted courtiers, crawled westward; their goal turned out to be the fortress of Alexandrovskaya Sloboda, about 100 miles from the capital. On the journey, Ivan composed a melodramatic will to explain his actions. "God's wrath has descended upon me," he wrote. "I am more vile and stinking in God's eyes for my loathsome deeds than a corpse."

This self-abasement was precisely calculated. A letter dispatched by Ivan to be read in public to the people of Moscow explained that he had abdicated because it was no longer possible to rule the ambitious, rebellious boyars. The merchants and common people, fearing the inevitable chaos of boyar rule, demanded Ivan's return. Bewildered and humiliated, the boyars themselves sent a delegation to Alexandrovskaya Sloboda, assuring Ivan complete authority. The czar, with apparent reluctance, agreed to resume office.

Ivan returned to Moscow in February 1565 with a plan designed to smash forever the power of the boyars and satisfy his overriding quest for security. He set aside large areas of the country as his own *oprichnina,* or "personal domain," which comprised parts of Moscow as well as some of Russia's richest estates; it eventually grew to include nearly half the state. In taking these properties, Ivan forcibly relocated thousands of wealthy families to the eastern frontier, replacing them with servicemen and *oprichniki,* as his own handpicked troops were called. These mounted men wore coarse, dark shirts and carried at their belts a quiver of arrows and a broom—a symbol of Ivan's determination to sweep the country clean of treason.

Those parts of the country that were not included in the oprichnina remained under the administration of the boyars, although Ivan reserved the right to overrule any boyar decision of which he disapproved, and he turned a blind eye to the routine plunder of boyar lands by the oprichniki. Russia was thus divided into two separate states, each with its own court, administration, and army. Such fragmentation caused great instability: Russia's ability to withstand the attacks of its enemies was weakened, and in order to maintain his artificially created state, Ivan was compelled to resort to extreme measures.

Within the oprichnina, experienced bureaucrats were replaced by the czar's sycophants and brutish hirelings, who enforced their rule by terror. Near the end of his life, Ivan confessed to more than 3,000 official executions. The most prominent victims suffered the full force of his ghoulish cruelty. One senior military commander, accused of plotting to overthrow the czar, was made to dress up in royal robes and ascend the throne. "You desired to take my place," mocked Ivan, kneeling before him. "Rejoice in the dominion you craved." Ivan's guards then stabbed the hapless general and dragged his body out into the street. Uncounted thousands of lesser opponents fell to the casual savagery of the oprichniki.

Apart from the czar's inner circle and his privileged oprichniki, there was almost universal opposition to the oprichnina policy; even Afanasii, Ivan's puppet metropolitan, retired to a monastery in protest. In addition, the Russian state was menaced not only in the west by Lithuania and Poland, and in the south by the Crimean khanate, but also by the Ottoman Turks, who were planning to build a canal linking

An icon commemorating Ivan the Terrible's seizure of the city of Kazan in 1552 and his triumphant return to Moscow celebrates Russia's ascendancy over its Mongol oppressors. On the left, the archangel Michael leads the Christian host into the heavenly city, while behind them Sodom burns. The central figure holding a crucifix represents Ivan; the warrior at the head of the lower column of troops is Alexander Nevsky, a Russian prince who fought the Mongols in the thirteenth century.

the Volga and Don rivers. Suspecting that his opponents were secretly conspiring with his enemies abroad, Ivan increased his personal guard from 1,000 to 1,500 and moved into a formidable new castle in an oprichnina district of Moscow. At the same time, he began planning his escape from Russia in the event of an armed rebellion, startling Queen Elizabeth of England with a request for asylum.

One of the few places in the kingdom where Ivan felt totally secure was Alexandrovskaya Sloboda. There, he organized his loyal oprichniki into a form of military religious order and subjected them to a severe monastic discipline. At four o'clock every morning, Ivan's trusted deputy, Maliuta Shkuratov—one of the most hated men in the country—rang the bell to summon all the brethren to prayer. Morning devotions lasted for six hours, followed by a spartan meal in a refectory. Alongside these ecclesiastical practices, however, the business of state terror continued. Prisoners taken by the oprichniki were tortured and executed by a variety of sadistic methods. On one occasion, for instance, seven monks who had aroused Ivan's anger were set down in a high-walled compound, into which wild bears that had been kept starving in cages were then unleashed.

The gaudy domes and cupolas of Saint Basil's Cathedral punctuate the Moscow skyline. Built outside the walls of the Kremlin as a monument to Ivan the Terrible's victory at Kazan in 1552, the cathedral was designed as eight separate chapels of alternating height clustered around a central altar. According to legend, when it was completed in 1560, Ivan had the architects blinded so that they could never again build anything so beautiful.

The peasantry, who had been little affected by Ivan's earlier policies against the boyars, began to suffer terribly. The cost of sustaining seemingly endless wars forced taxes to ruinous heights. Impoverished new proprietors belonging to the service class squeezed their tenants for all the money and produce they could extract. Then came two successive years of crop failure, followed, in 1570, by plague. Of the peasant families who survived these disasters, many left to pursue a new life in the frontier territories, where they could evade the tax collectors. The Novgorod and Pskov regions became a wasteland, and a traveler could ride for days through the once-populous farmland of northwest and central Russia without encountering another soul. In an attempt to stem the depopulation of fertile regions, Ivan passed temporary legislation that forbade any movement of the peasants whatsoever, even during the traditional Saint George's Day period.

Of all the cities in Russia, Novgorod in the northwest fared the worst. In 1571, having caught a slight whiff of treason coming from that independent-minded city, Ivan descended without warning and set his troops loose on the unsuspecting inhabitants, who had streamed out into the streets to welcome the royal party. Thousands of men, women, and children were killed. Some were thrown into the icy river to drown; others were roasted over fires. Warehouses were set alight, and melted wax and tallow flowed in the gutters of the streets along with the blood of the massacred citizens. Ivan reserved the more distinguished Novgorodians for show trials before torturing them to death. Nor did the Church escape the czar's displeasure. Visiting each of the local monasteries in turn, he tortured the abbots and monks until they consented to make huge contributions to the treasury.

A tragic defeat and a heroic victory helped bring the period of oprichnina to a close. In 1571, a huge Tatar army from Crimea invaded Russia's poorly defended southern territories, taking Ivan and his generals by surprise. The Tatars outflanked and defeated a hastily assembled oprichniki army, forcing Ivan to flee for his life. They then attacked Moscow with a fury reminiscent of the Mongol invasion three centuries earlier. Fanned by a gale, fires spread from the suburbs, leaping from wooden house to wooden house. So fast was Moscow's destruction that bodies lay three deep in the streets—Muscovites killed while attempting to escape heaped together with Tatars caught in the crush while trying to enter the city.

Elated by this victory, the khan of Crimea prepared for another attack the following year, confidently distributing Russian cities to his generals as booty in advance. The defeat of the Russian state seemed a mere formality when the Tatar army encountered a Russian force only one-third its size at the village of Molodi, about thirty miles from Moscow. But with their backs to Moscow, the oprichniki and troops loyal to the boyars at last forgot their differences and combined to rout the invading Tatars. No argument for a united Russia could have been more persuasive than this victory.

The oprichnina came to an end almost as suddenly as it had begun. The oprichniki were disbanded, and Ivan's personal domain was reintegrated with the rest of the state under the nominal administration of the boyar council. Anyone even mentioning the discredited policy would henceforth be publicly beaten, Ivan decreed, as if to obliterate the memory of the previous seven years. But the habit of terror was

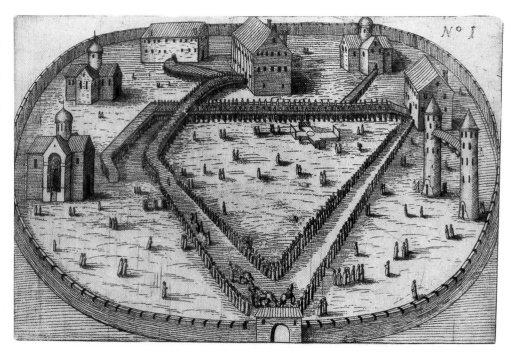

For seven years, beginning in 1565, the fortified village of Alexandrovskaya Sloboda—shown here in a sketch drawn by a Danish envoy in 1575—was the administrative center of the *oprichnina,* Ivan the Terrible's personal domain within Russia, which he ruled without boyar interference. As the location where Ivan and his handpicked guards systematically tortured and executed all who dared criticize his rule, it became known as "the bloody pit"; at the same time, Ivan's patronage established Alexandrovskaya as a cultural center that became renowned for its architecture, sacred music, and book printing.

harder to break. "That same year the czar hurled many of his lesser boyars in the Volkhov River, weighed down with stones," noted one chronicle. And when Ivan became suspicious of his own son—a youth in his early twenties, also named Ivan, who shared his father's taste for cruel pastimes—he struck out at all around him, killing many of his son's relatives and companions, although he left young Ivan alive.

Ivan had not finished astonishing his subjects. In 1575, he abdicated for a second time, installing in his place Simeon Bekbulatovich, a Tatar prince who had converted to Orthodox Christianity. Ivan Groznyi—Ivan the Terrible, a title he had earned during the oprichnina years—became plain Ivan Vasilyevich, "little Ivan of Moscow," as he was amused to call himself. But while Grand Prince Simeon presided over the boyar council and formally received visiting diplomats, the strings leading to the real source of power were clearly visible. Ivan continued to issue decrees and order assassinations through his willing mouthpiece; he also remained in command of a substantial private army and kept possession of several large estates. An able and ambitious young man named Boris Godunov, who had rapidly gained favor since entering the czar's service in about 1570, helped Ivan administer his territory.

Ivan had been careful never to invest Grand Prince Simeon as czar; and after about a year, tired of this performance, he pensioned off his supposed successor, resumed direct rule, and launched a vigorous fresh assault against Livonia. But this campaign foundered against the armies of Stefan Bathory, newly elected king of the combined state of Poland and Lithuania. With Sweden, Bathory regained much of the territory pillaged by the Russian troops, now little more than a strategically located wasteland; Bathory also reopened the war along the Lithuanian front, recapturing Polotsk and advancing with a huge army deep into Russian territory.

Faced with a new military crisis, Ivan took the uncharacteristic step of seeking a diplomatic solution. In an attempt to gain influence over the Catholic Bathory, he requested assistance from the pope, who sent Antonio Possevino, a skilled and patient diplomat, to arrange a truce. (So out of touch was the Vatican with Russian affairs that Possevino brought with him gifts for Czarina Anastasiya, who had been dead for twenty years.) These negotiations were ultimately successful, although it was not until 1583 that Russia signed an armistice with Bathory. The next year brought

Brandishing a severed head, Ivan the Terrible watches impassively as his henchmen go about their business of murder and extortion. Though not illustrating a specific event, this lithograph from 1582 accurately summarizes Ivan's treatment of the citizens of Novgorod in 1571, when rumors of treason attracted horrible retribution. More than 2,000 were formally executed; many thousands more fell victim to the brutality of Ivan's troops.

peace with Sweden, but at the expense of all of Russia's Livonian conquests. Twenty-five years of brutal warfare had resulted in nothing but a waste of life and resources.

Counterbalancing this disastrous failure was a success from an unexpected source. Russian colonists in the far northeast, employing an irregular army of frontier warriors, decisively defeated the Tatar tribes with whom they shared this neglected region. Suddenly much of Siberia was Russian territory. It was a success for which Ivan could claim no responsibility.

The lawless last decade of Ivan's reign was reflected in the chaos and violence of his personal life. His second wife died in 1569—poisoned, Ivan was later to insist. Two years later he took a new wife, but the marriage was never consummated and the czarina was dead within a month; again Ivan suspected foul play. His fourth and fifth wives—both called Anna—were dispatched to nunneries within the space of two years. A brief sixth marriage in 1574 left Ivan widowed again. In 1581, he took a seventh and last wife, Maria Nagaya; this marriage did not prevent him from proposing the following year to Mary Hastings, an English heiress. Queen Elizabeth of England—"the old virgin," as Ivan called her—had prudently refused his hand in marriage fifteen years earlier.

Not content with his own succession of wives, Ivan high-handedly managed the domestic life of his eldest son as well. He arranged two marriages for young Ivan, but then ordered both wives to nunneries. The czarevitch, who was growing increasingly antagonistic toward his father, chose his own third wife, Elena, from the family of a disgraced boyar. In 1581, Ivan came upon his pregnant daughter-in-law in a palace room at Alexandrovskaya Sloboda. Furious to see her wearing only one dress instead of the three dictated by court protocol, the czar savagely beat the young woman, causing her to miscarry. When young Ivan dared to remonstrate, his father furiously raised his long wooden staff and struck him on the head. The czarevitch died a few days later, leaving his father crazed with grief.

Irrationally, Ivan decreed that, henceforth, anyone slandering the boyars or offering false information about treasonous activities would be severely punished. Even the boyars trembled in anticipation of their ruler's next unpredictable move. But the czar was growing increasingly ill. Racked by an incurable bone disease, his body swelled and his skin peeled. Sensing that death was near, he appointed a regency council to govern the country in the name of Fyodor, his only surviving son by his first wife, a grown man too simpleminded to rule by himself.

On March 18, 1584, feeling refreshed after a long bath, Ivan sat down to play chess with Prince Bogdan Belsky. Suddenly he lost consciousness, falling backward to the floor. A crowd of anxious officials attempted to revive him, but the rule of Ivan the Terrible had finally come to an end.

After the turbulence of Ivan's reign, Russia enjoyed fourteen years of comparative peace and prosperity under Fyodor. In fact, the new czar—described by the English diplomat Giles Fletcher as "simple and slow-witted but very gentle and of an easy nature"—spent most of his time at prayer or on pilgrimages to monasteries or shrines, and left much of the business of government to his late father's favorite, Boris Godunov. A cautious and diplomatic man, Boris personally conducted Russia's foreign relations and held semiofficial receptions at his own court in the Kremlin. As the unquestioned ruler of all Russia, he had little difficulty in having himself proclaimed

Claiming to be the son of Ivan the Terrible and supported by a Polish army of invasion, the pretender Dmitry—who is portrayed here by a Polish artist—was proclaimed czar of Russia in 1605. Less than a year later, he was overthrown in a bloody coup and assassinated, and the country was once again plunged into a cycle of violence and anarchy. In 1607 and 1611, two other pretenders, both of whom called themselves Dmitry, claimed the Russian throne. One of them was murdered by his followers; the other pretender was betrayed and executed.

czar upon the death of the childless Fyodor in 1598. A rumor followed by a natural disaster put an end to the Indian summer that had prevailed since Ivan the Terrible's death. Soon after Czar Boris's coronation, it was whispered in the streets and council chambers that he had murdered the czarevitch, Dmitry, Ivan's son by his last marriage and Fyodor's successor. The seven-year-old had been found with his throat cut in 1591. Who but Boris, murmured his enemies, had gained by this cruel act?

In the minds of many ordinary Russians, the terrible famine that lasted from 1601 to 1603 added support to these damaging allegations. The land, which had recovered much of its productivity in the previous ten years, was now struck by successive crop failures. Thousands of peasants died; others survived only through banditry and cannibalism. Then a young man appeared in Poland who called himself Dmitry and claimed that he, not the child who had been found dead in 1591, was the true son of Czar Ivan; supported by the Poles, he advanced with his army into Russia, where he found a desperate and rebellious populous willing to give him support.

The sudden death of Czar Boris in 1605 plunged Russia into eight years of civil war and anarchy. The pretender Dmitry took Boris's place on the throne but was murdered a year later in a boyar coup. Leaders emerged and then sank again in a roiling sea of social disorder. It was as if all the aggressive energy of the Russian people—so long suppressed by the terror of Ivan's rule—had at last burst forth in internecine strife.

This "time of troubles," as it became known, was finally brought to an end by a patriotic appeal from the Orthodox church. In 1608, the Poles—Catholics owing their allegiance to the pope in Rome—established a blockade of Moscow and occupied vast areas of northeastern Russia; two years later, the boyars formed a provisional government with the aim of installing a Polish czar. Urging the people to banish these "eternal foes of Christianity," leaders of the Orthodox church inspired a volunteer army to drive out the foreigners, and in 1612, the Poles were forced to withdraw. The following year, at a national assembly comprising peasants, merchants, servicemen, and boyars, the Russian people voted for "the czar that the Lord would indicate to us." Their job was simplified by the war of attrition that Ivan had waged against the nobles throughout his reign. Of thirty-five families of royal blood competing for precedence in the mid-sixteenth century, only nine now survived. Sixteen-year-old Mikhail Romanov, a great-grandson of the father of Ivan the Terrible's first wife, Anastasiya, was the choice of the assembly.

The problems facing the new czar were immense. The combined effects of famine, civil anarchy, and Ivan the Terrible's futile wars had almost totally destroyed the economy of the fertile central and southwestern regions. In the process, the administrative reforms carried out in the early years of Ivan's reign had been largely canceled out. However, Ivan's legacy was not wholly negative: It was the institutions that he and his predecessors established that enabled the Russian state to survive. Most important of all was the powerful role of the czar himself in the government of the country. The boyars remained prominent despite Ivan's attempts to destroy them, but their status was dependent on the czar's favor. At the bottom of society, the peasants had become increasingly subject to comprehensive control: In a country vast in extent but ill endowed with natural resources, Ivan had seen fit to pass measures limiting their freedom of movement in order to ensure a reliable source of both revenue and labor. Midway through the seventeenth century, this gradual reduction of the peasants to the condition of serfdom was to culminate in laws that bound them forever to the estates where they lived.

By avoiding involvement in foreign conflicts, the government of Mikhail Romanov afforded Russia a sorely needed breathing space in which it could begin to recuperate. Gradually, the nightmare receded. Owing their tenure in part to Ivan the Terrible's ruthless centralization of power and his destruction of all opposition, the Romanov dynasty was to continue to rule Russia for 300 years.

An illustration from a seventeenth-century chronicle of the reign of Mikhail Romanov, who was elected czar in 1613, shows Russian dignitaries lining the road to Moscow as Mikhail and his father, Philaret, kneel to greet each other upon the latter's return from exile in Poland in 1619. Appointed patriarch of the Orthodox church, the sixty-six-year-old Philaret brought stability and a sense of purpose to the government of Russia, and by the time of his death in 1633, the authority of the new Romanov dynasty was firmly established.

# THE OTTOMAN ZENITH

**5** During the last days of August 1526, an army of Ottoman Turks marched through fog and rain across the desolate wilderness of the river marshes that cover a large part of southern Hungary. The Ottomans, a Muslim people originating in Anatolia, had in the course of the previous two centuries conquered an empire that included most of the Balkan lands of eastern Europe as well as extensive territories in the Middle East, and their present campaign—under the personal command of their sultan, Süleyman I—was intended to advance their northern frontier into the heart of western Christendom. Reaching at length the plain of Mohács on the Danube River, Süleyman was confronted by the forces of King Louis of Hungary. The first charge of the Hungarian cavalry, sweeping across the plain, in the words of a chronicler, "like an invasion of the shadows of the night," burst through the Ottoman front line and sent it reeling backward. Seeing his enemies apparently retreating in disarray, Louis launched a second onslaught to complete the rout. But as he did so, the Turks opened their ranks, and 300 cannon and several thousand muskets—invisible until that moment—unleashed at point-blank range a murderous hailstorm of iron balls and bullets.

The Hungarians fled for their lives, leaving more than 20,000 of their compatriots dead or dying on the plain. Louis was drowned when his horse slipped and fell on the muddy bank of a swollen stream. In early September, the Ottomans planted their crescent on the citadel at Buda, the Hungarian capital on the Danube, and a few days later, they crossed into the twin city of Pest on the opposite side of the river.

The swiftness and completeness of Süleyman's victory at Mohács—the battle lasted little more than two hours—revealed to a startled West as never before both the superior firepower and field tactics, and the formidable efficiency and discipline of the Ottoman war machine. In addition, the defeat of Hungary, the bulwark that had kept the Ottomans out of the heartlands of Europe for more than 100 years, created profound despondency throughout Christendom. Nor were the gloomy prognostications prevalent at the time without foundation. Süleyman was to rule for another forty years, and during that time, he would win many more victories on land and sea, vastly increase the size of the Ottoman domains, and far outshine in splendor, opulence, and glory his most ambitious and illustrious rivals. Only the logistical problems of sustaining an extended campaign without secure winter quarters prevented Süleyman from overrunning all of Europe.

Süleyman was the tenth Ottoman sultan. In acquiring the empire that he inherited, his forebears had displayed both fearlessness and ferocity in war, and an unusual talent for organization and administration. Their disciplined and well-armed infantry troops, the janissaries—from the Turkish *yeni ceri*, or "new force"—were a match for any army fielded against them; and among the Ottomans' subject peoples, Muslim

While fire ravages an outer tower of the fortress city of Belgrade on the Danube River, the Hungarian commander withdraws into the citadel and citizens call upon God to deliver them from their Muslim enemies. Their prayers were in vain: In August 1521, Belgrade fell to Süleyman I, sultan of the Ottoman Turks, and the route into the heart of Christian Europe lay open before him. The illustration is from a chronicle of Süleyman's reign, during which the Ottomans both vastly extended their domains and commemorated their achievement in artistic monuments whose splendor befitted an empire that spanned three continents.

The Ottoman Empire—which by 1520 already included Egypt, Syria, and the Balkan States of Europe in addition to Anatolia, the original Ottoman homeland—expanded during the sixteenth century along the southern coast of the Mediterranean, down the Red Sea, and into Iraq and Azerbaijan *(shaded yellow)*. The siege of Vienna in 1529 marked the farthest Ottoman advance into Europe under the empire's presiding genius, Süleyman the Magnificent, shown here *(inset)* in a portrait attributed to the Italian artist Titian.

as well as Christian, they had a reputation for just government. In 1453, their seizure of Constantinople, a bastion of Christianity for more than 1,000 years, had established them indisputably as a world power. From this city, known to the Ottomans as Istanbul, their power and influence extended far into both Asia and Europe.

Süleyman's two predecessors during the early years of the sixteenth century possessed starkly contrasting characters. Bajazet II, nicknamed the Mystic, had little thirst for world domination; he provided the Ottoman army with an effective artillery force, equipped the infantry with modern firearms, and greatly expanded the navy, but during his last years, the sultan's lack of bellicosity finally caused the janissaries

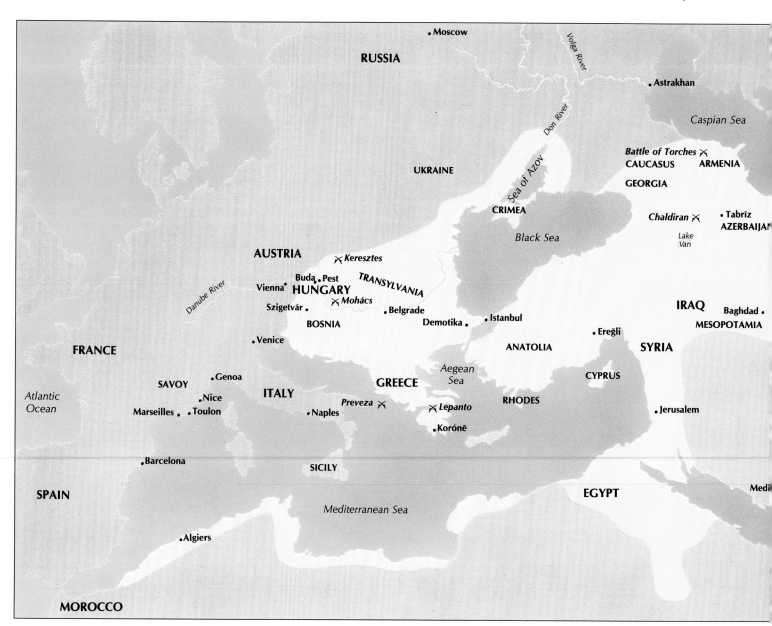

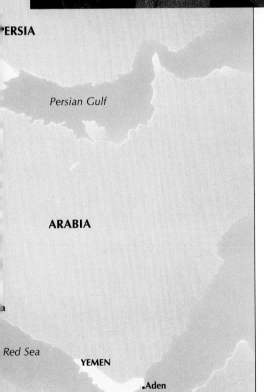

and household cavalry to mutiny and demand his abdication. In 1512, Bajazet acquiesced, declaring simply: "I cede the empire to my son Selim. God grant him a prosperous reign!" He died—perhaps from exhaustion and age, or possibly poisoned at Selim's instigation—while traveling to Demotika, the town in Greece where he had been born.

On the eve of his accession, Selim was described by the Venetian ambassador as "the most ferocious of men, who dreams of nothing but conquests and concerns himself solely with all that pertains to war." His stern demeanor and ruthless character were amply demonstrated at the start of his reign by his emphatic enforcement of the so-called Law of Fratricide, whereby the new sultan put to death his male relatives. The purpose of this macabre custom—which had been initiated in the late fourteenth century—was to prevent dynastic struggles and factional strife. Selim's two brothers and five nephews were ritually strangled with a silken bowstring.

Selim saw as his first task the defense of orthodox Sunni Islam against the teaching of the Shiites, followers of an alternative tradition of the faith who were gaining support in eastern Anatolia. He began by setting up an extensive network of spies and informers who compiled a detailed list of suspects. Upon the signal from Istanbul, mass arrests followed in every part of the empire. Some 40,000 members of Shiite sects were put to death or imprisoned. For this massacre Selim won from certain Ottoman historians the name of "the Just"; he became more widely known as Selim the Grim.

This domestic bloodletting was followed by a full-scale campaign against Persia, ruled since 1501 by the Shiite dynasty of the Safavids. In August 1514, Selim defeated the Safavid ruler, Shah Ismail, at Chaldiran, to the northeast of Lake Van, and then temporarily occupied the Safavid capital of Tabrīz. Although the shah retained most of his territories, Selim's success cowed Persia for the next twenty years.

In 1516, Selim turned his gaze on the rich dominions of the Mamluk sultans, rulers of Egypt and Syria. The Mamluks—who were in origin Turkish and Circassian slave troops but had long since overthrown their masters and provided sultans from their own ranks—were famous for their military prowess. Dissension among their leaders and the superiority of the Ottoman tactics, firearms, and artillery, however, proved the Mamluks' undoing. Within less than a year, Selim had annexed Syria and Egypt and part of Arabia.

Aside from the territorial gains, the benefit to the Ottoman treasury was colossal. Revenue from the spice trade would prove crucial in the financing of future wars against the Christians. The new conquests also brought with them control of Islam's three most sacred cities: Mecca, Medina, and Jerusalem. Selim removed the prophet Muhammad's supposed relics—his mantle, bow, and banner—to Istanbul and proclaimed himself the Protector of Islam. Thenceforth, the Ottoman sultans could claim to be the supreme sovereigns of the entire Muslim world.

Selim died in September 1520 at the age of fifty-four. His reign had been harsh and bloody: Summary executions were frequent, and the limited life expectancy of those close to the sultan gave rise to the popular curse, "May you be vizier to Sultan Selim!" Yet his military success laid a firm foundation for his son's celebrated career.

As the sole living heir to the throne, Süleyman was spared the need to inaugurate his reign by the wholesale slaughter of his male relatives. Already experienced in administration, thanks to governorships in the Crimea and Anatolia, the new sultan was blessed with personal dignity and grace, and a youthful vigor that commanded admiration. A Venetian resident in Istanbul described him as "tall but wiry and of a delicate complexion. His neck is a little too long, his face thin, and his nose aquiline. He has a light mustache and a small beard; nevertheless, he has a pleasant expression, though his skin tends to pallor. He is said to be a wise lord, fond of study, and all men hope for good from his rule."

Süleyman quickly gained the approbation of his subjects by deposing and executing certain corrupt officials, by generously rewarding the janissaries and other household troops for their loyalty, and by setting free several hundred Egyptian prisoners. But if his European enemies were hoping for similar clemency, their expectations were in vain. The prosecution of holy war against all Christian nations had been the guiding policy of the Ottomans since they had come to power in the fourteenth century, and Süleyman wasted no time in serving notice of his hostile intentions. He dispatched an ambassador to King Louis of Hungary to demand that he pay an annual tribute; when the envoy was treated with contempt, as Süleyman had probably expected, open warfare commenced.

An Ottoman campaign required months of planning and coordination. In December, a command for auxiliary troops would be sent to all the vassal rulers of the empire. Orders would also be sent to the cannon foundries for artillery, and to the iron, lead, and copper mines that supplied the metal for gun carriages, horseshoes, axes, and other tools. In the spring of the following year, all the components of the expeditionary force would be brought together at an assembly point outside the capital. In addition to the regular troops, these included herds of sheep and cattle for the provision of fresh meat; chains and cables for making pontoon bridges to cross rivers; oxen and buffaloes to drag the heavy guns, and camels and mules to carry the lighter baggage such as tents and ammunition; and numerous saddlers, butchers, bakers, and other members of the support train. West and east of Istanbul, the roads customarily followed by the Ottoman armies were kept constantly repaired. Discipline on the march was strict. Food requisitioned from the local population had to be paid for, as did damage to orchards or fields. Latrines were set up on every campsite, and drinking and gaming were forbidden. Together with the comprehensive training in fighting skills given to the troops, this rigorous organization was designed to ensure that, when the enemy was eventually encountered, the campaign could be swiftly brought to a conclusion before winter set in.

In 1521, Süleyman's forces advanced up the Danube and seized the great castle of Belgrade, then held by the Hungarians. In the next year, Rhodes was attacked, and the Knights of Saint John, members of a Christian military order, were driven out of the island. Both Belgrade and Rhodes had successfully withstood sieges by Süleyman's great-grandfather,

Mehmed the Conqueror. The removal of these formidable obstacles widened the Ottoman horizons: The capture of the fortress at Belgrade opened the road to central Europe, and the seizure of Rhodes made safe the sea route to Egypt and confirmed Ottoman dominance in the eastern Mediterranean.

Five years after the capture of Belgrade, the Ottomans won a decisive victory at Mohács. In the wake of the battle, Süleyman entrusted the country to János Zápolya, ruler of Transylvania, who in exchange recognized Ottoman suzerainty and agreed to pay tribute. This was the tactic that had often been applied to other Balkan kingdoms as a prelude to their absorption into the empire proper. But the Hapsburg archduke of Austria, Ferdinand I, also laid claim to the Hungarian crown, and expelled Zápolya from Buda. Clearly Süleyman could not allow the deposition of his vassal, and after dismissing Ferdinand's envoys in Istanbul with instructions to tell their master "to prepare himself for our visit," he set out with an army in May 1529.

Depicted by a sixteenth-century German artist, the commander of the sultan's elite troops *(opposite)* leads his senior officers *(right)* on parade. Established in the fourteenth century, the janissaries—called in Turkish the *yeni ceri*, or "new force"—were the first standing army in Europe. They were recruited as slaves in periodic levies of Christian boys in the Balkan States; taken to Istanbul, the youths were converted to Islam and given a rigorous military training. In Süleyman's time, they numbered around 12,000. Owing their loyalty exclusively to the sultan, they were a proud and turbulent body of men, and no Ottoman ruler could ascend or hold the throne without their support.

Having vowed that he would defeat Ferdinand on the plain of Mohács, and if not there in Pest, and failing that in the Austrian capital of Vienna, Süleyman advanced inexorably westward. Buda was retaken in early September, and Zápolya was crowned tributary king of Hungary. On September 29, Süleyman arrived before the walls of the Austrian capital, from which Ferdinand and his court had already fled.

Süleyman's vast army of more than 100,000 men encircled Vienna and for seventeen days and nights laid siege to the city. The defenders, who numbered some 25,000, had leveled the houses of the suburbs to deprive the enemy of cover, pulled off the wooden roofs of the buildings within the town as a precaution against fire, and even dug up the pavements to deaden the explosive effect of falling cannonballs. They had already raised a new rampart and ditch within the old walls and palisaded the banks of the Danube.

Bad weather and the poor state of the roads had prevented Süleyman from bringing with him any heavy siege guns, so he was forced to rely on tunneling and setting mines to breach the walls. Yet, although the Ottoman miners, famed for their expertise, succeeded in blowing great holes in the ramparts time after time, such was the intensity of the German and Spanish musket and cannon fire that the Ottomans ended only by filling the breaches with their own dead. One storming party after another hurled itself at the walls, and hand-to-hand fighting sometimes continued for several hours at a stretch; but without the aid of heavy artillery, all assaults appeared doomed to failure. The early onset of winter finally decided Süleyman to abandon the enterprise. In October, he gave the order to strike camp and turned for home, leaving his mounted irregulars to continue ravaging the countryside around Vienna.

Within the city, the Ottoman departure was greeted with a joyful ringing of bells and the solemn singing of the Te Deum in Saint Stephen's Cathedral. But the psychological shock of the siege of Vienna was deep and enduring: After it, Christendom was left in perpetual fear of a new and more far reaching Ottoman invasion.

During the next two years, Süleyman spent much of his time attending to domestic affairs. His residence when he was not on campaign was the Topkapi Saray, a palace built on a high wooded promontory at the eastern end of Istanbul shortly after the city had been conquered by the Ottomans in 1453. This superb site commanded views over the Golden Horn, the Sea of Marmara, and on the opposite side of the Bosporus, the shores of Asia. Parks and gardens adorned with pavilions and fountains were laid out on slopes falling away to the sea. The palace was not a single edifice but a collection of buildings grouped around a series of courtyards. The entrance to the sultan's own quarters was known as the Bab-i-Ali, translated by Westerners as the "Sublime Porte," a term that came to stand for the Ottoman court itself.

The sixteenth-century Florentine political writer Niccolò Machiavelli wrote of the Ottoman Empire that it was "ruled by one man: All the others are his servants," and nowhere was this more vividly seen than in the Topkapi Palace. The members of the palace establishment were divided into the Outer and Inner Services. The former included janissaries, household cavalry, gatekeepers, standard-bearers, musicians, artisans, physicians, astrologers, and gardeners; the latter comprised the sultan's eunuchs, personal attendants, pages, and valets. Every person wore a costume whose design and color proclaimed his rank, and all appointments ultimately depended on the sultan himself.

No less rigidly organized was the imperial harem, lodged in the Old Palace in the center of Istanbul, where the sultan could enjoy the company of his concubines uninterrupted by his household staff or ministers of state. Its members—in Süleyman's reign, probably around 200, of whom many were the concubines' children—had clearly defined ranks and positions. At the bottom were the novices, and above them a series of grades—the privileged ones, the favored, the fortunates—through which a young woman could rise according to her attractions and ability. If a fortunate bore the sultan a child, she earned the title of princess. The administration of the harem was supervised by a woman called the mistress of the household, but the supreme ruler was the princess mother, the mother of the reigning sultan.

Süleyman had already fathered a son by a woman named Gülbahar, or "Rose of the Spring," before he ascended the throne, but in the early 1520s, he fell passionately in love with a Ukrainian who, captured in an Ottoman raid, had entered the harem as a slave. Renamed Hürrem, or "the Smiling One," she was later to become known to Westerners as Roxelana, probably because of her Russian background. The Venetian ambassador described her as "young, not beautiful, but graceful and small." After a quarrel with Gülbahar—who referred to her rival as "sold meat"—

Hürrem quickly gained first place in the affections of the sultan, and in 1524, she bore him a son named Selim.

By fair means or foul, Hürrem managed to retain Süleyman's ardent devotion for the rest of her life. Customarily, an Ottoman sultan did not officially marry except for political reasons, to a princess of a foreign dynasty, and by the time of Süleyman's reign, such alliances were no longer necessary; but Hürrem proved an exception, even, it appears, withholding her favors to achieve her end. In the words of the French ambassador: "Passion on the one side and obstinacy on the other at last brought it about that Süleyman made her his wife." In 1541, after a serious fire in the Old Palace, the harem was moved to the Topkapi Palace, where Hürrem was able to exert greater influence on her husband.

The harem was not the only Ottoman institution in which it was possible for a slave to obtain a position of great power. Both in the city of Istanbul and throughout the empire, Ottoman society was broadly divided into two categories: the *askeri,* those citizens who did military service and were not required to pay taxes, and the *reaya,* those—both Muslim and Christian—who did not have military obligations but paid taxes instead. The former were in every respect the dominant or ruling class—nevertheless, the majority of officials who constituted the upper ranks of the askeri, including most of those who served in the Topkapi Saray, were of slave origin.

Some of these slaves were captured in battle or during campaigns, or seized in raids into Christian territory; others were purchased at slave markets within the Ottoman Empire or sent as gifts to the sultan and his officials. But the Ottomans also instituted an additional method of obtaining slave recruits: the *devshirme*. Meaning literally a "gathering," the devshirme consisted of a periodic levy of children from the Christian villages of the Balkans and Anatolia. Those selected by the sultan's officers were taken to Istanbul to be brought up as Muslims. Regularly assessed and examined during a thorough education and rigorous military training, some joined the ranks of the janissaries and household cavalry, and others were groomed in the palace school for positions in the administration. Since all promotions were made according to merit and achievement, an able soldier or bureaucrat might rise through the ranks to become a senior officer, general, or governor.

Although the devshirme must have caused great misery for many of the parents and children involved, it was not unknown for families to try to bribe the sultan's officials to select their sons. Their reasons were understandable: Enslavement was the means of elevation from subject to military status, and the devshirme a road to advancement, wealth, and power. Moreover, it was the slave institution that provided the officers who ran the efficient Ottoman bureaucracy and formed the backbone of the well-nigh invincible fighting force that for so long excited the admiration and dread of the sultan's adversaries. This fact never ceased to amaze European observers, coming as they did from rigidly hierarchical societies in which a person's place was usually decided by birth. As the Venetian ambassador to the Sublime Porte declared:

> It is in the highest degree remarkable that the wealth, the administration, the force, in short the whole body politic of the Ottoman Empire reposes upon and is entrusted to men born in the Christian faith, converted into slaves, and reared up Muhammadans.

The most spectacular example of a slave's rise to eminence was that of Ibrahim Pasha, the son of a Greek fisherman. He was captured by Turkish pirates and, after being sold as a slave, entered Süleyman's household as a page. Handsome, intelligent, and the same age as his master, he was promoted to chief falconer, married Süleyman's sister, and in 1523 was appointed to the post of grand vizier, the highest political office in the empire. As Süleyman's most trusted confidant, he personally conducted negotiations with foreign powers and led military campaigns.

During the second decade of his reign, Süleyman went on the attack in Asia and on the high seas. In 1533, he signed a truce with Ferdinand of Austria and Ferdinand's elder brother, Charles V, the Holy Roman emperor, to avoid the hazards of fighting a war on two fronts while he dealt with the old enemy, Persia. Not only were Shiite missionaries once again actively proselytizing in eastern Anatolia but Ismail's successor, Shah Tahmāsp, was in addition oppressing his own Sunni Muslim population. In Baghdad—Iraq at that time fell within the domains of the shah—Sunni teachers and believers were being persecuted and condemned to death and their holy places were being destroyed.

An Ottoman army under the command of Ibrahim, the grand vizier, marched on Baghdad in October 1533. Shah Tahmāsp retreated before him, having no intention of repeating his father's mistake of meeting the Ottomans head on, and the Sunnis of

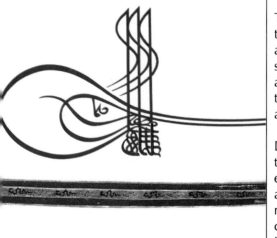

The boldly embellished calligraphy of Süleyman's imperial monogram *(left)* is a potent symbol of authority. The sultan's name *(above)* is woven into a formulaic phrase that reads in full: "Süleyman Shah, son of Selim Shah Khan, ever victorious." Such monograms were first used in the time of Orhan, the second Ottoman sultan, in the fourteenth century and became more elaborate in later reigns. They were inscribed at the head of official papers as a guarantee of authenticity; the decoration in this example was reserved for important documents such as grants of land to members of the sultan's family or high officials.

# THE SULTAN'S SEAGIRT PALACE

Built by Mehmed the Conqueror in the 1460s, soon after the Ottomans had made the city of Istanbul their capital, the sultan's palace stood on a high promontory overlooking the Golden Horn, the Bosporus, and the Sea of Marmara. It became known as the Topkapi Saray, or "Cannongate Palace," on account of its strongly armed portal in the sea walls. Grouped around a series of courtyards, its buildings included the royal residence as well as the center of government.

Some 20,000 slaves of the sultan served in the palace, of whom more than 4,000 lived within its walls. The first and most public courtyard was surrounded by the barracks of the janissaries, their armory, and an infirmary and bakery. Through the

In the second court of the Topkapi Palace, the sultan listens behind a curtained grille in a private kiosk *(below)* to the deliberations of his ministers. A eunuch peeps through the Gate of Felicity *(top right)*, the entrance to the sultan's private quarters.

Gate of Salutation, where errant officials were publicly beheaded, lay the hushed domain of the second court, containing the imperial council chamber and ministers' offices. In the third court stood the sultan's own apartments, the treasury, and the palace school, where slave recruits were trained for positions in the army and administration. Beginning in the 1540s, the several hundred women, children, and eunuchs of the sultan's harem were also lodged in the palace.

Gazelles, deer, and peacocks roamed at will over the lush lawns of the inner courtyards, and songbirds gathered in the trees. "Never," wrote an Ottoman courtier, "hath a more delightful residence been erected by the art of man."

Myriad domes roof the interlocking apartments of the harem—a center of intrigues that in the late sixteenth century increasingly overlapped with official affairs of state.

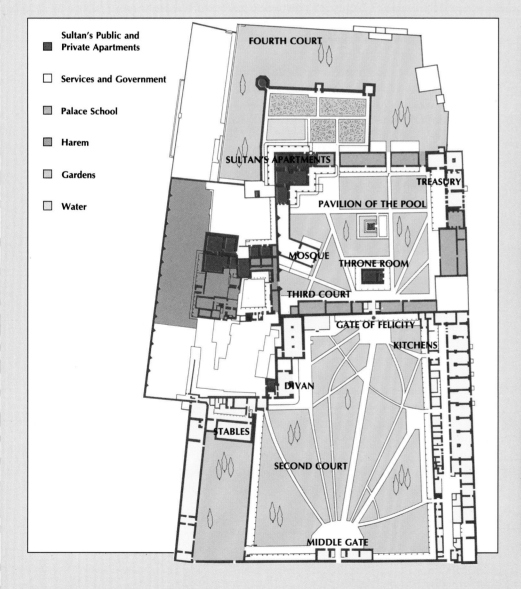

Sultan's Public and Private Apartments

Services and Government

Palace School

Harem

Gardens

Water

FOURTH COURT

SULTAN'S APARTMENTS

TREASURY

PAVILION OF THE POOL

MOSQUE

THRONE ROOM

THIRD COURT

GATE OF FELICITY

KITCHENS

DIVAN

STABLES

SECOND COURT

MIDDLE GATE

Baghdad rose up against their tormentors. Süleyman joined his troops for a grand ceremonial entry into the city, after which he spent the winter organizing the administration of the new province of Iraq. He also lavishly restored the damaged mausoleum of Abū Hanīfah, the founder of the Hanīfah school of law subscribed to by the Ottomans, and visited the important holy places of the region. This campaign, which at times took on the appearance of an armed pilgrimage, confirmed the Ottoman sultan's preeminence in the Islamic world; the Shiites had been roundly defeated, and orthodoxy in Iraq—the ancient seat of the Abbasid caliphs, the spiritual leaders of Islam—had been saved. In addition, with hardly a shot being fired, Süleyman gained vast new territories in Armenia, Azerbaijan, and Mesopotamia and brought the empire to the shores of the Persian Gulf.

Although this campaign greatly enhanced Süleyman's prestige, it led indirectly to the fall of his grand vizier. Ibrahim's personal enemies, who were jealous of his power, accused him of using his command of the army for his own ends and of accepting bribes from the Persians. Hürrem, who resented Ibrahim's influence over the sultan, supported these allegations. Fearing that his trusted vizier was now a threat to his own authority, Süleyman had him executed in Istanbul in 1536.

The situation on the empire's western frontiers was more complex. Although on land Süleyman had little difficulty in containing the threat posed by Charles V, at sea his position was decidedly less favorable. Charles had retained the services of the Genoese admiral Andrea Doria and, in 1530, had settled the Knights of Saint John in Malta. Three years later, after Doria had captured the ports of Korónē and Lepanto in southern Greece, Süleyman turned for assistance to an aging North African buccaneer named Khayr ad-Dīn and known in the West, because of the color of his hair, as Barbarossa (Redbeard). This pirate leader had been granted permission by Süleyman's father to recruit sailors in Anatolia and arm his ships with Ottoman cannon, and in 1529, he had seized the port of Algiers.

Süleyman received Barbarossa in Istanbul with the highest honors, entrusted him with the command of the Ottoman navy, and placed at his disposal the empire's harbors, arsenals, and foundries, as well as prodigious resources of manpower, timber, pitch, sailcloth, powder, and provisions to build and equip a new fleet. While Süleyman was engaged in the invasion of Iraq, Barbarossa recaptured the ports taken by Doria, conquered Tunis, and ravaged the coasts of Italy and Spain. In 1537, the year after Süleyman's return from Baghdad, Barbarossa seized most of Venice's remaining islands and fortresses in the Aegean, and in the following year, he defeated a combined Venetian, Spanish, and papal armada at the Battle of Preveza off the west coast of Greece. These victories established Ottoman supremacy in the Aegean and the eastern Mediterranean. Meanwhile, another Ottoman fleet operating in the Red Sea and the Indian Ocean, which had been fighting the Portuguese and establishing coastal strongholds in the region for several years, captured Aden and made an expedition as far as Gujarat in India.

The emergence of the Ottomans as a first-rate sea power increased diplomatic contact with the West. The nations of Europe, which only recently had been talking loudly of driving the accursed Turks back into the depths of Asia whence they had come, now vied with one another to establish cordial relations with the Ottoman court, hoping to protect their maritime interests. None, however, went as far as the French king Francis I, who in 1536 proposed a secret treaty with Süleyman directed against their common enemy, Charles V. In 1538, during peace negotiations follow-

Known to the Ottomans as Hürrem, or "the Smiling One," and to Westerners as Roxelana, Süleyman's consort is depicted by a Venetian artist who had only verbal descriptions to work from, since no foreigner was able to penetrate the jealously guarded seclusion of the Ottoman harem. Captured in a raid and sold as a slave in Istanbul, Roxelana bore Süleyman a daughter and five sons, including his successor, Selim. She used her wealth to endow mosques and charitable institutions; she also gained for herself and the harem a powerful influence over the government of the empire.

ing the Battle of Preveza, Francis's ambassador supplied Süleyman with valuable information about the intentions of his enemies, information that was obtained by French spies in Venice.

Süleyman did not otherwise find Francis a reliable or satisfactory ally, but in 1543, their accord led to an event that scandalized the whole of Christendom. At the invitation of the French king, Barbarossa arrived in Marseilles with a fleet of 110 galleys and 40 sailing ships to take part in joint operations with French squadrons. The town of Nice—then the possession of the dukes of Savoy—was sacked. Barbarossa spent the winter in Toulon, where he upbraided the French captains for the poor turnout of their vessels and general slovenliness; his own men, in spite of their fierce appearance, conducted themselves with perfect discipline. Setting sail in the spring, Barbarossa bombarded Barcelona and pillaged the coastal regions of Tuscany, Naples, and Sicily on his way back to Istanbul.

It was to be the great corsair's last voyage. He died in 1546, leaving most of his wealth to found a mosque and theological college.

During the latter half of Süleyman's reign, new conquests were made in Hungary, Transylvania, Georgia, and North Africa, but more resources were now employed in consolidating the immense new territories over which the sultan held sway. Throughout the empire, roads, bridges, aqueducts, baths, bazaars, caravansaries—hostels for traveling merchants—and fortresses were built, and everywhere the landscape was adorned by the graceful Ottoman domes and slender minarets that signaled to the traveler that he was entering the sultan's domains.

Not least among Süleyman's many building projects was the glorification and embellishment of his capital, Istanbul. The Topkapi Saray was expanded to receive the members of the harem; the central bazaar was enlarged to handle the rapidly increasing volume of commercial activity; the ancient aqueduct originally constructed by the Roman emperor Valens, which brought clean water into Istanbul, was rebuilt to allow the construction of numerous new fountains and baths; and mosques as well as other religious and public buildings were erected all over the city. In their midst there rose the magnificent Süleymaniye Mosque, the heart of a great complex of hospitals, schools, hostels, medical and theological colleges, public soup kitchens, and gardens. The skyline of Istanbul was altered forever.

The key figure in this vast enterprise was the imperial architect, Sinan. A Christian by birth, Sinan was brought to Istanbul in the devshirme, and in 1521, he entered the ranks of the janissaries. Having gained experience in the building of bridges and fortifications during campaigns in Hungary, Austria, and Iraq, he was appointed Architect of the Abode of Felicity in 1538 and given charge of the sultan's building projects. During the fifty years that he held this post, he was responsible for nearly 500 buildings. His military experience proved vital in overcoming the logistical problems posed by the scale of these projects, and his energy and dedication were as remarkable as his architectural originality.

The blossoming of Ottoman architecture was accompanied by a dramatic flowering in the decorative arts: Calligraphy, illumination, painting, engraving, stone carving, and ceramics all attained a peak of excellence in this epoch. The writing of history, geography, biography, and poetry also thrived. Like many of his royal forebears and successors, Süleyman was a poet—writing under the pen name Muhibbi, or "the Affectionate"—and a liberal patron of men of letters.

The monument for which Süleyman was held in highest esteem by his own subjects, however, was his system of law. A famous Islamic proverb states that "the world can go on with unbelief but not with injustice"; and on coming to the throne, Süleyman had given notice that the promulgation of justice was to be the overriding ambition of his reign. In theory, the only law in a Muslim state was that of the sharia, the holy law of Islam, which was derived from the Koran and the Traditions—the sayings and acts of the prophets—and interpreted by doctors of law. In practice, additional rules and regulations were required, which in the Ottoman state were known as *kanun*. Building on the kanun of his predecessors, and where necessary attempting to rationalize them and bring them into harmony with the sharia, the sultan personally drew up civil and criminal codes covering everything from taxes, land tenure, military privileges, and obligations to prices, wages, health regulations, and compensation for injuries. The implementation of this all-embracing system meant that for the first time, a more or less uniform system of justice operated throughout the empire. For this considerable achievement Süleyman won the appellation of Kanuni, the Lawgiver.

Süleyman's last years were clouded by a series of tragic events related to the vexed question of succession. As he approached his sixtieth year, three of his sons were still alive: the eldest, Mustafa, his son by Gülbahar, and Selim and Bajazet, his sons by Hürrem. In terms of qualities and accomplishments, Mustafa was the fittest to succeed; Hürrem, however, was determined that one of her own sons should inherit the throne—especially since, in the race for the sultanate, there could be only one winner, the losers facing instant execution. Hürrem had the support of the grand vizier, Rustem Pasha, to whom she had given her only daughter in marriage. Mustafa, on the other hand, had the support of the most powerful faction of all, the army—although this ultimately contributed to his downfall.

In 1553, Süleyman launched a new campaign against Persia, entrusting its leadership to Rustem Pasha. It was not intended that the sultan should take part personally in the expedition, but when the army reached eastern Anatolia, the grand vizier sent back disturbing reports that Mustafa was secretly conspiring with Shah Tahmāsp and elements in the army to overthrow his aging father. Even if the threatened rebellion was pure fabrication, Süleyman had reason to fear his son's potentially dangerous popularity with the janissaries, and his suspicions were encouraged by Hürrem.

Süleyman left Istanbul and hastened to join his forces in the east. At Ereğli, near Konya, Mustafa was summoned to pay his respects to his father. On entering Süleyman's tent, the prince was set upon by his father's men and, after a desperate struggle, strangled. His lifeless corpse was displayed outside Süleyman's tent.

This brutal act almost brought about the very uprising it was supposed to prevent. The janissaries in the camp were in uproar, and Süleyman was compelled to dismiss Rustem Pasha, whom they held responsible. The vizier was saved from execution only by the intervention of his wife, Hürrem's daughter.

The success of Hürrem's intrigues in eliminating the one prince of outstanding character and capabilities does not seem to have reduced Süleyman's adoration of his wife. When she died in 1558, he was overcome with grief. Her death precipitated a struggle between her surviving sons, from which Selim emerged the victor; Bajazet fled to Persia, where he and his children were later strangled by Selim's agents. In this manner, the most unworthy candidate, according to common consent, became the sole heir to the Ottoman throne.

It was said among the Ottomans that twelve times Süleyman led his army out of the gates of Istanbul, and twelve times he returned victorious. On May 1, 1566, he embarked on his thirteenth campaign, marching northward against the Hungarians. Falling ill during the siege of Szigetvár, a fortress in Hungary, he died in the early hours of September 6, two days before the stronghold fell to his troops. The Imperial Council kept the sultan's death secret to avoid disorder, while Selim traveled from his provincial governorate in Anatolia to the capital. Süleyman's heart was buried in Hungary, the scene of the triumphs of his youth. His body was conveyed in solemn procession to Istanbul and laid to rest in the mausoleum he had built for himself beside the Süleymaniye Mosque, close by that of his beloved Hürrem.

Süleyman, "sultan of sultans, king of kings, distributor of crowns to the princes of the world, the shadow of God on earth," left to his successors an empire extending from Austria to Aden, from the western Mediterranean to the Caspian Sea. Like the empire of ancient Rome, the Ottoman domains bestrode Europe, Asia, and Africa. Skilled in the arts of peace as well as of war, at once magnanimous and ruthless, Süleyman had presided over the apogee of Ottoman power and majesty.

Selim II, whose degenerate habits earned him the epithet of "the Sot," bore little resemblance to the great sultans who preceded him. In the words of the Venetian ambassador, he "preferred the society of eunuchs and of women, and the habits of the saray to the camp," and "wore away his days in sensual enjoyments, in drunkenness and indolence." Fortunately for the Ottoman state, he inherited an able grand vizier, Sokollu Mehmed Pasha, from his father.

For failing to clean the street outside his front door, a negligent citizen has the soles of his feet beaten with sticks. This punishment, bastinado, was summarily meted out for minor offenses such as assault and petty theft; more serious or complex cases were brought before a district judge. The Islamic code enforced throughout the Ottoman Empire was derived from the Koran and the sayings and actions of the prophet Muhammad, but many additional regulations were found necessary. For the Ottomans, one of Süleyman's greatest achievements was his comprehensive reorganization of the legal system to cover everything from land tenure and military service to wages and health measures.

The vision of Sokollu Mehmed was demonstrated in a grand plan to build a series of fortresses on the south Russian steppe and to dig a canal to join the Volga and the Don rivers, which at one point flowed within thirty miles of each other. This scheme had a threefold purpose: It would check the expansion of Russia under Ivan the Terrible; it would enable the Ottoman fleet to reach the Caspian Sea from the Sea of Azov, and so threaten Persia from the north; and it would facilitate communications with the Uzbek Turks of central Asia, who were allies of the Ottomans. In the event, the stout Russian defense of the fortress of Astrakhan against an Ottoman siege in 1569 prevented this plan from being carried out. But Ivan was effectively contained in this region, and a peace that lasted for the better part of a century was concluded between Moscow and Istanbul.

In 1571, the Ottomans captured Cyprus from the Venetians, but this success was followed by a naval defeat that restored a measure of pride to their Western enemies.

The craft guilds of the towel makers *(below)*, kebab makers, and millers *(opposite)* process before Murad III during the celebrations—which lasted fifty-two days and nights—held to mark the circumcision of the sultan's son in 1583. Every profession and social group in Ottoman society—even beggars, thieves, and lunatics—had its own guild. As well as fulfilling trade functions such as recruiting apprentices, maintaining prices and quality, and representing their members to the authorities, these organizations acted as social and religious fraternities and had their own esoteric ceremonies.

Sailing westward from Cyprus, the Ottoman fleet arrived in the Gulf of Patras and stopped to winter over in the port of Lepanto. On October 7, the crusading fleet of the Holy League—which comprised more than 200 Venetian, Spanish, and papal galleys under the command of Don John of Austria, a bastard son of Charles V—appeared at the entrance of the gulf. The Ottoman admiral, Muezzinzade Ali, re-

jecting the advice of his commanders, sailed out to meet the Christian fleet, and the opposing fleets clashed along a line approximately four miles long. There followed five hours of savage fighting. The crew members of one Ottoman vessel, having run out of ammunition, were reduced to hurling their supplies of oranges and lemons at the enemy—who threw them back amid derisive laughter. Eventually, after Muezzinzade Ali was killed by a musket ball and his flagship boarded by Don John, the Ottoman center gave way. Many of the Ottoman ships gallantly continued the fight, but their line was irreparably broken.

By evening, the Turkish fleet no longer existed. Approximately 90 Ottoman ships were sunk, and another 130 captured. Around 30,000 Muslims had been killed or captured, at the cost of 9,000 Christian casualties. The Spanish writer Miguel de Cervantes, who lost the use of his left hand as a result of wounds sustained at Lepanto, later wote in *Don Quixote:* "On that day so fortunate to Christendom, all nations were undeceived of the error of believing that the Turks were invincible at sea."

Although the battle at Lepanto, which was the last major naval engagement to be fought between galleys, was regarded in western Europe as a great Christian victory, its consequences for the Ottomans were far from devastating. The Holy League neglected to press home its advantage, and before long, it was disbanded in an atmosphere of mutual distrust. Selim, however, was able to rebuild his entire fleet over the course of the winter, supplementing its strength with several colossal warships. The island of Cyprus was not surrendered. Sokollu Mehmed made a grim observation to the Venetian ambassador:

*There is a great difference between your loss and ours. In seizing a kingdom from you, we have amputated an arm; but you, in defeating our fleet, have done no more than shave our beard. An arm cut off cannot grow again, whereas a beard shaved grows back stronger than ever.*

**D**rawing on both Islamic tradition and that of the Christian empire of Byzantium they had conquered in the fifteenth century, Ottoman architects developed a style distinctively their own. The larger mosques were adorned with cascades of domes of different sizes, vaulting arches, and as many as six slender minarets; within, in place of the Byzantine division of interiors by lines of columns, the architects sought to create a single unified space more suited to the needs of Muslim worship.

Under the reigns of Süleyman the Magnificent and his two successors, the post of imperial architect was held for fifty years by a former slave and janissary named Sinan. Working without ceasing until his death at the age of ninety-nine in 1588, Sinan was responsible for designing a large proportion of the mosques, caravansaries, public baths, schools, aqueducts, and mausoleums that were constructed throughout the Ottoman Empire to bear enduring witness to its golden age.

**S**oaring 230 feet into the sky, four minarets stand like sentinels around the dome of the Selimiye mosque in Edirne, the summer residence of the Ottoman sultans, which was a week's journey to the northeast of Istanbul. Designed by the architect Sinan, its airy interior *(left)* provides a serene setting for the mihrab— the prayer niche indicating the direction of Mecca, beyond the second arch from the left—and the triangular pulpit, from which a sermon was delivered at Friday prayers.

Selim the Sot died in 1574, following a drunken fall on the wet marble floor of the Topkapi baths. Both the Ottomans and foreign observers had high expectations of his serious and sober successor, Murad III, but these hopes were not to be fulfilled. Murad was dominated by his mother and by his consort, Princess Safiye; the former tirelessly maintained a supply of new concubines and their attendants for the sultan's harem, perhaps partly in an attempt to undermine the influence of her daughter-in-law. Murad is reputed to have changed the companion of his bed two or three times in a single night on some occasions, and his unceasing demand for beautiful slaves is reported to have grossly inflated the prices in the women's slave market. Under Murad's rule, both the size of the harem and its influence on the policies of state were greatly increased.

For the first years of Murad's reign, Sokollu Mehmed Pasha remained in office, providing some continuity with the era of Süleyman. The harem and other factions in the palace were jealous of his power, however, and conspired against him, and

Ottoman galleys, distinguished by the crescents on their banners, clash with Genoese and Venetian vessels at the battle of Lepanto, fought off the west coast of Greece in 1571. Surprised while preparing to lay up for the winter by the Christian armada of the Holy League, the Ottoman fleet was utterly routed. However, although Lepanto restored a measure of pride to the nations of western Europe after repeated reversals over decades, their victory was not decisive. In the course of the next winter, the Ottomans rebuilt their entire fleet, and they retained all their territories in the Mediterranean.

gradually the trusted and experienced members of his staff were banished from the capital or executed. The weak-willed Murad replaced them with talentless timeservers and court parasites. Sokollu Mehmed was stabbed to death in 1579 by an assassin hired by his enemies. In the remaining sixteen years of Murad's reign, the grand vizierate changed ten times.

Before his death, Sokollu Mehmed had encouraged initiatives that led to the opening of diplomatic relations with Elizabeth I of England and the granting of commercial privileges to English merchants. In the forging of this Anglo-Ottoman friendship, much play was made on both sides of their joint enmity toward the Catholics, and even of similarities between Protestantism and Islam. Elizabeth called herself in one letter "the unconquered and puissant defender of the True Faith against the idolators who falsely profess the name of Christ." The sultan assured her that in war "against the Spanish Infidels with whom you are ever in conflict and strife, with the help of God you will be victorious." On the eve of the dispatch of the Spanish Armada, Elizabeth's agent in Istanbul appealed to Murad to send Ottoman galleys to aid the English fleet in fighting off the threatened invasion.

Notwithstanding Murad's addiction to the delights of the harem, the Ottomans made advances in Georgia, Yemen, and Morocco; and in 1583, the Ottomans achieved a major victory against the Persians in the Caucasus at the Battle of Torches, so called because the conflict, which lasted almost a week, was fought by both day and night. But when war was resumed with Austria a decade later, the Ottomans found themselves unable to gain the upper hand with their accustomed ease. Writing in the 1590s, Hasan al-Kafi, a judge with experience of life on the frontier in Bosnia, attributed the Ottoman lack of success to the fact that the Christians were now better organized and disciplined, and equipped with up-to-date firearms, whereas the Ottomans, who in the past had always been open to innovations in weaponry, were now slow to adopt them and were not even properly trained in the use of their existing ones. This ominous failure to keep up with developments in science and technology was also illustrated by the fate of an astronomical observatory built by Murad in Istanbul, which was demolished—after the appearance of a comet had spread terror amid the populace—on the orders of the religious authorities.

Murad's death in January 1595 occasioned the worst fratricidal massacre in Ottoman history. All nineteen brothers of his heir, Mehmed III, were strangled, and fifteen slaves pregnant by Murad were also put to death. Mehmed's twenty-seven sisters and their attendants were banished to the Old Palace. After this, Mehmed seldom left the Topkapi Saray, where he followed the voluptuous and indolent lifestyle of his father. His mother, Princess Safiye, was now the head of the harem and dominated Mehmed just as she had previously controlled her husband.

The last years of the century were not happy ones for the empire. Inflation was rife, the value of silver—the staple currency—plummeting against that of gold, and the treasury was faced with a growing deficit after 1591. Perhaps because a sharp increase in the rural populace had not been matched by an equivalent increase in cultivable land in the Balkans and Anatolia, landless young peasants abounded. Deserting soldiers and peasants who had acquired horses and firearms roamed the country in gangs, living by banditry. At times the interior was reduced to a state of anarchy so serious that law-abiding folk were forced into a mass exodus from the land to seek the safety of fortified towns and cities.

Contemporary Ottoman observers recognized that all was not well and sought to account for the decline. Among their hypotheses were the failure of the sultan to take a personal interest in the day-to-day deliberations of his ministers; the meddling of the harem in politics; too-frequent changes of grand vizier; the treasury's failure to balance its books; the appointment of incompetent officials; the sale of offices, favoritism, nepotism, bribery, extortion, and the spread of corruption at every level of the state. But the frankness and courage of those who, knowing that they lived under a despotic monarchy, still voiced such harsh criticisms, indicated a healthy lack of complacency in some quarters at least.

Certainly one difficulty lay in the quality of the sultans themselves. For 250 years the Ottomans had produced, one after another, a whole series of exceptionally able and energetic rulers. The death of Süleyman, however, marked the beginning of a procession of weak, incompetent, degenerate, and even imbecile incumbents on the throne. Mehmed III was the last ruler to serve as a provincial governor before he became sultan. Because it was feared that the son of a sultan might take advantage of such a position to build up a personal power base, Mehmed's successors were confined to a group of buildings in the Topkapi grounds until the throne became vacant; instead of gaining valuable administrative experience, they idled away their hours with their slave girls and eunuchs. In the seventeenth century, the problem was further exacerbated by the accession of several underage rulers.

Mehmed himself was not totally devoid of the martial spirit and strength in adversity that had characterized his forebears. At the battle of Keresztes in Hungary in 1596, his refusal to flee when the Christian forces had broken through the Ottoman lines was instrumental in turning an apparent defeat into a complete rout of the enemy. And although they lacked leaders of excellence, the Ottomans displayed a resilience and capability for renewal that—despite the increasing military strength of their European enemies—sustained their empire into the first decades of the twentieth century. But almost from the time of Süleyman's death, his reign was looked back upon as a golden age. In the centuries that followed, he remained a source of inspiration to his compatriots, and of fascination and admiration to those beyond the borders of his wide domains, who gave him the name of "the Magnificent."

# THE PROUD DISPLAY OF PRIVILEGE

**W**hile fine clothes had advertised status and wealth in every age and every land, it was not until the sixteenth century that dress came to be ruled by fashion—at least in some societies. The development was confined to Europe, whose courts and capitals became centers of stylish extravagance. The contrast between the European appetite for eye-catching novelty and the more tradition-oriented garb that endured in many parts of Asia reflected deeper social and political differences.

In part, the European indulgence in finery was the direct result of foreign exploration and conquests. A greater variety of silks, brocades, and fine tissues reached Europe. New dyes such as cochineal, indigo, saffron, and henna became available. The injection of New World gold into the economy fueled spending on luxury goods. But social changes were equally significant. Thanks to the new wealth, the mercantile middle classes could now afford to outshine their so-called betters, and they engaged in a struggle for status that was most evident in the costumes they affected.

The old guard fought back by attempting to enforce laws that specified the dress proper to every rank of society. The purpose of this sumptuary legislation was to safeguard the traditionally exclusive rights of the ruling elite to luxury clothes and sometimes to protect local industries—such as the wool trade in England—from the competition of imports dictated by changing styles.

In the Muslim world, the development of national dress was strongly influenced by the expansion of the Ottoman Empire and the Mogul invasion of India. But where hierarchies remained constant, so did styles of dress. In China and Japan, clothes were no less important as a sign of rank than in Europe; in the Far East, however, the ordering of society was not changed by the fruits of exploration or by religious upheavals, and what both sovereigns and their subjects wore generally accorded with age-old conventions. To Eastern rulers, the changing fashions of the Europeans they encountered appeared fickle and frivolous; what they failed to recognize was that this restlessness was symptomatic of a new confidence and willingness to experiment that would soon pose a threat to their own more static societies.

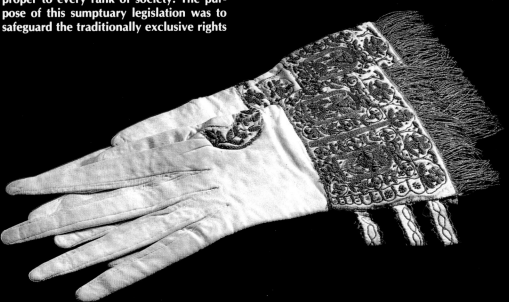

# THE CHANGING CONTOURS OF BEAUTY

Although each European country had its own fashions in women's dress, the clothes of the privileged showed many foreign influences thanks to international ties of marriage, diplomacy, and commerce. The Italian contribution reflected Renaissance ideas of beauty and harmony, which gave women a fluid grace in voluminous dresses of rich materials. The bright ornamentation of a Germanic style spread to the English and French courts and there encouraged a colorful extravagance. In the latter half of the century, the Spanish taste for somber splendor and an increasingly exaggerated artificiality spread throughout Europe. Rigid corsets imposed a narrow, elongated line on the body, and skirts were worn over metal frames known as farthingales.

Black silk embroidery on white linen—shown here on the frilled cuffs of a chemise—originated in Spain and was popularized in England by Catherine of Aragon, Henry VIII's first wife.

Worn over a gold-tinsel cap, this German-style black velvet hat provides a setting for a plume and gold ornaments studded with jewels and pearls.

In a portrait painted around 1545, an English lady wears a curved, jeweled French hood and a French gown of ivory silk brocade with silver thread. The lynx fur on the funnel-shaped sleeves was a material restricted by law to women of the highest rank. A Spanish-type triangular bodice and conical farthingale accentuate the narrow waistline.

skirt fringed with silver and supported by a wheel-shaped farthingale. The pointed stomacher and padded sleeves—balancing the width of the farthingale—are embroidered with a pattern of gold-and-black carnations and hops, matching the gold honeysuckle on the black gown that frames the outfit.

Above this typically Italian low, square-cut bodice and ample sleeve, the wearer's bare shoulder is covered with silk gauze woven with gold thread.

The front of this stiff, richly bordered Spanish dress is closed with tags known as aglets. The horizontal pleat above the upper aglet allowed the dress to fold down when the wearer was seated, modestly concealing her feet.

MARY COVNTESs. RIVERS.

Lace ruffs originated in Spain but were adopted throughout Europe. The more elaborate ruffs were supported by wire frames to prevent them from being blown out of shape out-of-doors.

His elbows thrust out and his hands resting on his hip and sword hilt, this mid-century Englishman's swaggering posture is emphasized by the wide shoulders and puffed sleeves of his short gown. Beneath the gown he wears a matching jerkin and an embroidered shirt with flared cuffs. The ostrich plume in the broad-brimmed cap, the long tassel hanging from the dagger, and the jewels that stud the shoes all contribute to the extrovert character of the costume.

Slashing, a fashion demonstrated by the rows of slits in this German costume, originated on the battlefield of Grandson in 1476, when German mercenaries copied Swiss troops who mended their torn clothes with strips of silk from plundered tents.

A gold-embroidered codpiece, a pouch worn at the crotch, projects through the jerkin in a detail from a French portrait painted in 1550. Often thickly padded and richly decorated, the codpiece became an object of mockery and was out of fashion by the

In their rich fabrics and embroidery, men's fashions at European courts reached an even more extreme degree of ostentation than women's. An arrogant masculinity with exaggeratedly broad shoulders and puffed trunk hose typified the first half of the century; thereafter, as Spain's New World wealth brought it ever-greater prestige, the somber colors and severe lines of Spanish costume predominated, with much padding to achieve a faultlessly smooth surface. The more dashing styles came in for ridicule: Three young Venetians who visited Spain in 1581 reported that their ornate lace ruffs, wider than was usual in Spain, were derided as "enormous lettuces."

This end-of-the-century costume worn by an English diplomat is dominated by the stiff, elongated shape of the padded doublet, a more austere style of dress than that seen earlier in the century. A Dutch-style cloak of dark green velvet embroidered with parallel panels of gold braid is draped over the shoulders.

An Italian noble sports headgear typical of his country: a pleated red hat adorned with a Saint Christopher's medal, worn over a turbanlike coif.

Slung from an ornamented belt on the left hip—so it could be drawn with the right hand—a sword with an ornate hilt was an ac-

In northern India, where a Muslim ruling class originating in central Asia prevailed over a mainly Hindu population, styles of dress varied according to racial origin and local religious tradition and climate. Rank, however, was a decisive factor in all regions, and courtiers were adorned in the finest silk, muslin, and cashmere fabrics. Keenly aware of the political significance of dress, the Mogul emperor Akbar—at whose court thousands of costumes were made and distributed each year at imperial ceremonies—enacted laws reserving certain colors, materials, and styles for the ruling elite. The traditional Muslim turban, coat, and footwear were adapted to conform with local Hindu conventions, and Muslim women adopted the styles of dress worn by Akbar's Rajput wives, minimizing differences between the cultures.

A Muslim sultan from central India wears headgear typical of his region and a jama—the coatlike outer garment that became the basic male garment after the establishment of Muslim power in India—of diaphanous muslin. His shawl is made of cashmere, a fine wool woven in the territory of Kashmir.

The style of this dagger tucked into the sash of a grandee at Akbar's Muslim court proclaims its wearer to be a Hindu of the Rajput warrior caste.

part in a hunting expedition is dressed in a full-skirted jama embroidered with appropriate scenes of animals and birds in a landscape. On his head he wears a lightweight turban specifically designed for the hot climate of India.

The central Asian head-gear worn by this musician and the Persian influence evident in the painting of his face demonstrate the cosmopolitan character of Emperor Humāyūn's court.

## Ottoman Opulence

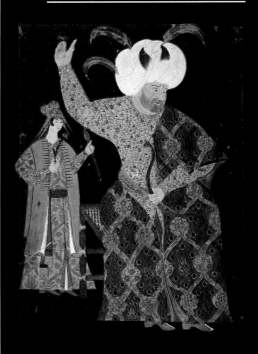

In the Ottoman Empire, the size of a turban denoted its wearer's rank and its color his religious adherence: white for Muslims, yellow for Jews, blue for Christians. In the painting above, Sultan Selim II wears a giant turban adorned with feathers reserved for royalty. His caftan—the basic garment for both men and women—and his single-sleeved mantle are made of brocaded silks woven with arabesque patterns. Muslim women in the Ottoman Empire wore multi-layered variations of men's clothes, including trailing underskirts; in obedience to the Koranic instruction that they conceal their bodies from public view, women covered their faces with veils or with scarves.

Imperial dress in Japan changed so slowly that in the sixteenth century, when European missionaries reached the islands, courtiers were wearing a costume that was recognizably a naturalized form of the costume borrowed from China some eight centuries before. Although fewer layers of clothing were worn in the sixteenth century than previously, both men and women still dressed in loose, long-sleeved silk gowns; the men's silks were so stiff that their sleeves stood out like sails. Women covered their heads when out-of-doors. Samurai warriors wore the same baggy trousers as courtiers, but with a broad-shouldered sleeveless coat that was easy to slip on over armor for warmth. To European visitors, one of the most surprising indicators of high rank was the Japanese custom of artificially blackening the teeth with a paste containing black iron oxide.

A samurai warrior wears a sleeveless jacket patterned with scattered pine needles over a green kimono. Tucked into the folds of his clothing are the two swords that samurai were required to carry.

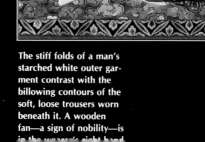

The stiff folds of a man's starched white outer garment contrast with the billowing contours of the soft, loose trousers worn beneath it. A wooden fan—a sign of nobility—is in the wearer's right hand.

Under an outer blue robe, the contrasting blocks of color on the inner garment represent the many layers of clothing traditionally worn.

# China's Timeless Robes

In the rigidly formalized hierarchy of the Ming dynasty, every item of clothing denoted status: shoes, belt, hat, dagger, and above all, the flowing robes of silk that had formed the basis of court dress for more than 1,000 years. The crimson "dragon robes" worn by the government official shown on the left were bestowed only on the highest functionaries, and strict protocol governed which way the dragons should face for each wearer. The black silk cap with horizontal projections was reserved for ceremonial occasions. The emblems woven into the robes of lesser officials—birds for the ten civilian ranks, animals for the nine military ranks—accorded with similar regulations. Women had their feet tightly bound in bandages from girlhood; originally a symbol of chastity, bound feet were considered a sign of both privilege—indicating that the woman did not have to work—and sensuousness.

The formal cap worn by a Japanese feudal lord was made of stiff paper covered with black silk gauze and coated with lacquer. It was held in place by cords of paper string tied under the chin.

A Japanese noblewoman wears a flowing mantle over a plain white kimono tied with a red sash embroidered with gold. The designs on the mantle were produced by a combination of dyeing, embroidery, and appliquéd gold foil—a substitute for expensive imported brocades. The woman's hair is worn loose, echoing the style of her dress.

# THE MOGULS ASCENDANT

In January 1505, a band of horsemen set out from the Afghan city of Kabul, riding eastward. They left behind the snow-covered summits of the Hindu Kush mountains and descended toward the foothills. In a few days they reached the lowland district of Ningnahar, which marked the beginning of the great northern Indian plain. Bābur, the twenty-one-year-old leader of the expedition, had never before seen this border region or experienced the warm climate of India. "In Ningnahar," he later wrote, "another world came into view: the grasses, the trees, the animals, the birds, the manners and customs of the people—everything was different. We were amazed, and in truth there was much to be amazed at."

Bābur's route from the barren mountains of central Asia through the passes of the North-West Frontier had been followed by many earlier invaders, and all had shared his wonder at the abundant fertility of northern India. On this occasion, the aggressors had come to raid, not occupy: For three months, Bābur's cavalry ranged along the western banks of the Indus River, seizing sheep, cattle, and horses, and then, when the heat became oppressive and the sun blistered their skin, they retired with their plunder to Kabul. But the new world that Bābur had seen, and the promise of riches it held, preyed on his mind, and a determination grew within him to make it his own. Two decades later, he was to return with an army of invasion to occupy the lands of the sultan of Delhi, chief ruler of Hindustan—a northern region of India.

Under Bābur's son and successor, his gains were all but lost. But under his grandson Akbar, whose reign began in 1556, the fortunes of the young empire were gloriously revived. The end of the century would see its territories vastly extended, its government efficient, its culture a creative intermingling of international talent and influences. Under the firm rule of foreign invaders, India would be changed forever.

All of this came about, it seemed, almost by chance: Bābur's early years had been plagued by disappointments, and until 1505, the possibility of founding an empire in India had never occurred to him. One of the few advantages he enjoyed was his pedigree: He was descended on his father's side from the fourteenth-century Mongol warrior Timur, known to the West as Tamerlane, whose ferocious campaigns had won him a short-lived but massive empire in central Asia; and on his mother's side, he could trace his ancestry back to the world-conquering Mongol Genghis Khan, who in the twelfth century had laid the foundations of the largest empire known to man. Bābur himself was thus nominally a Mongol, but his immediate forebears had long since been absorbed into the culture of the Turkish-speaking peoples of central Asia, and Bābur had no great respect for those of pure Mongol blood. He spoke of "those Mogul wretches"—Mogul being the term used among his people for Mongol—and complained that "mischief and devastation must always be expected from the Mogul

As the ruler of an expanding Muslim empire in India, the Mogul emperor Akbar gained the allegiance of his subjects as much by his sensitivity toward their differing religious traditions as by his military skill, and he is shown in this detail from a sixteenth-century painting in a characteristic attitude of compassion. The picture records an incident on a hunt in 1578, when Akbar experienced a mystical vision and ordered the slaughter of animals by his huntsmen to cease; during the following years, the emperor devised a syncretic faith that fused tenets of Islam, Christianity, and Hinduism.

horde.'' It was only in the seventeenth century that Bābur's descendants began to style themselves Moguls, harking back to their distant nomad forebear Genghis Khan.

For Bābur, it was his descent through Tamerlane that counted when it came to legitimizing his claims to kingship. After Tamerlane's death in 1405, his empire had rapidly declined in power and extent, so that by the end of the century, the Timurid princes—as his descendants were called—controlled only the territories to the north, south, and west of the mountain chain of the Hindu Kush. (Lands that are now divided among Iran, Afghanistan, and the Muslim republics of the Soviet Union.) In this region of rugged mountain, steppe, and desert dotted with oases, borders were ill

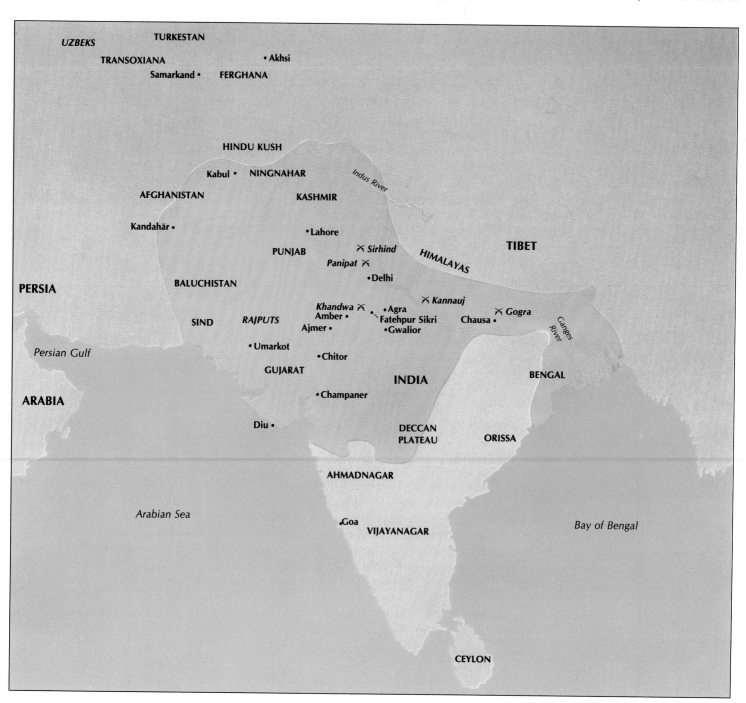

defined, and the Timurid rulers—all blood relatives through their common ancestor—were in perpetual conflict as they struggled for precedence and expansion.

Bābur, a great-great-great-grandson of Tamerlane, was born on February 14, 1483, in the Timurid state of Ferghana. Lying to the north of the Hindu Kush, about 250 miles east of Samarkand, Ferghana was, in Bābur's words, "a small country abounding in grain and fruits, girt 'round by mountains except on the west." The fortified palace of Bābur's father, Umar, stood on the edge of a precipitous ravine; and here, one day in 1494, Umar was watching his pigeons fly to and fro when suddenly the terrace on which he was sitting gave way, the prince plunging with the falling masonry into the abyss. By this strange accident, Bābur acceded to the throne of Ferghana when he was only a boy of eleven.

Bābur inherited his father's enemies along with his throne. Paternal and maternal uncles, the rulers of neighboring kingdoms, attempted to wrest Ferghana from him, and at home he was beset with plots and intrigues. Undeterred, the youth nurtured his own ambitions, in particular that of seizing the city of Samarkand, which in the fourteenth century had been the capital of Tamerlane's empire.

Three times Bābur succeeded in capturing Samarkand, but on each occasion he held it only briefly. Against his own factious relatives, Bābur was able to gain the upper hand with little difficulty; but he also had to contend with the Uzbeks, a Muslim people from Turkestan who were gradually advancing southward and overrunning the fragmented Timurid kingdoms. In 1500, Bābur faced complete obscurity: Having surrendered Samarkand to the Uzbeks, he found that his own kingdom of Ferghana had been taken from him in his absence by his younger brother, and he was reduced to the condition of a barefoot fugitive.

For several years, Bābur wandered the remote uplands in search of a home. Gradually, however, his band of followers was swelled by refugees fleeing before the Uzbek onslaught. Drawn to the prince by his fame and illustrious family name, whole clans and companies of fighters presented themselves at his camp.

Needing a secure base from which to operate, Bābur led his soldiers southward through the high passes and in 1505 descended on the city of Kabul, catching it unawares. The taking of Kabul was dictated by expediency, but the consequences were far-reaching. From here, Bābur was able to make a number of raiding expeditions into Hindustan. And when he realized that, because the Uzbeks were now firmly entrenched in the old Timurid domains, his hope of founding an empire in central Asia was an impossible dream, Bābur determined to make Kabul the springboard for a full-scale invasion of India.

Hot, dusty, and rugged but fertile, well populated, and immensely wealthy, Hindustan offered prospects of unlimited booty. About its civilization, Bābur was less than complimentary: "Its people have no good looks; of social intercourse, paying and receiving visits, there is none; of genius and capacity, none; of manners, none; in handicrafts and work there is no form or symmetry, method or quality." Furthermore, he complained that "there are no good horses, no good dogs, no grapes, muskmelons or first-rate fruits, no ice or cold water, no good bread and cooked food in the bazaars, no hot baths, no colleges, no candles, torches or candlesticks." But fruit and candles were not what he was interested in: "It is a large country and has masses of gold and silver," and "unnumbered and endless workmen of every kind."

Northern India had been controlled for the past 300 years by Muslim dynasties

A sixteenth-century Indian painting depicts Mogul warriors in pursuit of the sultan of Delhi's fleeing army at Panipat in April 1526. Bābur's superior tactics and weaponry—especially the artillery that he had brought with him from Kabul—enabled him to defeat an army four times the size of his own, and on the day after his victory, he was proclaimed emperor of Hindustan in Delhi. Thirty years later, Bābur's grandson Akbar also fought against seemingly insurmountable odds at Panipat and also rode victorious into Delhi.

founded in the wake of invasions by Afghan and Turkish peoples from central Asia; for a brief period at the end of the fourteenth century, it had been ruled by Tamerlane himself. Over this time, Hindu subjects and Muslim overlords had learned to live together in relative harmony, but the northwestern region of Rajputana was still dominated by a fiercely independent Hindu warrior caste known as the Rajputs. Far to the south, the Hindu empire of Vijayanagar staunchly defended its borders against Muslim incursions. The most recent newcomers to the subcontinent were the Portuguese, who in 1510 had established control of the port of Goa on the west coast, from where they sought to control the maritime trade of the Indian Ocean.

In 1519, when Bābur heard of the death of the sultan of Delhi, he sent a goshawk to his successor, Ibrahim, and demanded the return of those lands that, Bābur claimed, rightfully belonged to the descendants of Tamerlane. Ibrahim did not deign to reply, and a few years later, when the governor of Lahore quarreled with Sultan Ibrahim and appealed to Kabul for help, Bābur led his army into Hindustan. After destroying an army sent to oppose him outside Lahore, Bābur was forced to go home to deal with Uzbek activities on his northern border, but he then returned and marched on Delhi. Ibrahim's forces advanced from their capital to meet the invaders, and the armies came face to face on the plain of Panipat in April 1526.

The Moguls numbered some 25,000, as against Ibrahim's forces of 100,000 men and 1,000 elephants. Bābur took up a defensive position, digging ditches, making barricades out of branches, and lashing together several hundred carts, with gaps at intervals to allow his cavalry to sally forth. Behind this protective wall, he positioned his infantry, armed with muskets, and also field artillery recently acquired from the Ottoman Turks, who controlled an expanding empire in the Middle East.

After a week of skirmishing, Ibrahim launched a full-scale attack, but his frontal assault proved unequal to the invader's superior tactics. Attacked on both flanks by mounted archers, Ibrahim's troops were mowed down from the front by Bābur's artillery and muskets. Ibrahim was killed and his head was brought to Bābur.

On the day after his victory at Panipat, Bābur entered the city of Delhi. On April 27, 1526, in the Grand Mosque, Bābur's name was read in the Khutba—the prayer said for the sovereign at Friday worship—and he was declared emperor of Hindustan. He proceeded to divest himself of vast quantities of money and loot with prodigal generosity. His officers and soldiers were laden with gifts, and rich presents were dispatched to his wives and relations at home and to his friends in central Asia who had aided him in his "throneless times," as he called them. "The treasures of five kings fell into his hands," Bābur's daughter recounted. "He gave everything away."

Two more battles had to be fought and won before Bābur could consolidate his authority in Hindustan. The first was against Rānā Sāngā Singh, the acknowledged leader of the Rajputs, who in the spring of 1527 advanced with an enormous army to Khandwa, a village about forty miles from Agra. Outnumbered several times over, and already greatly disturbed by tales of the Rajputs' invincibility, the Moguls were cast into the deepest dejection when one of their camp astrologers publicly predicted a Muslim defeat. In an attempt to restore morale, Bābur reminded his troops that they were now fighting a holy war against the infidel; also, on the eve of the battle, he proved himself a good Muslim by renouncing wine, of which he was greatly fond. Three hundred nobles and troops followed their leader in taking the pledge.

At Khandwa, Bābur again adopted a defensive strategy, placing his artillery and musketeers behind a barricade of chained carts. Knowing that they were in hostile

Protected by a wall from wind and dust, the Garden of Fidelity in Kabul is sectioned into quarters by irrigation channels running from a central fountain and shaded by orange and pomegranate trees. In the foreground, gardeners tend borders with mattock and spade. Bābur preferred the more refreshing climate of Afghanistan to that of India, and of the many gardens he laid out in the territories he conquered, this was his favorite.

territory, and that defeat would spell annihilation, Bābur's infantry fought with desperate courage to repel wave after wave of Rajput soldiers. His cavalry, meanwhile, using skill and dash, wreaked havoc on the wings, and after ten hours of fighting, the Moguls emerged victorious. Rānā Sāngā was one of the few chiefs to escape alive, only to die of his wounds within a year.

But Bābur's troubles were not at an end. Encouraged by Bābur's clemency after Panipat, many of the chiefs who had served under Sultan Ibrahim had sworn allegiance to the conqueror, but others had fled east and rallied behind Ibrahim's brother Mahmud. The defeat of this army at Gogra on the banks of the Ganges, in May 1527, was Bābur's third great victory.

In the winning of his empire, Bābur's ability to inspire loyalty and genuine affection in his followers had been at least as important as his brilliant generalship. His memoirs, based upon diaries that he kept throughout his life, included detailed descriptions of the landscapes and people he encountered as well as his campaigns. He wrote poetry in Persian and laid out lavish gardens in the cities he conquered. Unfortunately, the time in which he could enjoy the arts of peace was now limited, for he was exhausted by years of campaigning and weakened by the uncongenial Indian climate, and his health was in decline. A letter sent to a friend in Kabul bore poignant witness to his longing for the shady groves and orchards, running waters, and snowcapped peaks of the land he had left behind: "Boundless and infinite is my desire to go to those parts."

Bābur died on December 26, 1530, and was buried at Agra. A few years later, his body was taken to Kabul and, according to his wishes, laid to rest in a garden overlooking the city in a roofless tomb open to the snow, wind, and rain.

Having conquered Hindustan in just four years, Bābur had had no time to establish a proper system of administration, and the throne inherited by his son, Humāyūn, was by no means secure. In addition to his three younger half brothers, who constantly plotted against him, two enemies threatened Humāyūn's precarious hold in India: the Afghan chief Shēr Khan in the east and Bahādur Shah of Gujarat to the south.

Dealing first with Bahādur, Humāyūn forced the Gujarati ruler to abandon his army and flee to the coast, from where he made his escape by sea to the Portuguese port of Diu. Humāyūn then stormed Champaner, a stronghold held by Bahādur's supporters, and celebrated his victory with weeks of feasting and entertertainments.

This was the first of many occasions when advantages won by vigorous activity were dissipated in pleasure and idleness. Though brave, intelligent, and resourceful, Humāyūn lacked his father's sense of purpose and self-discipline, and this flaw in his character was exacerbated by his excessive dependence on wine and opium. Gujarat was eventually left in the charge of one of Humāyūn's brothers, who alienated the local chiefs and abandoned his post, allowing Bahādur Shah to reoccupy his kingdom with the help of the Portuguese and a company of African slaves.

A similar lack of resolution followed Humāyūn's initial successes against Shēr Khan, who was now well established in eastern Hindustan. Having taken key citadels and towns, Humāyūn, in the words of his personal servant, "unaccountably shut himself up for a considerable time in his harem and abandoned himself to every kind of indulgence and luxury."

Presently, news arrived that another of Humāyūn's brothers had declared himself emperor at Agra. Returning to deal with this rebellion, Humāyūn and his army were cut off by Shēr Khan at Chausa on the Ganges River. Humāyūn opened negotiations with Shēr Khan. Lulled into a false sense of security by the parley, his forces were utterly routed by a dawn attack on June 26, 1539. The Moguls were driven into the river, and Humāyūn managed to escape only with the aid of an inflated animal skin lent to him by a water carrier. Following this victory, Shēr Khan struck coins and had the Khutba read in his name—the two prerogatives of an independent Muslim sovereign—and adopted the title Shēr Shah.

Mustering an army of some 40,000 soldiers and 60,000 retainers, the beleaguered emperor confronted Shēr Shah again in May 1540, on the banks of the Ganges at Kannauj. Shēr Shah's 10,000 horsemen, by adroit maneuvering on the wings, forced the Mogul cavalry into the center, rendering the use of their artillery impossible. Once again, Humāyūn's forces were driven into the river and thousands were killed, drowned, or captured. Humāyūn reached Agra with a tiny band of mounted survivors, but with Shēr Shah hard on his heels, he hastily set off for Lahore, passing through Sirhind on the way.

When Shēr Shah reached this last town, Humāyūn sent word to him from Lahore:

In northern India, a line of ducks marches eternally along the tile facade of Gwalior Palace, built by the Rajput ruler Raja Man Singh in the early sixteenth century. The Rajputs, an alliance of clans of the warrior caste, had maintained their independence in northwest India despite successive Muslim invasions that began in the ninth century, but their army was routed by Bābur at Khandwa in 1527. In the second half of the sixteenth century, Akbar's conciliatory policies won the loyalty of the Rajput leaders, many of whom served as governors and military commanders in the Mogul empire.

"What justice is there in this? I have left you the whole of Hindustan. Leave Lahore alone and let Sirhind, where you are, be a boundary between you and me." Shēr Shah replied: "I have left you Kabul. You should go there."

The emperor, however, was not left with even this alternative, since his brother in Kabul refused to offer him asylum. With Shēr Shah only hours away, Lahore was abandoned amid appalling scenes of panic and disorder. Humāyūn fled south into the deserts of Sind. It appeared that the Mogul empire in India had been lost forever.

Having chased the Moguls out of Hindustan, Shēr Shah proved more than a match for the Rajput rulers who opposed him. He was also a skilled administrator: He introduced an efficient system for setting and collecting revenues, and he built several major roads across Hindustan with fruit trees planted along the way. Numerous caravansaries were established to provide accommodation for traveling merchants; each had separate kitchens for Muslims and Hindus, as well as post horses to provide rapid transit for official mail. During this time of peace and justice, a contemporary chronicler wrote, "a decrepit old woman might place a basketful of gold ornaments on her head and go on a journey, and no thief or robber would come near her."

Though an orthodox Muslim, Shēr Shah was open-minded and tolerant, and he was perhaps the only Afghan ruler who managed to instill discipline in the turbulent clans over which he presided, convincing them of the wisdom of taking a national rather than a factional view. But his career was tragically cut short in 1545, the fifth year of his reign, when he was wounded by an explosion while he was besieging a Hindu fort. Seriously burned, Shēr Shah continued to direct the siege; upon learning that the fort had fallen, however, he died. He was succeeded by his son Islam Shah.

Meanwhile, Humāyūn's experiences in the wilderness of Sind were proving reminiscent of his father Bābur's "throneless times." Many of his followers died of heat and thirst in a series of desert treks. During this time, Humāyūn fell in love with Hamida, the fourteen-year-old daughter of a spiritual adviser, and married her. In October 1542, Hamida gave birth to a son, the future emperor, Akbar.

Recognizing the hopelessness of his position in Sind, Humāyūn eventually sought refuge with Shah Tahmāsp of Persia. Over the course of his year and a half at the Persian court, he was by turns well treated, bullied, and ignored by the shah. Eventually, however, he persuaded the shah to lend him 12,000 troops, and with their help, he reentered his lost domains and captured Kandahār. He then marched on Kabul and took it from his brother in November 1545.

During eight years of relentless campaigns against both the Uzbeks and the brother from whom he had retaken Kabul, Humāyūn reestablished himself as the undisputed leader of the Moguls. He then devoted himself to the recovery of his former kingdom in India. Shēr Shah's successors there lacked the exceptional qualities of their dynasty's founder, and their tyrannical rule had weakened Afghan solidarity and power. Fifteen years after his flight, Humāyūn crossed the Indus and reentered Hindustan. In May 1555, though greatly outnumbered, he defeated the Afghans in a closely contested battle at Sirhind. He reached Delhi in July and again ascended the throne.

Yet Humāyūn's second reign in India was to last barely six months. On January 23, 1556, he climbed onto the roof of his library to observe the rising of Venus. As he was about to descend, he was momentarily distracted by the dawn call to prayer, lost his footing, and fell down the steep stone stairs. He died of his injuries a few days later.

When Akbar learned of his father's demise, he was campaigning against the Af-

Depicting the Muslim prophet Elias rescuing a young prince from the sea, this manuscript painting is the work of one of two gifted artists who were brought to India from the Persian court, where Emperor Humāyūn spent some eighteen months in self-imposed exile. Both Humāyūn and his son Akbar were tutored by these artists, and Akbar appointed them to direct the painting workshops he established. The fusion of native Indian traditions with the Persian mastery of fine detail created a distinctive Mogul style of painting.

ghans in the Punjab under the guidance of Humāyūn's general Bayram Khan. Just thirteen years old, Akbar was a headstrong and precocious child, as brave and reckless as any of his forebears. His favorite pastimes were field sports and hunting, and he loved riding uncontrollable camels and, later, the most ferocious fighting elephants. He had seen action at Humāyūn's side and had been present at the battle of Sirhind. Surprisingly, in view of his father's and grandfather's passion for books, he was illiterate and the despair of his tutors. It may be that he suffered from some form of dyslexia, or that, having failed to master the skills of reading and writing during an unsettled and peripatetic childhood, he was unwilling to reveal his poor level of competence. But he had a prodigious memory, and in later life, when he had scribes to read to him and take down his words, his illiteracy proved no serious inconvenience.

In the first years of Akbar's reign, it seemed that the Moguls were again about to be driven from India. The city of Delhi was captured by Himu, a Hindu, and many of Akbar's supporters clamored for a hasty retreat to Kabul. Himu was of humble origin, having been a market trader in saltpeter, but he had risen through the ranks of the recently overthrown regime of Shēr Shah, and he could now muster an army of 100,000 men and 1,500 elephants. Akbar's forces totaled only 20,000. Going against the advice of all the other Mogul counselors, Bayram Khan proposed chancing everything on a confrontation with Himu, a plan enthusiastically endorsed by Akbar.

The Moguls met Himu's forces on the field of Panipat, north of Delhi, the site of Bābur's first major victory in India thirty years before. The odds on this occasion were even less favorable to the Moguls, who were all but swamped by the vast Hindu army. But as Himu, mounted on an elephant, led his troops forward to deal the last crushing blow, he was struck in the eye by an arrow with such force that the tip projected from the back of his head, killing him instantly. His army broke up in panic, many of his men being slaughtered by the Moguls as they fled.

Delhi was reoccupied and Mogul rule restored. At first, Bayram Khan acted as Akbar's regent, ordering the affairs of state and hiring a Persian tutor to continue his ward's education. This tutor was no more successful than his predecessors in improving Akbar's literacy but did instill in him the principle of *sulh-i kull,* or "universal toleration," which influenced his later policies.

By the time Akbar was eighteen, he was impatient to rule his kingdom on his own account. His resentment of Bayram Khan's power was fanned by his mother and the other women of the imperial harem who had nursed him in his infancy and who were now jealous of the minister's unique position of authority and privilege. The bond

The two-story exterior of Akbar's private audience hall *(above)* belies its single interior space *(left)*, dominated by a central pillar on which the emperor's throne was placed. Its roof afforded views across the palace complex *(top)*.

The towering Gate of Victory *(near right)* leads into the mosque, which contains the white marble tomb of Salim Chisti *(bottom right)*. Viewed across a paved courtyard from within the tomb's arcade is the west gate *(top right)*.

Following the birth of a male heir in 1569, Emperor Akbar commanded that a new imperial city be constructed about twenty-five miles west of Agra on the site of the hermitage of Sheik Salim Chisti, a holy man who had predicted this joyous event. Five years later, on his triumphal homecoming after the conquest of Gujarat, Akbar named his new capital Fatehpur Sikri, or "City of Victory." Rising up the barren flanks of a hill overlooking a lake, its grand pavilions, palaces, and audience halls—all fashioned in red sandstone and carved with intricate motifs—were compared by a contemporary historian to "paradise on the brink of a precipice." Its beauty notwithstanding, Fatehpur Sikri remained the hub of the Mogul empire for little more than a decade: In the late 1580s, the entire capital complex was abandoned, probably because of the failure of the water supply.

between a child and its foster mother is held by all Muslims to be an especially affectionate one; and as this relationship was seen to extend to the families of—in Akbar's case, numerous—foster mothers, the group constituted a sizable party.

The women of the harem seized every opportunity to denigrate Bayram Khan, even insinuating that he wanted the throne for himself. Despite all provocations, Bayram Khan remained loyal to Akbar, but at length this proud and distinguished soldier and statesman agreed to remove himself from the scene by making a pilgrimage to Mecca. En route, he was stabbed to death in Gujarat by a gang of Afghans. According to a contemporary historian, Bayram Khan deserved a better end: "In wisdom, generosity, sincerity, goodness of disposition, submissiveness and humility he surpassed all," he wrote. "The second conquest of Hindustan and the building up of the empire were due to his strenuous efforts, his valor and his far-sighted policy."

Bayram Khan's death strengthened the hand of the harem faction, which for two years maintained a dominant influence over Akbar. Maham Anga, Akbar's chief foster mother, was particularly powerful. This ambitious woman was ruthless in the promotion of her son Adham Khan, who so envied the power of Akbar's chief minister that in 1562 he had him murdered by a band of ruffians. Roused to anger by this brutal act, Akbar cursed Adham Khan and hit him in the face with his fist, knocking him unconscious. Akbar then had Adham Khan hurled over the parapet of the palace. When he was found still breathing, Akbar had him brought up and thrown down again. Akbar himself broke the news to Maham Anga, who said, "You did well," but she died of grief forty days later. Thereafter, Akbar took care to suppress all backstairs influences that threatened to compromise his rule.

In the same year, while Akbar was traveling on a pilgrimage to a Muslim shrine at Ajmer, about 220 miles southwest of Agra, the Rajput raja of Amber (modern Jaipur) came to pay court to the emperor. The Hindu invited Akbar to take his daughter as a wife. Akbar accepted, and on the return journey, his marriage to the woman who was to be the mother of his successor was celebrated. A number of the raja's other relatives were given positions at court and in the army. This alliance put an end to the longstanding animosity that had existed between the Rajputs and the Moguls, and Akbar's subsequent integration of many other Rajputs into the Mogul hierarchy brought a new stability to his imperial enterprise.

Akbar's success in subduing his external enemies was chiefly attributable to the efficiency and discipline of the Mogul army, in which were combined both traditional strengths and the advantages of modern weapons. The backbone of the army consisted of archers mounted on swift horses, who could fire off arrows with the same speed and accuracy as the Mongol warriors who had won for Genghis Khan his world empire in the thirteenth century. Of lowlier status but equally deadly, the infantry's fighting arm consisted of archers, spearmen, and some 12,000 musketeers. As in Bābur's time, light and heavy artillery, still officered by Ottoman and other foreign experts, were decisive in gaining many victories. Stone and iron shot were used, and sometimes cannons were loaded with rough copper coins, which at close quarters had devastating results. The Lord of Fire, as the commander of artillery was styled, also had at his disposal weapons capable of firing rockets that exploded on impact.

Elephants had been used in warfare in India for centuries, and Akbar continued this tradition, often employing hundreds of them in combat. The spectacle of these large and immensely strong beasts—heavily armored, and bearing archers and musketeers on their backs—was calculated to strike terror into the hearts of the enemy. It was also recognized, of course, that elephants running out of control could do as much damage to their own side as to the opposition. But Akbar himself was particularly fond of riding elephants and watching them fight, and his enthusiasm led him to make more extensive use of them than was strictly justified on military grounds.

The years 1562 to 1579 were ones of ceaseless military and diplomatic activity. Several campaigns were entrusted to Akbar's Mogul and Rajput generals, but when the emperor did take personal command of the army, he never hesitated to throw himself into the heart of the fray. In 1573, for example, when about to set off to conquer Bengal, Akbar learned of a revolt on the other side of the subcontinent, in Gujarat. With a force of 3,000 horsemen, he rode more than 400 miles in eleven days and, without pausing for rest, swam a river with an advance party. He fought two battles on the same day, both against heavy odds, and put down the rebellion before it had time to consolidate. In 1579, Akbar finally succeeded in annexing Bengal, which gave him mastery over virtually the whole of northern India, from the Arabian Sea to the Bay of Bengal, from the Himalayas to the Deccan plateau.

The military origins of the Mogul state were reflected in the titles Akbar gave to his adminstrators and courtiers. The governor of a province was a commander in chief, that of a subdistrict a commandant, and so on. All senior officials, military and civil, were rated as cavalry commanders; one nominally at the head of 500 to 2,500 horses was considered an *amir,* or "noble," and one with more than 2,500 horses an *amir-i kabir,* or "great noble." The court historian, Abū Fazl, was graded in the hierarchy as the commander of 2,500 horses; the Hindu poet and wit Raja Bir Bar, commander of 1,000. There were thirty-three grades in all.

Akbar inherited the Indian military system of handing out fiefs to commanders, the revenue from which was used by each officer to finance and equip a given number of horses and men. These fiefs were not hereditary, and fief holders could be promoted or demoted by being moved to larger or smaller fiefs in different parts of the country. Transfers were made as a matter of course to prevent officers from building up independent local power bases and threatening the unity of the empire.

In 1574, Akbar decreed that he would assume direct control of all lands, and that officers would be paid in cash directly from the treasury according to their rank. This innovation proved very unpopular, not least because many fief holders were accustomed to enriching themselves at the state's expense. The practice was nevertheless introduced in the state's central provinces, although the old fief system continued in frontier regions and in provinces that were not fully integrated into the empire.

Akbar also tried to change the age-old system of collecting revenue by eliminating the middlemen

Sketched around 1605, the year in which Akbar died, this intimate portrait captures the emperor in meditative mood. Akbar had brought the Mogul empire to the pinnacle of its glory, but his last years were clouded by family discord. All three of his sons were addicted to alcohol; two of them died when they were about thirty, and the third threatened rebellion for five years before being reconciled with his father.

# TREASURES FROM THE IMPERIAL WORKSHOPS

Paintings, manuscripts, textiles, ceramics, perfumes, metalwork—Akbar's appreciation of beautiful objects was comprehensive and extended to cultures well beyond those of the Mogul empire. His library included Persian, Greek, and Arabic volumes and was continually enlarged through the painstaking labors of the calligraphers, translators, illuminators, and bookbinders in his employ. In the workshops that he established at his new capital city of Fatehpur Sikri and elsewhere, Persian and other foreign craftsmen worked side by side with artisans from all over northern India; even an English jeweler, who happened to arrive in Fatehpur Sikri in 1583, was pressed into service. Their collaborative work and the influence of imported objects—including porcelain from China and prints and engravings from Europe—were to revitalize the arts of India.

A detail from a painting executed around 1585 shows artists of different nationalities—one of whom is wearing spectacles—at work on manuscript illustrations.

This white-jade wine cup, carved in the shape of a gourd with its handle tapering to a finely detailed goat's head, is believed to have been made for the emperor Shah Jahān, Akbar's grandson.

Animals, both real and fantastic, stampede across a late-sixteenth-century carpet featuring hunting vignettes (left). Mogul weavers often shunned symmetry in favor of more lively compositions.

A gold spoon set with rubies, emeralds, and diamonds combines European influence in its shape with Persian decoration.

who set and gathered taxes, remitting money later to the ruler. Expanding trade with the West had led to an influx of South American silver, so the peasants who formed the majority of Akbar's subjects were increasingly able to pay taxes in coin rather than kind. But changes in the system were opposed by vested interests and applied only in the central provinces and a large quantity of revenue never reached the treasury.

Some of Akbar's reforms were motivated by humane considerations. He forbade the enslavement of women and children captured by the army, ordering his soldiers "to permit them to go freely to their homes and relations." He opposed the Hindu practice of sati, the burning of widows on the deaths of their husbands. He could not keep women from throwing themselves onto the funeral pyres, but he appointed inspectors in every city and district to prevent anyone from being forcibly burned.

In 1563, not long after his first marriage to a Hindu princess, Akbar put a stop to the collection of pilgrim taxes levied at Hindu holy places. And the year after, at enormous cost to the treasury, he abolished the bitterly resented poll tax that had been raised on non-Muslims, an imposition sanctioned by the Koran. These practical measures designed to conciliate the Rajputs and other Hindus to their Muslim rulers reflected a sensitivity to India's indigenous religion that was increasingly mirrored in Akbar's personal habits. He sometimes wore Hindu dress and decorated his forehead with a colored caste mark. He let his hair grow long, instead of shaving his head in the central Asian fashion, and he wore a Rajput-like turban. Hindu festivals were celebrated at court, and Akbar even began to follow the Hindu custom of abjuring meat, disliking the idea of making his body "a tomb for beasts."

In 1569, Akbar's first Hindu wife gave birth to a son, Jahāngīr, in a holy man's hermitage at Sikri, a village about twenty-five miles west of Agra, where she had gone for her confinement. To celebrate, Akbar ordered the building of a new capital at Sikri, and in less than four years, a magnificent city sprang up where the hermitage stood. Returning from a triumphant campaign in Gujarat in 1574, Akbar found his capital ready to occupy and named it Fatehpur Sikri, or "City of Victory."

When residing at his new royal palace, Akbar kept to a strict routine. Rising at dawn, he appeared after sunrise at a window on the first floor of the palace to show himself to the people. Afterward, Akbar held open court to which people of every degree—rich and poor, men and women, Hindu and Muslim—were admitted to present petitions and have their cases decided by the emperor. At around midday, he retired to the women's quarters to deal with the business of the harem, granting requests and settling disputes. During this time he also ate and rested. In the afternoon, Akbar held a full court session in his audience hall. Here regular state business was attended to, orders given, appointments made and confirmed, financial matters discussed, and the notes of the previous day's business presented for Akbar's approval. He then went out to inspect the royal stables, elephants, horses, and other animals, and visited the royal factories and workshops where both military equipment and cultural artifacts such as paintings and manuscripts were produced by skilled artisans. Having bathed in the late afternoon, Akbar met in a smaller private chamber with ministers and trusted advisers to transact confidential and secret affairs.

The official day drew to a close at sunset, when lamps were ceremoniously lighted and prayers for the long life of the sovereign and the empire recited. At this time a cheerful and congenial atmosphere was encouraged, often to the accompaniment of music and other entertainments. Akbar's personal involvement in the administration of the empire contributed much to its smooth and efficient running, and the daily routine he established was one of his most important legacies to his successors.

Following the fall of Bayram Khan in the early years of his reign, Akbar made sure that never again would so much influence be concentrated in the hands of any one of his counselors. After 1564, he divided civil and financial responsibilities among different ministers, and even kept the post of prime minister vacant for years at a time. He was much aided by a number of men of exceptional ability. Raja Todar Mal, a man of Hindu merchant caste, proved a brilliant finance minister. Another courtier, Abdul Fadl, was responsible for compiling the *Institutes of Akbar,* a monumental compendium of statistical, economic, geographical, legal, social, and administrative data embracing the whole empire. Never before had a ruler of India been in possession of so much information on which to base his decisions.

Stimulated by his early teachers, Akbar was intensely interested in religious matters, and he spent many hours in theological discussion with holy men and the learned Muslim doctors of law. At Fatehpur Sikri, he constructed an edifice called the House of Worship, which in fact turned out to be more of a debating hall. At first, only Muslims were allowed to take part in the proceedings, but disillusioned by the bigotry of the principal Muslim contributors, Akbar later opened them to men of all religions, even asking the Portuguese viceroy at Goa to send Jesuit missionaries.

The Jesuits arrived with high hopes of converting the emperor to Christianity but were frustrated by his insistence that there was good in all religions. Moreover, as Akbar knew well, if he accepted Christianity he would have to put away all but one of his wives. Given that he had assiduously married dozens of Rajput and other royal wives for dynastic reasons, and that these alliances maintained the stability of the state, to dismiss his harem would have been political suicide. Nevertheless, the Jesuits were impressed by Akbar's demeanor and authority, and one of them wrote a vivid account of the emperor in his prime:

> *His brow was broad and open, and his eyes sparkled as does the sea when lighted by the sun. He had in his body, which is very well made, and neither thin and meager nor fat and gross, much courage and strength. When he laughs he is distorted, but when he is tranquil and serene he has a noble mien and great dignity. In his wrath he is majestic.*

Far from searching for an existing faith to convert to, Akbar was creating a new one. While out hunting in 1578, he experienced a mystical vision. "A strange ecstasy," reported a chronicler, "and a strong sense of attraction to God came upon the emperor . . . and at once he ordered the hunt to be stopped." As a consequence of this vision, Akbar determined to concentrate both temporal and spiritual authority in his own person. He enacted a Decree of Infallibility, which made him the ultimate arbiter of all religious questions, and in 1582, he announced to the world a new faith.

Dubbed the Divine Faith, this religion was a synthesis of Hindu, Christian, and Muslim doctrines and was designed to unify all Akbar's peoples under his own quasi-divine leadership. It was at once an expression of Akbar's own mystical cast of mind and a pragmatic instrument of state policy. However,

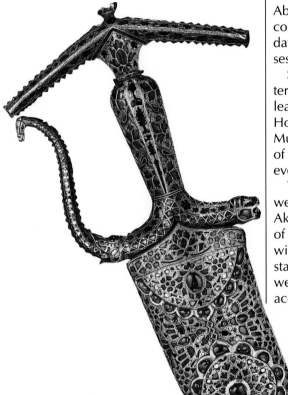

This intricately worked gold dagger and sheath encrusted with jewels was commissioned in 1619 by Emperor Jahāngīr, who continued his father's patronage of the arts. Of such a dagger, Jahāngīr recorded in his memoirs that it was "so delicate that I never wish it to be apart from me for a moment," and the emperor rewarded its makers with an elephant and other lavish gifts.

although it was not unusual for Oriental monarchs to claim godlike qualities, the new faith failed to win wide acceptance. A handful of converts were made at court, but they were motivated by a desire to please their sovereign or gain advancement rather than by spiritual fervor. The vast majority of Akbar's subjects remained blissfully unaware of the new religion, and after his death, it was to be quietly forgotten.

During the final decade of the century, renewed military campaigns and triumphs enlarged and made secure the empire that Akbar was to bequeath to his successors. The final subjection of Sind, Baluchistan, Kandahār, and Kashmir, and the agreement of the Uzbeks to make the Hindu Kush the frontier between themselves and the Moguls, gave Akbar a strong, continuous western border stretching from the Arabian Sea to the Himalayas. The eastern flank of the empire was stabilized by the pacification of the kingdom of Orissa. Stronger than ever, Akbar was able to turn his attention to the unfulfilled dream of many a north Indian dynasty, the conquest of the south. Invading the Deccan kingdom of Ahmadnagar, the Moguls found themselves up against one of their most redoubtable opponents, the warrior queen Chand Bibi. Twice she beat back their attacks on her capital, on the second occasion in 1595 recklessly exposing herself to enemy fire while directing the repair of a section of wall damaged by mine. But in 1600, this brave queen was killed by one of her eunuchs, and the Moguls were at last able to gain a firm foothold in her domains.

Akbar died on October 26, 1605, just a few weeks short of the fiftieth anniversary of his coming to the throne. During his reign, he had transformed a brittle young state, vulnerable to enemies both within and outside its borders, into a powerful, flourishing empire whose magnificence was the envy of every traveler who described it. His genius lay in using his personal qualities—his courage in battle, his toleration of strangers—to serve a larger purpose. The empire had been won by military victories; it survived because Akbar had ensured that the loyalty of its subjects to their ruler overrode all religious and cultural differences.

Akbar's son Jahāngīr continued his father's evenhanded treatment of all his subjects, as did the next emperor, Shah Jahān. In the second half of the seventeenth century, under Aurangzeb, the empire was to reach the apogee of its territorial extent, with only the tip of India remaining outside its domains. Aurangzeb, however, was a religious bigot, and by generally reversing the wise and successful principles of Akbar, he set the empire on the path of decline. The intricate balance of forces that had sustained the Moguls for so long—military strength, efficient administration, conciliatory policies toward subjects of different faiths, and the competence of the emperors themselves—was now lost. And as the Moguls began to lose their grip, the European powers moved in, eagerly competing for the wealthy resources of India that the Moguls had made known to the wider world. First came the merchants, then the soldiers; and in 1857, three centuries after Humāyūn's founding of the second empire in Hindustan, the last Mogul emperor was exiled by the British to Burma.

When Bābur inherited the tiny kingdom of Ferghana at the close of the fifteenth century, his dynasty was facing extinction. He arrived in India almost by accident, having been prevented from achieving his imperial ambitions elsewhere, but in the end, his inspiration gave rise to an empire more enduring than that of his ancestor Tamerlane. Other Muslim conquerors before Bābur had developed policies that allowed them to live in relative harmony with their Hindu subjects; the Moguls went a stage further, and by adjusting their own cultural identity to that of the country they ruled, they presided over a new civilization.

A monument to Shah Jahān's enduring love for his favorite wife, Mumtāz Mahal, who died in 1631 giving birth to her fourteenth child, the Taj Mahal is mirrored in the tranquil water of a formal pool. Fashioned entirely of white marble, the octagonal mausoleum took more than two decades to complete; its surfaces were lavishly inscribed with verses from the Koran and adorned with inlays of semiprecious stones.

| | 1500-1510 | 1510-1520 | 1520-1530 | 1530-1540 | 1540-1550 |
|---|---|---|---|---|---|
| **EUROPE** | Henry VIII succeeds Henry VII as king of England and marries Catherine of Aragon (1509). | Charles V becomes king of Spain (1516) and inherits Hapsburg domains in Burgundy, the Netherlands, and southern Italy.<br><br>The German monk Martin Luther attacks papal indulgences in his Ninety-five Theses (1517).<br><br>Charles V is elected Holy Roman emperor (1519). | Luther is condemned as a heretic at the Diet of Worms (1521).<br><br>The Hungarian fortress of Belgrade falls to the Ottoman Turks (1521).<br><br>A peasants' revolt in Germany is brutally suppressed (1525).<br><br>The Hungarian army is defeated by the Ottomans at Mohács (1526).<br><br>Lutheran national churches are established in Sweden (1527) and Finland (1528).<br><br>Vienna holds out against an Ottoman siege (1529). | Protestant German princes form the Schmalkaldic League to defend the Reformation (1530).<br><br>Henry VIII of England breaks with Rome and establishes the Anglican church (1534).<br><br>Denmark (1536) and Norway (1539) adopt Lutheranism. | The Society of Jesus, dedicated to revitalizing the Church of Rome, receives the pope's blessing (1540).<br><br>The French preacher John Calvin founds a reformed church Geneva (1541).<br><br>The Council of Trent, an assembly of prelates charged with reforming the Roman church, is convoked (1545).<br><br>Martin Luther dies (1546).<br><br>Edward VI succeeds Henry VIII as king of England (1547). |
| **THE AMERICAS** | The first slaves from Africa are sent to Spanish colonies in the Caribbean (c.1510). | The Spanish conquistador Hernán Cortés sets out from Cuba to conquer the Aztec empire of Mexico (1519).<br><br>The first Spanish settlement on the Pacific is founded at Panama (1519).<br><br>The Portuguese navigator Ferdinand Magellan crosses the Pacific (1520). | After the death of the Aztec emperor Montezuma, Cortés is forced to flee from the Aztec capital of Tenochtitlán (1520), but he returns the next year to capture the city. | The Spanish conquistador Francisco Pizarro sails from Panama to conquer the Inca empire of Peru (1530).<br><br>Atahualpa, the Inca emperor, is killed by Pizarro (1533).<br><br>Pizarro founds the city of Lima on the coast of Peru (1535).<br><br>The Spanish establish a viceregal administration in Mexico, called New Spain (1535). | Pizarro is assassinated in Lima (1541).<br><br>The Portuguese found the administrative capital of Bahia on the coast of Brazil (1549). |
| **RUSSIA** | Ivan III, who has brought the state of Muscovy to prominence following the decline of Mongol power, is succeeded by Vasily III (1505). | | | Vasily III dies and is succeeded by his three-year-old son, Ivan IV (1533); Russia is effectively ruled by the boyars, the state's hereditary nobles. | Ivan IV, the Terrible, is crowned czar of Russia (1547). |
| **THE MIDDLE EAST AND INDIA** | In Persia, Shah Ismail founds the Safavid dynasty, following the minority Shiite tradition of Islam (1501).<br><br>Bābur, a central Asian prince, seizes Kabul (1505) and leads raiding expeditions into northern India. | Selim the Grim succeeds Bajazet II as Ottoman sultan in Istanbul (1512).<br><br>Selim defeats the Persian Safavids at the Battle of Chaldiran (1514) and annexes Syria, Egypt, and much of Arabia (1516-1517).<br><br>Selim dies and is succeeded by his son Süleyman I (1520). | Bābur defeats the sultan of Delhi at the battle of Panipat and occupies Delhi and Agra (1526).<br><br>Bābur defeats the Hindu army of the Rajputs at Khandwa (1527).<br><br>The North African pirate Barbarossa seizes Algiers with Ottoman aid (1529).<br><br>Bābur dies and is succeeded by his son Humāyūn (1530). | Süleyman seizes Baghdad and occupies Iraq (1533).<br><br>Barbarossa captures Tunis and defeats a Venetian, Genoese, and papal fleet at the Battle of Preveza (1538).<br><br>An Ottoman fleet in the Red Sea captures Aden (1538). | Defeated by Shēr Shah at Kannauj on the Ganges (1540), Humāyūn flees India and seek refuge at the Persian court (1544). |

# TimeFrame AD 1500-1600

| 50-1560 | 1560-1570 | 1570-1580 | 1580-1590 | 1590-1600 |
|---|---|---|---|---|
| ...ard VI of England dies and ...cceeded by Mary Tudor ...3).<br><br>...Peace of Augsburg grants ...ation to Lutherans in Ger-...y (1555).<br><br>...les V abdicates and retires ...monastery in Spain (1555); ...on, Philip II, becomes ruler ...pain, the Netherlands, and ...s of Italy and the Americas.<br><br>...beth I succeeds Mary as ...en of England (1558). | In France, warfare breaks out between Protestant and Roman Catholic factions (1562).<br><br>A rebellion of Catholic nobles in the north of England is defeated (1569-1570). | Thousands of French Protestants are killed in the Massacre of Saint Bartholomew's Day (1572).<br><br>Protestants in the Netherlands revolt against Spanish rule (1572).<br><br>The English mariner Francis Drake sails around the world (1577-1580). | The crowns of Spain and Portugal are united, and Spain acquires all of Portugal's overseas territories (1580).<br><br>The northern provinces of the Netherlands declare themselves an independent republic (1581).<br><br>Mary Queen of Scots, held prisoner by Elizabeth I in England, is beheaded (1587).<br><br>The Spanish Armada is defeated by the English navy (1588). | The Globe Theatre is built in London by a company of actors performing plays by Shakespeare (1599). |
| | The Spanish introduce a convoy system of armed escort ships to protect their treasure fleets carrying silver, the principal American export, across the Atlantic (1564).<br><br>The Portuguese found the Brazilian city of Rio de Janeiro (1567).<br><br>The Spanish viceroy attacks an English expedition led by John Hawkins in the Mexican port of San Juan de Ulúa (1568). | | Roanoke Island in North America is claimed by an English expedition and named Virginia by Sir Walter Raleigh (1584). | A relief expedition to Roanoke Island discovers no trace of the original settlers (1591).<br><br>Sir Walter Raleigh sails up the Orinoco River in South America in search of El Dorado, a legendary city of gold (1595). |
| ...n conquers the Tatar city of ...an (1552) and the khanate of ...rakhan (1556), extending ...sian territory to the east and ...theast.<br><br>...r breaks out between Russia ... the states of Livonia, Lithua-... and Poland to the west ...58). | Seeking to rid himself of all obstruction by the boyars, Ivan establishes the *oprichnina*, his personal domain within Russia, which he rules by terror (1565). | Ivan sacks the city of Novgorod (1571).<br><br>Needing a united army to defend Russia against a Tatar invasion, Ivan dissolves the oprichnina (1572). | Ivan makes peace with Stefan Bathory of Poland and Lithuania (1583).<br><br>Ivan dies and is succeeded by his son Fyodor (1584). | On the death of the childless Fyodor, Boris Godunov, a former favorite of Ivan the Terrible, is proclaimed czar (1598). |
| ...eyman has his eldest son, ...stafa, killed (1553).<br><br>...māyūn defeats Shēr Shah's ...cessor at the battle of Sirhind ...55) and regains Mogul do-...ins in India.<br><br>...māyūn dies and is succeeded ...his son Akbar (1556), who ...eats a Hindu army at the sec-...d battle of Panipat. | Akbar marries the daughter of a Rajput ruler (1562) and proceeds to assimilate Rajputs into the Mogul hierarchy.<br><br>Süleyman dies while besieging the Hungarian fortress of Szigetvár and is succeeded as Ottoman sultan by Selim II (1566). | The Ottomans capture Cyprus from the Venetians (1571). Their fleet is routed by a Christian armada at the battle of Lepanto in the same year, but it is quickly rebuilt.<br><br>Akbar founds a new capital at Fatehpur Sikri near Delhi (1574).<br><br>Selim II dies and is succeeded by Murad III (1574).<br><br>Bengal is incorporated into the Mogul empire (1579). | Akbar proclaims the Divine Faith, a new religion combining Hindu, Christian, and Muslim doctrines (1582).<br><br>The Ottomans defeat the Persians at the Battle of Torches (1583). | Murad III dies and is succeeded by Mehmed III (1595).<br><br>The Ottomans win the battle of Keresztes in Hungary (1596) but fail to advance their frontiers in Europe.<br><br>Akbar commences war against the Deccan principalities to the south and captures Ahmadnagar (1600). |

# ACKNOWLEDGMENTS

The following materials have been reprinted with the kind permission of the publishers: Page 21: "Churches are to be built wide and strong . . .," quoted in *The Reformation in the Cities,* by Steven E. Ozment, New Haven, Connecticut: Yale University Press, 1975. Page 63: "The queen poor, the realm exhausted . . .," quoted in *Elizabeth: A Study in Power and Intellect,* by Paul Johnson, London: Weidenfeld and Nicolson, 1974. Page 120: "Tall but wiry and of a delicate complexion . . .," quoted in *Suleiman the Magnificent,* by Antony Bridge, London: Granada, 1983.

The editors also wish to thank the following individuals and institutions for their valuable assistance in the preparation of this volume:
**England:** Cambridge—Robert Scribner, Clare College. London—Douglas Amrine; Elizabeth Baquedano; Warwick Bray, Institute of Archaeology, University College; Elizabeth Clarke, Thames and Hudson; Rosemary Crill, Indian Department, Victoria & Albert Museum; Theo Crosby, Pentagram Design; Tim Fraser; Madeleine Ginsburg; Godfrey Goodwin, Royal Asiatic Society; Jon Greenfield, Pentagram Design; Victor Harris, Department of Japanese Antiquities, British Museum; Liz Hodgson; Caroline Manyon;

Jackie Matthews; Christopher Rawlings, Photographic Services, British Library; Eugénie Romer; Anthony Shelton, Curator (American Collections) of the Ethnography Department, British Museum; Brian A. Tremain, Photographic Services, British Museum. Oxford—John Man; Linda Proud. Reading—Andrew Gurr, Faculty of Letters and Social Sciences, University of Reading.
**France:** Paris—François Avril, Conservateur, Département des Manuscrits, Bibliothèque Nationale.
**Japan:** Tokyo—Mieko Ikeda.
**Turkey:** Istanbul—Ara Güler.

# PICTURE CREDITS

# BIBLIOGRAPHY

## THE REFORMATION

**Dickens,** A. G.:
*The Counter Reformation.* London: Thames and Hudson, 1968.
*The German Nation and Martin Luther.* London: Edward Arnold, 1974.
*Reformation and Society in Sixteenth-Century Europe.* London: Thames and Hudson, 1966.

**Fernández Alvarez,** Manuel, *Charles V: Elected Emperor and Hereditary Ruler.* Transl. by J. A. Lalagunal. London: Thames and Hudson, 1976.

**Green,** V. H. H., *Luther and the Reformation.* London: B. T. Batsford, 1964.

**Hillerbrand,** Hans J., *The Reformation in Its Own Words.* London: SCM Press, 1964.

**Ozment,** Steven E., *The Reformation in the Cities.* New Haven, Connecticut: Yale University Press, 1975.

**Parker,** T. H. L., *John Calvin: A Biography.* London: J. M. Dent & Sons, 1975.

**Rodríguez-Salgado,** M. J., *The Changing Face of Empire: Charles V, Philip II and Habsburg Authority, 1551-1559.* Cambridge: Cambridge University Press, 1988.

**Rupp,** E. G., and Benjamin Drewery, *Documents of Modern History: Martin Luther.* London: Edward Arnold, 1972.

**Scribner,** R. W.:
*For the Sake of Simple Folk: Popular Propaganda for the German Reformation.* Cambridge: Cambridge University Press, 1981.
*The German Reformation.* London: Macmillan, 1986.

**Simon,** Edith, and the Editors of Time-Life Books, *The Reformation* (Great Ages of Man series). Alexandria, Virginia: Time-Life Books, 1977.

**Simpson,** Leonard Francis, transl., *The Autobiography of Charles V.* London: Longman, Green, 1862.

## SPANISH AMERICA

**Bray,** Warwick, ed., *The Gold of El Dorado.* London: Times Newspapers, 1978.

**Burland,** C. A., *Montezuma: Lord of the Aztecs.* London: Weidenfeld and Nicolson, 1973.

**Carrasco,** Davíd, *Quetzalcoatl and the Irony of Empire: Myths and Prophecies in the Aztec Tradition.* Chicago: University of Chicago Press, 1982.

**Cheetham,** Nicolas, *New Spain: The Birth of Modern Mexico.* London: Victor Gollancz, 1974.

**Díaz del Castillo,** Bernal, *The Conquest of Mexico.* Transl. by J. H. Cohen. London: Penguin, 1963.

**Elliott,** J. H., *Imperial Spain: 1469-1716.* Harmondsworth, Middlesex: Penguin, 1970.

**Fuentes,** Patricia de, transl. and ed., *The Conquistadors: First-Person Accounts of the Conquest of Mexico.* London: Cassell, 1964.

**Hemming,** John:
*The Conquest of the Incas.* London: Macmillan, 1970.
*The Search for El Dorado.* London: Michael Joseph, 1978.

**Innes,** Hammond, *The Conquistadors.* London: William Collins, 1969.

**McNeill,** William, *Plagues and Peoples.* Oxford: Basil Blackwell, 1977.

**Nicholson,** H. B., with Eloise Quiñones Keber, *Art of Aztec Mexico: Treasures of Tenochtitlan.* Washington, D.C.: National Gallery of Art, 1983.

**Parry,** J. H., *The Discovery of South America.* London: Paul Elek, 1979.

## ENGLAND

**Andrews,** K. R., *Trade, Plunder and Settlement.* Cambridge: Cambridge University Press, 1984.

**Archer,** Ian, Caroline Barron, and Vanessa Harding, eds., *Hugh Alley's Caveat: The Markets of London in 1598.* London: London Topographical Society, 1988.

**Beier,** A. L., *Masterless Men: The Vagrancy Problem in England, 1560-1640.* London: Methuen, 1985.

**Briggs,** Asa, *A Social History of England.* London: Weidenfeld and Nicolson, 1983.

**Dods,** A. H., *Elizabethan England.* London: B. T. Batsford, 1973.

**Doran,** Susan, *England and Europe: 1485-1603.* London: Longman, 1986.

**Fox,** Levi, ed., *The Shakespeare Handbook.* Boston: G. K. Hall, 1987.

**Gurr,** Andrew, with John Orrell, *Rebuilding Shakespeare's Globe.* London: Weidenfeld and Nicolson, 1989.

**Haigh,** C., ed., *The English Reformation Revised.* Cambridge: Cambridge University Press, 1987.

**Hakluyt,** Richard, *Hakluyt's Voyages.* Ed. by I. R. Blacker. New York: Viking, 1965.

**Harrison,** G. B., *The Elizabethan Journals.* New York: Doubleday, 1965.

**Harrison,** William, *The Description of England.* Ed. by G. Edelen. Ithaca, New York: Cornell University Press, 1968.

**Hurstfield,** Joel, *Elizabeth I and the Unity of England.* London: English Universities Press, 1960.

**Hurstfield,** Joel, and A. G. R. Smith, eds., *Elizabethan People.* London: Edward Arnold, 1972.

**Johnson,** Paul, *Elizabeth: A Study in Power and Intellect.* London: Weidenfeld and Nicolson, 1974.

**Judges,** A. V., ed., *The Elizabethan Underworld.* London: Routledge & Kegan Paul, 1930.

**Martin,** Colin, "The Atlantic Adventures." *Queen Elizabeth I: Most Politick Princess,* ed. by Simon Adams. London: History Today, no date.

**Martin,** Colin, and Geoffrey Parker, *The Spanish Armada.* London: Hamish Hamilton, 1988.

**Nashe,** Thomas, *The Unfortunate Traveller.* Ed. by J. B. Steane. London: Penguin, 1972.

**Norris,** Herbert, *The Tudors.* Vol. 3 of *Costume & Fashion.* London: J. M. Dent & Sons, 1938.

**Rodríguez-Salgado,** M. J., and the Staff of the National Maritime Museum, *Armada: 1588-1988.* London: Penguin, 1988.

**Rowse,** A. L.:
*The Elizabethan Renaissance.* London: Sphere Books, 1974.
*The Expansion of Elizabethan England.* London: Macmillan, 1955.

**Smith,** A. G. R.: *The Emergence of a Nation-State.* London: Longman, 1984.

**Strong,** Roy:
*Artists of the Tudor Court.* London: Victoria & Albert Museum, 1983.
*The Cult of Elizabeth.* London: Thames and Hudson, 1977.
*The English Renaissance Miniature.* London: Thames and Hudson, 1984.
*Gloriana: The Portraits of Queen Elizabeth I.* London: Thames and Hudson, 1987.

**Williams,** Neville, *All the Queen's Men.* London: Sphere Books, 1974.

**Yates,** Frances, *Astraea.* London: Routledge & Kegan Paul, 1975.

**Youings,** Joyce, *Sixteenth Century England.* London: Penguin, 1984.

## RUSSIA

**Alpatov,** M. V., *Art Treasures of Russia.* London: Thames and Hudson, 1968.

**Auty,** Robert, and Dimitri Obolensky, *An Introduction to Russian History.* Cambridge: Cambridge University Press, 1976.

**Barbour,** Philip L., *Dimitry, Called the Pretender.* London: Macmillan, 1967.

**Berry,** Lloyd E., and Robert O. Crummey, *Rude and Barbarous Kingdom.* Madison, Wisconsin: University of Wisconsin Press, 1968.

**Berton,** Kathleen, *Moscow: An Architectural History.* London: Cassell & Collier Macmillan, 1977.

**Blum,** Jerome, *Lord and Peasant in Russia.* Princeton, New Jersey: Princeton University Press, 1961.

**Bond,** Edward A., ed., *Russia at the Close of the Sixteenth Century: Comprising "Of the Russe Common Wealth," by Dr. Giles Fletcher and the Travels of Sir Jerome Horsey.* London: Hakluyt Society, 1856.

**Crummey,** Robert O., *The Formation of Muscovy: 1304-1613.* London: Longman, 1987.

**Herberstein,** Sigmund von, *Description of Moscow and Muscovy: 1557.* Ed. by Bertold Picard, transl. by J. B. C. Grundy. London: J. M. Dent & Sons, 1969.

**Hoetzsch,** Otto, *The Evolution of Russia.* London: Thames and Hudson, 1966.

**Rodimzeva,** Irina, *The Kremlin and Its Art Treasures.* New York: Rizzoli International Publications, 1987.

**Rogov,** A., *Alexandrov.* Leningrad: Aurora Art Publishers, 1979.

**Skrynnikov,** Ruslan G., *Ivan the Terrible.* Ed. and transl. by Hugh F. Graham. Gulf Breeze, Florida: Academic International Press, 1981.

**Smith,** R. E. F., *Peasant Farming in Muscovy.* Cambridge: Cambridge University Press, 1977.

**Troyat,** Henri, *Ivan the Terrible.* London: New English Library, 1985.

**Vernadsky,** George, *A Source Book for Russian History from Early Times to 1917.* New Haven, Connecticut: Yale University Press, 1972.

**Wittram,** Reinhard, *Russia and Europe.* London: Thames and Hudson, 1973.

## OTTOMAN EMPIRE

**Bridge,** Antony, *Suleiman the Magnificent.* London: Granada, 1983.

**Coles,** Paul, *The Ottoman Impact on Europe.* London: Thames and Hudson, 1968.

**Goodwin,** Godfrey, *A History of Ottoman Architecture.* London: Thames and Hudson, 1971.

**Holt,** P. M., Ann K. S. Lambton, and Bernard Lewis, *Cambridge History of Islam.* Vol. 1. Cambridge: Cambridge University Press, 1970.

**Inalcik,** Halil, *The Ottoman Empire: The Classical Age, 1300-1600.* London: Weidenfeld and Nicolson, 1973.

**Ipşiroğlu,** Mazhar S., *Masterpieces from the Topkapi Museum.* London: Thames and Hudson, 1980.

**Lewis,** Bernard, et al., *The World of Islam.* London: Thames and Hudson, 1976.

**Parry,** V. J., *A History of the Ottoman Empire to 1730.* Cambridge: Cambridge University Press, 1976.

**Penzer,** N. M., *The Harem.* London: Spring Books, 1966.

**Petsopoulos,** Yanni, ed., *Tulips, Arabesques and Turbans: Decorative Arts from the Ottoman Empire.* London: Alexandria Press, 1982.

**Rogers,** J. M., and R. M. Ward, *Süleyman the Magnificent.* London: British Museum Publications, 1988.

**Scarce,** Jennifer, *Women's Costume of the Near and Middle East.* London: Unwin Hyman, 1987.

**Shaw,** Stanford, *History of the Ottoman Empire and Modern Turkey.* Vol. 1. Cambridge: Cambridge University Press, 1976.

## INDIA

**Abul Fazl,** *Ain-i Akbari.* Transl. by H. Blochmann and H. S. Jarrett. Calcutta: Royal Asiatic Society of Bengal, 1873-1894.

**Babur,** *Baburnama.* Transl. by Annette Beveridge. London: Luzac, 1921.

**Badauni,** *Muntakhab al-Tawarikh.* Transl. by Ranking, Lowe, and Haig. Calcutta: Royal Asiatic Society of Bengal, 1884-1925.

**Beveridge,** H., transl. *Akbarnama.* Calcutta: Royal Asiatic Society of Bengal, 1907-1939.

**Bhushan,** *The Costumes and Textiles of India.* Bombay: D. B. Taraporevala Sons, 1958.

**Bosworth,** C. E., *The Islamic Dynasties.* Edinburgh: Edinburgh University Press, 1980.

**Brand,** Michael, and Glenn D. Lowry, *Akbar's India: Art from the Mughal City of Victory.* New York: The Asia Society Galleries, 1985.

**Crowe,** Sylvia, et al., *The Gardens of Mughal India.* London: Thames and Hudson, 1972.

**Dar,** S. N., *Costumes of India and Pakistan.* Bombay: D. B. Taraporevala Sons, 1969.

**Elliot,** H. M., and J. Dowson, *The History of India As Told by Its Own Historians.* London: Trubner, 1867-1877.

**Foster,** W., ed., *Early Travels in India.* London: Oxford University Press, 1921.

**Gascoigne,** Bamber, *The Great Moghuls.* London: Jonathan Cape, 1971.

**Gulbadan Begum,** *Humayun-nama.* Transl. by Annette Beveridge. London: Oriental Translation Fund, 1902.

**Haig,** W., ed., *The Mughal Period.* Vol. 4 of *The Cambridge History of India.* Cambridge: Cambridge University Press, 1937.

**Ibn Hasan,** *The Central Structure of the Mughal Empire.* London: Oxford University Press, 1936.

***The Indian Heritage:*** *Court Life & Arts under Mughal Rule.* London: Victoria & Albert Museum, 1982.

**Lane-Poole,** S., *Medieval India: AD 712-1764.* London: Fisher Unwin, 1903.

**Pal,** Pratapaditya, *Court Paintings of India: 16th-19th Centuries.* New York: Navin Kumar, 1983.

**Rizvi,** S. A. A., *The Wonder That Was India.* Vol. 2. London: Sidgwick & Jackson, 1987.

**Smith,** Vincent A., *Akbar the Great Mogul.* Oxford: Oxford University Press, 1927.

**Spear,** Percival, *A History of India.* Vol. 2. London: Penguin, 1978.

**Welch,** Stuart Cary, *Imperial Mughal Painting.* London: Chatto & Windus, 1978.

**Yule,** R. E., and A. C. Burnell, *Hobson-Jobson: A Glossary of Anglo-Indian Words and Phrases.* London: John Murray, 1903.

## GENERAL

**Ashelford,** Jane, *A Visual History of Costume: The Sixteenth Century.* London: B. T. Batsford, 1983.

**Boucher,** François, *A History of Costume in the West.* London: Thames and Hudson, 1967.

**Braudel,** Fernand:
*Civilization and Capitalism: 15th-18th Century.* Vols. 1, 2, and 3. London: Collins, 1981, 1982, 1984.
*The Mediterranean and the Mediterranean World in the Age of Philip II.* Vol. 1. London: Collins, 1972.

**Cammann,** Schuyler, *China's Dragon Robes.* New York: Ronald Press, 1952.

**Chou,** Hsuu, *5000 Years of Chinese Costume.* Hong Kong: Commercial Press, 1987.

**Hale,** J. R., *Renaissance War Studies.* London: The Hambledon Press, 1983.

**Hashimoto,** Sumika, *Japanese Accessories.* Tokyo: Japan Travel Bureau, 1962.

**Held,** Robert, *The Age of Firearms: A Pictorial History.* London: Cassell, 1959.

**McNeill,** William H., *The Pursuit of Power: Technology, Armed Force, and Society since A.D. 1000.* Chicago: University of Chicago Press, 1982.

**Minnich,** Helen, *Japanese Costume.* Tokyo: Charles E. Tuttle, 1963.

**Oman,** Sir Charles, *A History of the Art of War in the Sixteenth Century.* London: Methuen, 1937.

**Parker,** Geoffrey, *The Military Revolution: Military Innovation and the Rise of the West, 1500-1800.* Cambridge: Cambridge University Press, 1988.

**Roach,** Mary Ellen, and J. B. Eicher, *Dress, Adornment and the Social Order.* New York: John Wiley and Sons, 1965.

**Rogers,** Colonel H. C. B., *Artillery through the Ages.* London: Seeley Service, 1972.

**Shimizu,** Yoshiaki, ed., *Japan: The Shaping of Daimyo Culture, 1185-1868.* Washington, D.C.: National Gallery of Art, 1988.

**Squire,** Geoffrey, *Dress, Art and Society.* London: Studio Vista, 1974.

# INDEX

*Numerals in italics indicate an illustration of the subject mentioned.*

## A

**Abdul Fadl** (Mogul courtier): *Institutes of Akbar,* 165
**Abū Fazl,** (Mogul historian), 161
**Abū Hanīfah,** 128
**Act of Supremacy,** 63-64
**Act of Uniformity,** 63-64
*Adam and Eve* (Michelangelo), 26-27
**Adashev,** Alexei, 101-104, 106
**"Address to the German Nobility, The"** (Luther), 15
**Adham Khan,** 160
**Aegean Sea,** 128
**Afanasii,** Metropolitan, 107-108
**Africa,** 30, 57, 70
**"Against the Murdering, Thieving Hordes of Peasants"** (Luther), 23
**Agra** (Indian city), 155, 159, 160
**Agriculture:** Aztec, 42; in England, 64, 67-68, 81-83; in Germany, 23; Inca, 50; in Ottoman Empire, 137; in Russia, 103, 110, 114
**Ahmadnagar,** kingdom of, 150, 167
**Ajmer** (Muslim shrine), 160
**Akbar** (Mogul emperor), 86, *148,* 149, 150, *161;* birth of, 156; and court intrigues, 157-160; Decree of Infallibility by, 165-167; enlightened government of, 164-165; military campaigns of, 157, 160-161; palace of, *158;* quoted, 164
**Albert** (archbishop of Mainz), 12-14
**Albert of Hohenzollern** (duke of Prussia), 25
**Alexander VI,** Pope, 39
**Alexandrovskaya Sloboda** (Russian fortress), 107, 109, *111,* 113
**Almagro,** Diego de, 50-51, 53
**Alvarado,** Pedro de, 47
**Anatolia,** 117, 120, 125, 128, 131, 137
**Andes,** 51-53
**Anglican church,** 25, 61, 62, 63-64
**Anne of Cleves** (queen of England), 62
**Ansbach,** 23
**Antichrist,** 17, *18-19*
**Antwerp,** *28-29,* 69
**Arabian Sea,** 167
**Architecture:** in England, 69, 76-77, 80; in Hindustan, *155, 166;* Inca, 50; military, *88-89;* Mogul, *158-159;* Ottoman Turk, *123,* 129, *134-135*
**Armenia,** 128
**Art:** African, *91;* Andean gold, *54-56;* Aztec, *40, 41, 44-45;* German, 17; icons, *94, 102, 108-109;* of India, 86, *152, 162-163;* Japanese, 30, *90-91;* Mogul, *157;* Ottoman Turks, *124-125, 132-133;* Protestant, *18-19, 20, 21, 24;* Roman Catholic, *26, 27;* Sinu, *55;* Spanish, *92;* Tudor, *78. See also individual artists*
**Asia,** 30, 80
**Astrakhan,** khanate of, 105, 132
**Atahualpa** (Inca ruler), 37, *50-51,* 51-52
**Augsburg,** 9, 14; Confession of, 22; Peace of, 31
**Augustinians,** 11-12, 14, 56
**Aurangzeb** (Mogul emperor), 150, 167
**Austria,** 137
**Axayacatl** (father of Montezuma), 46, 48

**Azerbaijan,** 128
**Azov,** Sea of, 132
**Aztecs:** architecture, *43;* artisans, *44-45;* government, *40;* human sacrifices, 42-43, 49; legend of white-skinned god, 37; rabbit fertility god, *41*

## B

**Bābur** (Mogul emperor): birth of, 151; and conquest of Hindustan, 153-154; death of, 154; quoted, 149-151, 153, 154
**"Babylonian Captivity of the Church, The"** (Luther), 15
**Baghdad,** 125-128
**Bahādur Shah** (ruler of Gujarat), 154-156
**Bahia,** *map 49*
**Baja,** 56
**Bajazet** (son of Süleyman), 130
**Bajazet II** (Ottoman emperor), quoted, 118
**Balboa.** *See* Núñez de Balboa, Vasco
**Balkans,** 125, 137
**Baltic Sea,** 97, 106
**Baluchistan,** 167
**Barbarossa** (Redbeard), 128-129
**Barcelona,** 129
**Bathory,** Stefan. *See* Stefan Bathory
**Bayram Khan** (Mogul general), 157-160, 165
**Bekbulatovich,** Prince Simeon, 111-112
**Belgrade,** *116,* 120
**Belsky,** Prince Bogdan, 113
**Bengal,** 161
**Bess of Hardwick** (countess of Shrewsbury), 68-69
**Bir Bar,** Raja (Hindu poet), 161
**Black Forest,** 23
**Black Sea,** 95
**Bloody Mary.** *See* Mary I (queen of England)
**Boleyn,** Anne (queen of England), 61, *62*
**Bora,** Katharina von (wife of Martin Luther), 29
**Bosch,** Hieronymus, *Ship of Fools, 8*
**Bosnia,** 137
**Boyars** (Russian nobles), *98-99,* 101-102, 106-113
**Brazil,** *map 49,* 70
**Buda** (Hungarian city), 121
**Burghley House,** *76-77*
**Byzantium,** 97

## C

**Cabot,** John, 70
**Cabral,** Pedro Álvars, 49
**Cajamarca** (Inca city), 51
**Cajetan,** Cardinal, 14
**Calais,** 77
**Calvin,** John, 10, *24,* 25-28, 60
**Calvinism,** *24,* 25, 28, 31
**Cambridge University,** 67
**Canada,** 80

**Cape Verde Islands,** 49
**Carey,** George (cousin of Queen Elizabeth I), quoted, 84
**Caribbean** (islands), 70-71
**Caspian Sea,** 95, 132
**Cathedral of the Dormition,** 101
**Catherine of Aragon** (queen of England), 25, 61, *62,* 140
**Catholicism.** *See* Roman Catholic church
**Cecil,** Sir William, 63, 76
**Celtis,** Conradus (German poet), quoted, 11
**Cervantes,** Miguel de, *Don Quixote,* 133
**Chaldiran** (Turkish city), 119
**Chancellor,** Richard, quoted, 103
**Chand Bibi** (queen of Ahmadnagar), 167
**Charlemagne,** 18, 33
**Charles V** (Holy Roman emperor), 22-23, 32-35, 39, 56, 90; bust, shield, and coat of arms of, *33-35;* defeat of Schmalkaldic League by, 30; and Diet of Speyer, 25; and Diet of Worms, 17-19; election of, 14; and Ottoman Turks, 25, 125, 128-129; and Peace of Augsburg, 31; quoted, 34
**Charles VIII** (king of France), 85
**Chausa,** battle of, 155
**China,** fashions in, *147*
**Cholula** (Aztec city), 45
**Christ,** *18-19,* 102
**Christian Armada,** *132-133, 136-137*
**Church of England.** *See* Anglican church
**Clothing.** *See* Fashions
**Columbus,** Christopher, 39
**Conquistadors,** 37; brutality of, *46-47;* quoted, 57; weapons of, 41, 45
**Constantine I** (emperor of Rome), 122
**Constantine IX Monomachus** (emperor of Byzantium), 101; crown of, *96-97*
**Constantinople.** *See* Istanbul
**Cortés,** Hernán, 37, *38,* 42, 51, 53; arrest of Montezuma by, *46-47;* death of, 56; described, 39; quoted, 57; rule of, over Aztecs, 47-53
**Cranach,** Lucas the Elder, painting by, *11*
**Cranach,** Lucas the Younger, painting by, *16*
**Cranmer,** Thomas (archbishop of Canterbury), 61
**Crimea,** khanate of, *96-97,* 106-108, 111, 120
**Cuba,** 38, 39, 42, 48
**Cuitlahuac** (brother of Montezuma), 48
**Cuzco** (Inca capital), 50, 52
**Cyprus,** 132

## D

**Danube River,** 117, 120
**Delhi,** 150, 153, 157
**Denmark,** 25, 106
*Description of England* (Harrison), 69
**de Soto,** Hernando, 51
**Devereux,** Robert, (earl of Essex), 78, 83
**Díaz del Castillo,** Bernal, 48-49; quoted, 39, 42, 46, 48
**Dmitry,** Czar (usurper of Russian throne), *114*

**Dmitry,** Prince (first son of Ivan IV), 105-106
**Dmitry,** Prince (last son of Ivan IV), 114
**Dnieper River,** 95
*Dr. Faustus* (Marlowe), 79
**Dominicans,** 9, 50, 56
**Don John** (son of Charles V), 133
*Don Quixote* (Cervantes), 133
**Don River,** 109
**Doria,** Andrea (Genoese admiral), 128
**Dowland,** John, *First Booke of Songes or Ayres,* 80
**Drake,** Sir Francis, *81;* and attack on harbor of Cadiz, 73-76; and circumnavigation of globe, 71-72, 80; knighted, 72
**Drama.** *See* Theater
**Dublin,** 83
**Dudley,** Lord Robert (earl of Leicester), 66, 83
**Dürer,** Albrecht, engraving by, *13*

## E

**Eberlin,** Johann, quoted, 21
**Eck,** Johann, 14-15
**Economics:** in England, 63-64, *72,* 81-83; in New Spain, 56; in Ottoman Empire, 137-138
**Ecuador,** 50
**Edward VI** (king of England), 59, 61
**Egypt,** 119
**Eisenach** (German city), 19-20
**Eisleben** (German city), 11
**El Dorado,** legend of, 54
**Elena** (daughter-in-law of Ivan IV), 113
**Elias** (Muslim prophet), *157*
**Elizabethan Age,** 79-84
**Elizabeth I,** (queen of England), *58, 67, 68-69;* death of, 83-84; described, 62; education of, 61-63; excommunicated, 72; and execution of Mary Queen of Scots, 73; government of, 63-65; and Ivan IV, 109, 113; and naval build-up, 73-76; and Ottoman Empire, 137; quoted, 65, 66, 137; and Sir Francis Drake, 71; suitors of, 65-66; as Virgin Queen, 79
**England,** 10, 17, 25, *map 60,* 64-65; agriculture, 81-83; architecture, 76-77, 80; defeat of Spanish Armada by, 79-79, *82-83;* economics, *72,* 81-83; expansion by, 82-84; family life in, 69; fashions, *140-143;* government, 63-65; under Henry VIII, 59-61; music in, 80; navy, 73-76, *92;* royalty, 68-69; as rural agrarian society, 67-69; theater and music, 66-67, 79; travel in, *73;* war with Ireland, 83
**Erasmus,** Desiderius, 11, *13,* 29, 79; quoted, 18

## F

*Faerie Queene, The* (Spenser), 79
**Fashions,** *139-147;* China, *147;* England, *140-143;* Germany, *140, 142;* India, *144;* Islam, *145;* Italy, *141-143;* Japan, *146-147;* Ottoman Empire, *145;* Spain, *140-141*

**Fatehpur Sikri** (Mogul capital), *158-159,* 164
**Ferdinand** (king of Spain), 29
**Ferdinand I** (archduke of Austria), 121-122, 125
**Ferghana,** kingdom of, 151, 167
**Field of Cloth of Gold,** *64-65*
**Filofei** (Russian monk), quoted, 97
**Finland,** 25
*First Booke of Songes or Ayres* (Dowland), 80
**Fletcher,** Giles, quoted, 95, 113
**Fotheringhay Castle,** 73
**France,** 25, *map* 60, 64; Calvinism in, 28; as enemy of England, 59-61; Massacre of Saint Bartholomew's Day, 31; Reformation in, 11; royal pavilion, *64-65;* treaty with England, 64-65
**Franciscans,** 56
**Francis I** (king of France), 32, 34, 65, 90, 128-129
**Frankenhausen,** battle of, 23
**Frederick** (elector of Saxony), 12, *16, 18, 22-23,* 23-25; as protector of Luther, 14, 19-20
**Frobisher,** Martin, 80
**Fugger** (German banking house), 9, 14
**Fydor I,** Czar (son of Ivan IV), 113-114

## G

**Ganges River,** 154, 155
**Garden of Fidelity** (Kabul), *154*
**Geneva,** 10, 24, 25, 60
**Genghis Khan,** 149-150
**Germany:** Calvinism in, 24; censorship in, 17; fashions, *140, 142;* nationalism in, 10-11, 20-25; Peasants' War, 23; the Reformation in, 20-31; and Thirty Years' War, 31
**Ghent** (Flemish city), 32
**Gibraltar,** Strait of, 69
**Gilbert,** Humphrey, 80
**Glinskaya,** Czarina Elena, 97-98
**Globe Theatre,** *74-75*
**Goa** (Portuguese port), 153, 165
**Godunov,** Czar Boris, 101, 112, 113-114
**Gogra,** battle at, 154
*Golden Hind,* 71-72
**Golden Horde.** *See* Mongol Empire
**Golden Horn,** 122, 123, 125
**Golden Man.** *See* El Dorado
**Good Hope,** Cape of, 171
**Government:** Aztec, *40,* 42; of Charles V, 33-35; in England, 63-65; in Germany, 10-11, 20-21, 23; in Holy Roman Empire, 10-11, 14; in Mogul empire, 146, 161-165; in Ottoman Empire, 123-125; and the Reformation, 31; in Russia, 101-104, 107-109
**Granada,** 39
**Grand Mosque** (Delhi), 153
**Gravelines,** battle of, 77, *82-83*
**Greece,** ancient, 79
**Greek Orthodox church,** 122
**Gresham,** Sir Thomas, 63
**Guatavita** (lake), 54
**Gujarat,** 128, 159, 160, 161
**Gülbahar** (mistress of Süleyman I), 123, 130

**Gunpowder,** *85-91,* 122-123
**Gwalior Palace** (Rajputna), *155*

## H

**Habichtsburg** (German castle), 32
**Hamburg,** 23
**Hamida** (wife of Humāyūn), 156-160
**Hapsburgs,** 32-35
**Harems,** 129; in Mogul empire, 154-155; in Ottoman Empire, 123-125, *127,* 136; political power of, 157-160
**Harrison,** William, *Description of England,* 69
**Hasan al-Kafi,** 137
**Hastings,** Mary, 113
**Hawkins,** John (Caribbean slave trader), 70-71, 80
**Hawkins,** William, 70
**Henry II** (king of France), 31
**Henry VIII** (king of England), 63, 64, 65, 72, 83; building of royal navy by, 73; formation of Anglican church by, 25; last years of, 59-61
**Herberstein,** Sigmund von, *104-105;* quoted, 105
**Hilliard,** Nicholas, 80; miniature portrait by, *78*
**Himu** (Hindu general), 157
**Hinduism,** 156, 164-165
**Hindu Kush** (mountains), 149, 167
**Hindustan,** 149, 151, 153
**Hispaniola,** 39
**Holbein,** Hans the Younger, painting by, *63*
**Holy League,** 132-133, *136-137*
**Holy Roman Empire,** *map* 10, 10-11, 25, 30-35
**Horsey,** Jerome, quoted, 95, 101
**Howard,** Catherine (queen of England), *62*
**Howard,** Charles (lord high admiral of England), *68-69*
**Huáscar,** (son of Inca emperor), 51, 53
**Huayna Capac** (Inca emperor), 51, 53
**Humāyūn** (Mogul emperor), 150, 154-157
**Hungary,** 117, 129, 131, 138
**Hürrem** (Roxelana), 123, 124, 128, *129,* 130
**Hus,** Jan, 14

## I

**Ibrahim,** (sultan of Delhi), 153-154
**Ibrahim Pasha** (Ottoman grand vizier), 125-128
**Incas,** 36, 50; culture, 50; legend of white-skinned god, 37; warfare with Spaniards, 52-56
**India,** 57, *144,* 149, *map* 150, 161
**Indian Ocean,** 128, 153
**Indus River,** 149
**Ingolstadt,** University of, 11
**Inquisition,** 14, 29
*Institutes of Akbar* (Abdul Fadl), 165
**Ioasaf,** Metropolitan, 99
**Ireland,** 60, 77, 83
**Isabella** (queen of Spain), 29
**Islam,** 165; architecture of, *134-135;*

and Christian slaves, 125; code of, *131;* fashions, *145;* in India, 151-154, 156; law, 129-130; and poll taxes, 164; Shiite and Sunni sects of, 119, 125-128
**Islam Shah** (Afghan chief), 156
**Istanbul,** 118, *122,* 123, 129
**Italy,** 25; battle of Pavia, *90;* fashions, *141;* ravaged by Barbarossa, 128; Reformation in, 11; Roman Catholicism in, 10; Spanish soldiers in, 39
**Ivan,** Czarevitch (second son of Ivan IV), 111, 113
**Ivan III,** Czar (the Great), 97, 98
**Ivan IV,** Czar (the Terrible), *86, 94, 108-109;* birth of, 97; cruelty of, 98-101, 107-113, *112;* death of, 113; domains under, *map* 96; and marriage proposal to Queen Elizabeth, 113; military campaigns of, 104-105, 106, 110-113; and Ottoman Turks, 132; political reforms under, 101-104, 107-109; quoted, 101, 105, 106, 107, 108, 111, 113

## J

**Jahāngīr** (Mogul emperor), 164-167; dagger of, *165*
**James VI** (king of England), 84
**Janissaries** (Ottoman infantry), 117, 123, 125-126, 130
**Japan,** *90-91, 146-147*
**Jerome,** Saint, 20
**Jesuits,** 29, *30,* 73, 165
**Jews,** 31
**Jonson,** Ben, quoted, 79
**Julius II,** Pope, 26
**Jüterborg** (German city), 9

## K

**Kabul,** 149, 153, 154, 156
**Kandahār,** 156, 167
**Kannauj,** battle at, 155
**Karlstadt,** Andreas, 21-22
**Kashmir,** 167
**Kazan,** khanate of, *86,* 97, 104-105, *108-109*
**Keresztes,** battle at, 138
**Khandwa,** battle at, 153-154
**Khayr ad-Dīn.** *See* Barbarossa
**Kiev,** 95
**Kirillov** (monastery), 106
**Knights of Saint John,** 120, 128
**Knox,** John, 31
**Korean turtleship,** *92-93*
**Koróne** (Greek port), 128
**Kremlin,** 97, 99, *100,* 101, 102, 113
**Kulikovo** (Russian city), 96

## L

**Lahore,** 153
**La Noche Triste,** 48
**Latin Vulgate,** 20, 26
**Le Havre,** 64-65
**Leo X,** Pope, 9, 12-14, 17-19, 20;

quoted, 14
**Lepanto,** 128, 132-133, *136-137*
**Lima,** 53
**Lisbon,** 77
**Literature:** in England, 80; Lutheran, 9-10, 14, 15-17, 20, 23; Ottoman, 129
**Lithuania,** 97, 106-108, 112-113
**Livonia,** 97, 106-108, 112-113
**London,** *map 70-71,* 80
**Lord Admiral's Men** (theater company), 80
**Lord Chamberlain's Men** (theater company), 74, 80
**Louis** (king of Hungary), 117
**Loyola,** Ignatius, 30
**Luque,** Hernando de, 50, 51
**Luther,** Hans (father of Martin), 11-12
**Luther,** Martin, 9, *11, 16,* 60; "The Address to the German Nobility," 15; "Against the Murdering, Thieving Hordes of Peasants," 23; "The Babylonian Captivity of the Church," 15; as Catholic monk, 11-12; and Charles V, 34; on divorce, 29; excommunication of, 17-19; on the family, 29; as lecturer, 9-10, 12-14; Ninety-five Theses, 9, 14, 20; other reformers and, 20-23; quoted, 11, 15, 18-19, 22, 23, 29; seven sacraments attacked by, 15-17; as translator, 20; on women, 29
**Lutheranism:** as a capital offense, 18; and Confession of Augsburg, 22; and Peace of Augsburg, 31; rise of, 23; spread of, 25-28

# M

**Macarius,** Metropolitan, 100, 101, 106-107
**Machiavelli,** Niccolò, quoted, 123
**Magellan,** Strait of, 71
**Maham Anga,** 160
**Mahmud** (brother of Ibrahim), 154
**Mainz,** 17
**Malta,** 128
**Mamluks,** 119
**Manco** (son of Inca emperor), 53
**Marina,** Doña (Aztec mistress of Cortés), 42, 45, 47
**Marlowe,** Christopher: *Dr. Faustus,* 79; *Tamburlaine the Great,* 79
**Marmara,** Sea of, 123, 125
**Marseilles,** 129
**Mary I** (queen of England), 59, 61, 62, 63-64, 65
*Mary Rose* (English warship), 92
**Mary Stuart** (queen of Scotland), 31, 72-73, 84
**Matsumoto Castle** (Japan), *88-89*
**Maximilian I** (Holy Roman emperor), 14, 32, 87
**Mecca,** 134, 160
**Medina-Sidonia,** duke of, 77
**Mediterranean** (area), 25, 69, 121, 128
**Mehmed II** (Ottoman emperor), 120-121, 125
**Mehmed III,** 137-138
**Melanchthon,** Philipp, 9, 16, 23
**Mendoza,** Antonio de (first viceroy of New Spain), 40
**Mexico,** 37, 39, 47, 57; new Spanish city of, 50; rule of Spain in, 50, 53, 56

**Michael** (the archangel), *108-109*
**Michelangelo:** *Adam and Eve, 26-27; Moses, 26*
**Mildmay,** Sir Walter, quoted, 67
**Mining,** 37, 39, *53,* 56, 69, 120
**Mogul empire,** *map* 150; art, *162-163;* battle of Panipat, *152,* 157; decline of, 167; discipline of army, 160-161; government, 156, 161-165; religion, 164; slavery, 164; trade, 156, 164; warriors, *152;* wars with Hindustan, 153-154, 155-157
**Mohács,** battle at, 117, 121
**Molodi** (Russian city), 111
**Mongol Empire,** 95-97, 104, 113, 149-150; invasion of Russia by, 110-111
**Montezuma,** 37, 43, 46-48, 52
**More,** Sir Thomas, 79
**Moscow,** 95-97, 102, 103-104, *108-109,* 110-111, 114
*Moses* (Michelangelo), 26
**Muezzinzade Ali** (Ottoman admiral), 133
**Muhammadans.** See Islam
**Mühlberg,** battle of, 30
**Muisca,** 54
**Mumtāz** (wife of Shah Jahān), 167
**Münzer,** Thomas, 22-23
**Murad III** (Ottoman emperor), *136-137;* quoted, 137
**Muscovy.** See Moscow; Russia
**Muscovy Company,** 70
**Music:** and Calvinism, 25; in England, 66-67, 80; in the Reformation, 21
**Muslims.** See Islam
**Mustafa** (son of Süleyman I), 130

# N

**Nagashino,** battle of, *90-91*
**Nahuatl** (Aztec language), 40, 42
**Narva** (Baltic port), 106
**Naval warfare:** English navy, 73-79; Korean turtleship, *92-93;* Ottoman galleys, 128-129, 132-133; Spanish Armada, 73-79, *82-83;* use of cannon, *92-93*
**Negaya,** Maria (last wife of Ivan IV), 113
**Netherlands,** 18, 77; and Calvinism, 28; trade, *28-29;* war with England, 60; war with Spain, 31, 69, 73
**Nevsky,** Prince Alexander, *108-109*
**New Castile,** 38, 51, 56
**Newfoundland,** 70, 80
**New Spain,** 38, 50, 56
**New Testament,** 20, 25, *102*
**New World,** 49, 50, 80
**Ninety-five Theses** (Luther), 9, 14, 20
**North Africa,** 39, 129
**North America,** 80, 83
**Nova Scotia,** 70
**Novgorod,** 97, 101, 110, *112*
**Núñez de Balboa,** Vasco, 50
**Nuremberg,** 23

# O

**Obolensky,** Prince, 98, 99
**Oka River,** 95-96

**Old Testament,** 15, 20, 25
**Oliver,** Isaac, painting by, 67
**O'Neill,** Hugh (earl of Tyrone), 83
**Oprichniki** (personal guard of Ivan IV), 107-111
**Oprichnina** (personal domains of Ivan IV), 107-111
**Orhan** (Ottoman emperor), 125
**Orissas,** kingdom of, 167
**Ortegualla** (Cortés's page), 49
**Ottoman Empire,** 33-34, 108, *map* 118-119; agriculture, 137; architecture, *134-135;* arts and literature, 129; astronomy, 137; bastinado, *131;* cavalry officers, *120-121;* craft guilds, *132-133;* economics, 137-138; fashions, *145;* fratricide, 137; government, 125; harems, 123-125; janissaries, 117, 123, 125-126, 130; navy, 132-133; and Russia, 132-133; social divisions in, 124-125; trade, 119; wars, 25, *116,* 119, 128-129, 137
**Otumba,** battle of, 48
**Oxford University,** 67

# P

**Panama,** 39, 50
**Panipat,** battle of, *152, 153,* 157
**Parliament,** English, 63, 66, 67, 73, 84
**Parma,** duke of, 77
**Parr,** Catherine (queen of England), 62
**Patras,** Gulf of, 133
**Paul,** Saint, quoted, 12
**Paul III,** Pope, 29-30
**Pavia,** battle of, *90*
**Peasants' War,** *21,* 28
**Persia,** 119, 125, 130, 132, 137
**Persian Gulf,** 57
**Peru,** 37, 57
**Pest** (Hungarian city), 122
**Philaret** (father of Czar Mikhail Romanov), *115*
**Philip** (landgrave of Hesse), 25, 29
**Philip II** (king of Spain), 35, 61, 65, 71-73
**Philippines,** 57
**Pius V,** Pope, 72
**Pizarro,** Francisco, 37, *38,* 39, *50;* death of, 56; expedition of, 50-51; rule of, over Incas, 53
**Pizarro,** Hernando (brother of Francisco), 51, 53
**Plymouth** (English port), 71, *80-81*
**Poland,** 106, 108, 112
**Polotsk** (Polish city), 106, 112
**Popocatépetl** (mountain), 46
**Portugal,** 10, 91, 153, 154, 165
**Possevino,** Antonio, 112
**Potosí** (mountain), *53*
**Presbyterian church.** See Calvinism
**Preveza,** Battle of, 128-129
**Printing:** in England, 80; in Germany, 17; in New Spain, 40; during the Reformation, *18-19*
**Privy Council,** English, 63, 67
**Protestantism.** See individual denominations
**Prussia,** 25
**Pskov,** 97, 101, 110
**Purgatory,** 12
**Puritans,** 80

# Q

**Quesada,** Gonzalo Jiménez de, 54
**Quetzalcoatl** (Aztec sun god), *36,* 37, 43, 46

# R

**Raja Man Singh** (Rajput ruler), 155
**Rajputs** (Hindu warrior caste), 153, 160-161
**Raleigh,** Sir Walter, 54, 67, 77-79, *80,* 83
**Rānā Sāngā** (Rajput chief), 154
**Raphael,** 26
**Red Sea,** 128
**Reformation,** *map* 10, 73; background of, 9-14; in England, 79-81; in Germany, 20-31, 23-25; and the Jesuits, 30; in Switzerland, 21; and women, 29
**Religion.** See *individual denominations*
**Renaissance,** 11, 12, 13, 78, 79, 140
**Rhodes,** 120
*Richard II* (Shakespeare), 32
**Roman Catholic church:** in the Caribbean, 39; converts to, *30;* corruption in, *8, 11, 18-19;* Diet of Speyer, 25; Diet of Worms, 17-19; and divorce, 29; in England, 63-65, 73, 83; and excommunication of Martin Luther, 17-19; and Henry VIII, 59-61; and the Inquisition, 29; and Islam, 137; in New Castile and New Spain, 42, 56; and Orthodox Christianity, 114; and Peace of Augsburg, 31; revitalization of, 29-30; and the rise of Lutheranism, 20-25, 110; and sale of indulgences, 9, 12-14
**Romanov,** Czar Mikhail, 114-115, *115*
**Romanov,** Czarina Anastasiya, 101, 106, 112, 114
**Rotterdam,** 11
**Russia,** *map* 96; agriculture, 103, 110; architecture, 111; cavalry tactics, 104-105; civil war, 114; economics, 101-103, 110, 114; government, 101-104; invasion of, by Mongol Empire, 110-111; music, 111; rise of, 95-98; trade, 70; warfare, *108-109*
**Russian Orthodox church,** 95, 99, 111; and civil war in Russia, 114; and Ivan IV, 100-101, 110; Moscow as seat of, 96, 102
**Rustem Pasha** (Ottoman grand vizier), 130

# S

**Safavids** (Shiite Muslim dynasty), 119
**Safiye,** Princess (consort to Murad III), 136, 137
**Saint Augustine** (Florida), 89
**Saint Bartholomew's Day,** Massacre of, 31
**Saint Basil's Cathedral,** *110*
**Saint George's Day,** 103, 110
**Saint Peter's Basilica,** 12-14, 26

**Saint Stephen's Cathedral** (Vienna), 123
**Salim Chisti,** Sheik, tomb of, *159*
**Samarkand,** 151
**Samurai warrior,** *146*
**San Juan de Ulúa,** 42, 43, 70-71
**San Miguel,** 51
**Santa Cruz,** marquis of, 77
**Santiago de Baracoa,** (Cuban capital), 39
**Sarai** (Mongol capital), 95
**Scheldt River,** 69
**Schmalkaldic League,** 25, 30
**Scotland,** *map* 60, 64; Calvinism in, 28, 31; and England, 59-61, 64-65
**Selim** (Ottoman emperor), 119
**Selim II** (Ottoman emperor), 124, 130-136, 145
**Selimiye mosque,** *134-135*
**Seymour,** Jane (queen of England), 61, *62*
**Shah Ismail** (Safavid ruler), 119
**Shah Jahān,** (Mogul emperor), 163, 167
**Shah Tahmāsp,** (Safavid ruler), 125-128, 130, 156
**Shakespeare,** William, 35, *74*, 79; *Richard II, 32*
**Shēr Khan** (Afghan chief), 154-157
*Ship of Fools* (Bosch), *8*
**Shisky,** Prince Andrei, 99
**Shkuratov,** Maliuta, 107
**Siberia,** 113
**Silvester,** 101, 106
**Sinan** (Ottoman architect), 129, 134
**Sind,** 156, 167
**Sirhind,** battle at, 156-157
**Sixtus IV,** Pope, 12
**Slavery:** of Africans, 41-42, 49, 70-71, 91, 154; of Caribbean Indians, 39; of children, 125, 164; harems, 123-125, 129, 136, 154-155, 157-160; in Ottoman Empire, 125-126; of women, 42, 164
**Smallpox,** 42, 48, 51, 57
**Smolensk,** 97
**Society of Jesus.** *See* Jesuits
**Sodom,** *108-109*
**Sokollu Mehmed Pasha** (Ottoman grand vizier), 131-132, 136-137; quoted, 133
**Spain,** 10, 17, 25; American territories, 57; atrocities in Mexico, *46-47;* Caribbean colonies, 39; and England, 59-61, 70-71, 76-79; fashions, *140-141;* Islamic faith in, 35; ravaged by Barbarossa, 128; rule in Mexico, 50, 53, 56; trade, 37; treasure fleets, 56
**Spanish Armada,** 76-79, *82-83, 92,* 137
**Spenser,** Edmund: *The Faerie Queene,* 79; quoted, 79
**Speyer,** Diet of, 25
**Staritsky,** Prince Vladimir, 108
**Stefan Bathory** (king of Poland and Lithuania), 112
**Strasbourg,** 23
**Stratford-on-Avon,** 74
**Süleyman I** (Ottoman emperor), *87,* 119, 129; death of, 131; described, 120; government of, 123-125; heirs of, 130; imperial monogram of, *124-125;* law

under, 129-130; military campaigns of, 117, 120-123, 125-130; quoted, 121
**Süleymaniye Mosque,** *122,* 129
**Sweden,** 25, 106, 112-113
**Switzerland,** 21, 29
**Szigetvár,** siege of, 131

# T

**Tabascans,** 41-42
**Tabrīz,** (Safavid capital), 119
**Taj Mahal,** *166*
*Tamburlaine the Great* (Marlowe), 79
**Tamerlane** (Timur), 96, 149-151, 153, 167
**Tatars.** *See* Mongol Empire
**Temiukovna,** Czarina Maria, 107
**Tenochtitlán** (Aztec capital), *map 43,* 45, 46, 47-50
**Tetzel,** Johann, 12-14; quoted, 9
**Texcoco,** Lake, 42, 46, 48-49
**Thames River,** *70-71,* 74, 76
**Theater:** in England, 66-67, 79-80; Globe Theatre, *74-75;* and Puritans, 80; and Roman Catholic church, 79
**Theology.** *See individual denominations*
**Thirty Years' War,** 31
**Timurid empire,** 149-151
**Titian,** 26; painting attributed to, *119*
**Tlaxcala,** 45, 48
**Todar Mal,** Raja, 165
**Topkapi Saray** (imperial Ottoman palace), 123, 124, *126-127,* 129, 136, 137
**Torches,** Battle of, 137
**Tordesillas,** Treaty of, 49
**Totomacs,** 45
**Toulon,** 129
**Tower of London,** *70-71;* earl of Essex beheaded in, 83; Elizabeth I confined to, 62-63; Sir Walter Raleigh imprisoned in, 67
**Trade:** in England, 67, 69-72; in Hindustan, 156; in Mogul empire, 164; in the Netherlands, *28-29;* in the Ottoman Empire, 119; Portuguese sugarcane, 49; routes to New World, 80; in Russia, 96-97; Spanish treasure fleets, 56
**Transylvania,** 129
**Trent,** Council of, 29-30
**Tumbes,** 50, 51
**Tyndale,** William, 60

# U

**Umar** (Mogul emperor), 151
**Uzbeks,** 132, 153, 167

# V

**Valens** (Roman emperor), 129
**Vasily III,** Czar, 97
**Vatican,** 73, 112
**Velásquez de Cuéllar,** Diego, (governor of Cuba), 39-41, 47, 48
**Veracruz,** 43-45, 47
**Vienna,** 25, 122-123
**Vijayanagar,** 153
**Vilcabamba,** 57

**Viracocha** (Inca god), 37
**Virginia** (North American colony), 83
**Volga River,** 104-105, 109
**Volkhov River,** 111
**Vorontsov,** Fyodor, 99

# W

**Warfare:** Aztec, 42-43, 47-50; effect of gunpowder on, *85-91;* English, 73-79, 83, *92;* German, 23, 31; Holy Roman Empire, 23, 30, *90;* Irish, 83; Japanese, *88-89, 90-91, 146;* Mogul, *152,* 153-154, 155, 156-157, 160-161; Ottoman, *116, 120-121,* 122-123, 128-129, 132-133, *136-137,* 138; Russian, 96, 104-105, *108-109,* 110-113, 114; Spanish, 37-39, *45,* 47-53, 73-79, *82-83;* use of elephants in, 153, 157, 160-161; warrior queen Chand Bibi, 167. *See also* Naval warfare
**Wartburg** (castle), 19-20
**Weapons:** bows, 160; of conquistadors, 41; daggers, *144, 165;* English guns, 77, *82-83, 92;* hand-held firearms, 77, 85, *90-91,* 123, 137, 153, 160; Inca, 52; Korean guns, 92-93; Mogul guns, *86,* 152-153, 155, 160; Ottoman, 120; Ottoman guns, *87,* 117-119, 122-123, 128-129; Spanish, 57, 77; Spanish guns, 45, 51-52, *92;* swords, *142-143, 146;* Tabascan, 41
**West Indies,** 70
**Westminster,** *70-71*
**White Sea,** 106
**Wittenberg,** University of, 9, 11-14, 17, 19, 21-22, 29
**Women:** fashions, *139-141, 145, 147;* as harem slaves, 123-125, *127,* 129, 136, 154-155, 157-160; Martin Luther on, 29; and poverty in England, 81-83
**Worms,** Diet of, 17-19
**Worms,** Edict of, 19

# X

**Xerez,** Francisco de (Pizarro's secretary), 50; quoted, 51

# Y

**Yaroslavl,** 97
**Yucatán peninsula,** 39
**Yuri** (brother of Ivan IV), 98-99
**Yuste,** 32, 35

# Z

**Zápolya,** János, (ruler of Transylvania), 121-122
**Zempoala** (Totomac city), 45, 47
**Zurich,** 10, 29
**Zwingli,** Huldrych (Swiss pastor), 21, 29